IMAGES
of America

COTTON ON THE SOUTH PLAINS

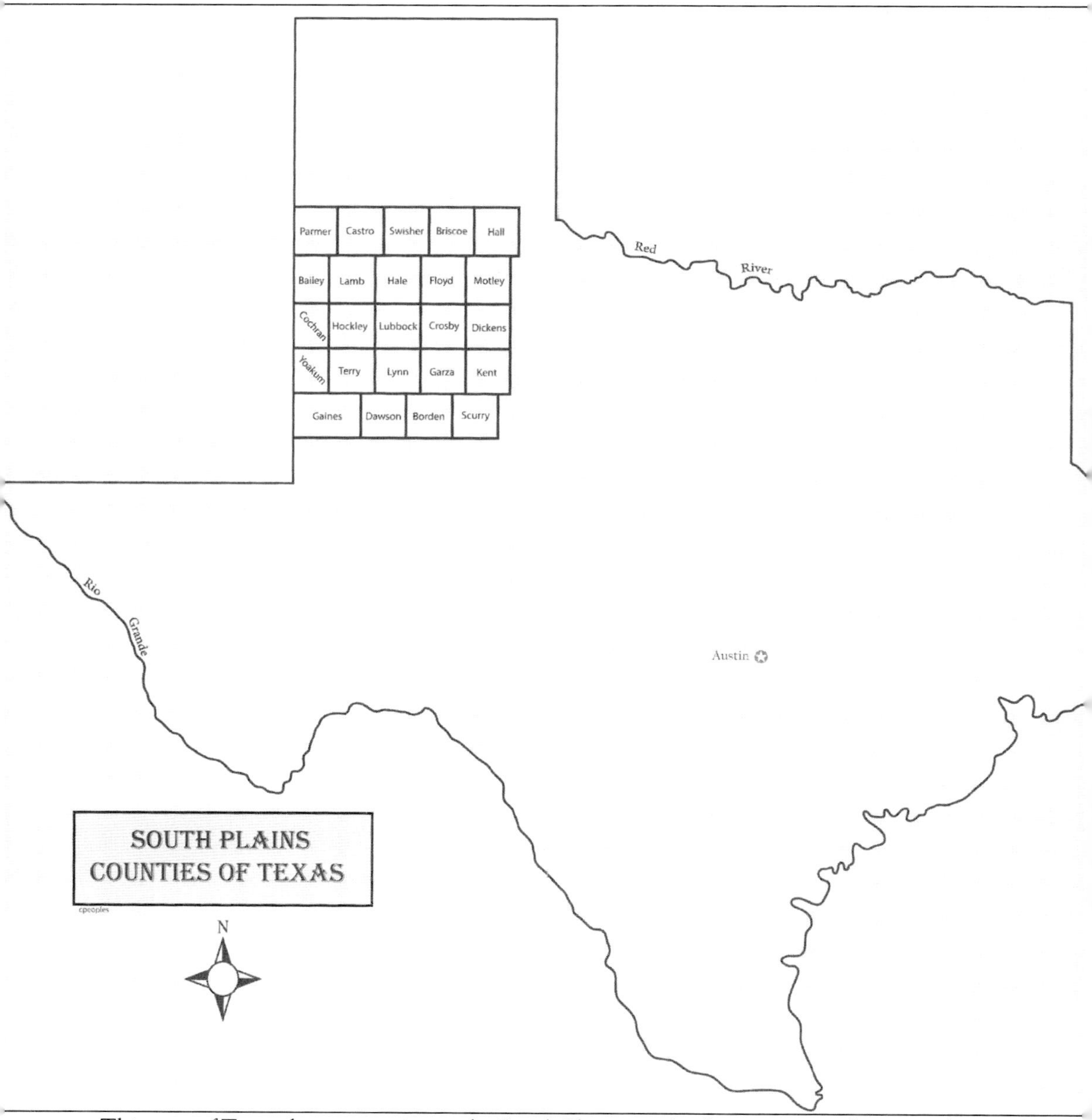

This map of Texas shows counties on the South Plains involved in cotton production. The South Plains region, besides being the largest cotton-producing region in the world, is also a leader in the production of cattle, hogs and pigs, corn, wheat, and milo as well as a major producer of gas, oil, and wind energy. (Map illustration by Curtis Peoples.)

On the Cover: Taken in 1947, this photograph most likely shows Bracero workers picking cotton in Lubbock. Notice the hats for shading their faces from the sun and the bags hanging on their shoulders. The development of mechanical harvesters put an end to hand harvesting on the South Plains and the migration of workers. Nevertheless, cotton remains king on the South Plains. (Photograph from the Winston Reeves Photograph Collection, courtesy of the Southwest Collection/Special Collections Library, Texas Tech University.)

IMAGES
of America

COTTON ON THE SOUTH PLAINS

John T. "Jack" Becker, Innocent Awasom,
and Cynthia Henry

ARCADIA
PUBLISHING

ISBN 978-0-7385-9585-6

Published by Arcadia Publishing
Charleston, South Carolina

Printed in the United States of America

Library of Congress Control Number: 2012937144

For all general information, please contact Arcadia Publishing:
Telephone 843-853-2070
Fax 843-853-0044
E-mail sales@arcadiapublishing.com
For customer service and orders:
Toll-Free 1-888-313-2665

Visit us on the Internet at www.arcadiapublishing.com

This book is dedicated to the hardworking cotton farmers of the South Plains of Texas.

Contents

ACKNOWLEDGMENTS

The cotton industry on the South Plains is the result of many years of hard work performed anonymously by many thousands of people. It is also the story of people working collectively to create an industry that efficiently produces a quality product. The authors would like to recognize that this spirit still exists in many of the people who still labor in the cotton industry and helped us put this book together. First and foremost, we would like to thank Dan Taylor, Wendell Dean "Buzz" Vardeman, and Carol and Powell Adams, who generously gave of their time, advice, and use of their personal photograph collections.

Lynette Wilson with the Plains Cotton Cooperative Association and Neva Haney, who works at the Texas AgriLife Research and Extension Center, both of Lubbock, were also forthcoming with help, images, and contacts. Michael Sierra, the safety director at the Littlefield Denim Mills, helped us tremendously by taking the time to explain the complicated cotton-milling process.

Thanks go to several South Plains museums, historical associations, curators, newspaper reporters, and individuals who shared with us their knowledge and photographs. They are DeLoyce Montgomery, Ralls Historical Museum; Richard Porter, Wayland Baptist University and the *Plainview Daily Herald*; John Rigg, *Hockley County News-Press*; Henry Reiff, Hale County Farm and Ranch Museum; Janet Milam and Dorothy Turner, Floyd County Historical Museum; Randy Vance, Texas Tech University, Southwest Collection/Special Collection; and Kimberly Vardeman. And, last but not least, thanks go to Emerson Tucker, who helped us in numerous small ways.

INTRODUCTION

The South Plains of Texas is a flat, semiarid, and an almost featureless region that makes up the 36 southernmost counties of the Texas Panhandle. In 24 counties, on three million acres, farmers produce over 40 percent of Texas's annual upland cotton crop or about one-quarter of all cotton grown annually in the United States. In most years, the economic impact of cotton-growing in the region exceeds $5 billion. Lubbock, Texas, is considered the center of this prolific cotton producing area. Critics say that Lubbock sits in the middle of a giant cotton field, and there is some truth to that statement. If one were to travel 60 miles in any direction from the city of Lubbock, he or she would not lose sight of a cotton field. However, this did not happen overnight, it took over a century of hard work, cooperation, and innovation to achieve.

Less than 150 years ago, the area was an enormous short-grass prairie, home to enormous herds of buffalo and nomadic tribes of Comanche and Kiowa Indians. Considered part of the vast Great American Desert, and unfit for agriculture, the South Plains of Texas was the last extended area in the continental United States to be settled. Nevertheless, the counties in the Texas Panhandle are today some of the most agriculturally productive areas in the United States, if not the world. The Panhandle is a leader in the production of cattle and calves, cattle on feed, hogs and pigs, wheat, sorghum, milk, and, of course, cotton.

Raising cotton on the South Plains has gone through many changes in the past 100 years. In the early 20th century, cotton was grown by hand and almost exclusively by farmers owning small farms (most less than a quarter section, or 165 acres) along with other crops and livestock. These small farmers planted the cottonseed by hand (sometimes two or three times in one year), weeded and thinned the young plants by hand, carrying hoes, and cultivated the cotton by horse- or mule-drawn cultivators. If an insect infestation attacked the crop, the invading insects were picked off the cotton or were sprayed with insecticide by hand. At harvest time, the cotton was picked (actually pulled) by hand. It would not be until World War I that cotton became a crop grown by South Plains farmers exclusive of all others.

Cotton-growing on the South Plains got its first boost before World War I when railroads extended lines into every corner of the region, thus allowing Texas farmers to ship their crops more easily to ports like Houston and Galveston and into the world market. World War I created a huge demand for South Plains cotton, and area farmers enjoyed high prices and good crop years all during the war and for several years afterwards. During this period, it became obvious to many that small-scale, general farming as practiced was not suited to the climate of the South Plains. Despite the high prices, many small landowning farmers left the area for opportunities elsewhere, and the land became consolidated in fewer but larger farms, a trend that continues to the present.

The widespread use of tractors after World War II accelerated the consolidation of small farms into bigger ones, as tractor-powered machinery allowed one farmer to do the work of several, thus making it possible to cultivate a larger area than before. But even with tractors, cotton farmers of the 1940s, 1950s, and 1960s could not cultivate more than four rows of cotton at a time. Cotton production was limited in another way, as well—chiefly because the majority of cotton was still harvested by hand and hauled to local gins in wagons or carts.

Today, cotton is grown without being touched by human hands. Huge tractors pull 16-row planters across fields often over a mile in length to plant seeds precisely at the depth and spacing farmers require. Later, cultivators—some of which can cultivate up to eight rows at a time—and sprayers attack any pests that may find their way into the cotton patch. At harvest time, eight-row strippers strip in one day what 240 people use to pull in the same amount of time. At one time, thousands of people migrated to the South Plains to pull cotton. Some would remain after the harvest was finished to work in local gins, which at peak times operated 24 hours a day. Most workers came from the Rio Grande valley in Mexico or from other cotton-growing states of the South. Many workers from Mexico, part of the Bracero Program, came to the South Plains and harvested their way north, pulling cotton as it matured.

Cotton harvested by hand in the South Plains was pulled, or broken off the plant, bur and all—unlike in other areas, where the cotton was actually pulled out of the bur. This process gave South Plains cotton a bad reputation, as upland cotton was harvested along with the bur and needed extra ginning to be cleaned. When mechanical harvest became common, mechanical harvesters stripped the entire cotton plant, including burs and lint, along with some dried leaves and stems. But, again, advances in strippers and ginning technology cleaned upland cotton to manufacturers specifications. Profitable markets were found for cotton gin by-products. Cotton seeds have a long history of use, as livestock feed, oil, and food additives and in cosmetics. The leftover trash is made into animal feed, mulch, and in some cases (and grades) into currency. An average pound of cotton produces more by-products (by weight) than lint, so the sale of by-products has become increasingly important.

One of the last major problems preventing the timely production and harvesting of cotton was finally solved in the early 1970s, with the development of module builders, which made it possible to temporarily store cotton in the field. Until the development of module builders, whether the cotton was pulled by hand or stripped mechanically, it was dumped into a trailer so that it could be hauled to the gin for processing. During the harvest, farmers often waited for days for the gin to unload the cotton from farmers' trailers, making it impossible for the farmer to continue harvesting.

Today, the stripped cotton is taken to a module builder, located in the cotton field, where it is compressed into large modules, weighing up to 15,000 pounds and equaling 10 to 12 bales. The cotton remains in the module, near the field where it was grown, until specially designed trucks using GPS technology move it to the gin. There is no more hauling the cotton to the gin in wagons or trailers and waiting on the gin to empty them; the farmer can harvest continually until the entire field is stripped clean of cotton. This allows cotton to be harvested when the quality of the cotton is optimal.

Throughout the growing season, the cotton is watered, fertilized, and protected from pests by means of irrigated water that can be put over (or under) the plants at a moment's notice. Cotton production on the South Plains has gone high-tech. But that has not always been the case. Irrigation, more than anything else created by man, has made cotton-growing on the South Plains as productive as it is, although about half of all cotton grown in the area is dryland cotton. In the early days of irrigation, water was pumped onto cotton fields with little concern to where it ran or to the amount of water wasted in the process. It seemed the Ogallala Aquifer, which lay just beneath the surface, held an endless supply of water. The water was easy to get to and cheap to use, and in some areas of the South Plains, the aquifer could be found less than 200 feet below the surface of the ground. But as the level of the water dropped, it become more expensive to use, thus creating the need for conservation.

Today, center-pivot irrigation systems spread water evenly over a cotton fields up to 165 acres in size. Equipped with drop nozzles, a center-pivot system will deliver the water directly over the plant or on the ground, thus eliminating loss to blowing wind and runoff. A promising new technology is inground drip irrigation, which is currently being used by some farmers and has the ability to conserve even more water than other irrigation systems.

Other innovations in the irrigation of cotton are the use of computers and satellite technology. With these innovations, a South Plains farmer can irrigate his cotton from his home or from his truck if he has a wireless connection. New imaging software can show the farmer pictures of his cotton taken by satellites hundreds of miles in space. The new technology allows the farmer to look at his cotton fields, check weather conditions, and then communicate with the center pivot to apply the correct amount of moister on his cotton. In addition, the pictures can tell the farmer if his cotton is being stressed by insect pests or a chemical deficiency, both of which can be taken care of by putting the correct agricultural chemicals in the water in the correct amounts.

The type of cotton grown on the South Plains is upland cotton, which is a short-staple cotton with fibers that measure from 13/16 to 1 and 1/4 inches in length. In ideal conditions, the cotton plant will germinate in about five to ten days after planting. As the cotton plant grows, it sets out leaves, but it is not until about two to four weeks that it sets out its first true leaves. In about five to seven weeks, the plant puts out its first squares, a small flower bud. As the square develops, the bud swells and becomes a flower. After the flower pollinates, it dies and falls off the plant, revealing an immature boll beneath. As the boll grows, the fibers inside grow and thicken, eventually becoming the size of a walnut. An average boll will contain up to 500,000 fibers, and each plant can produce up to 100 bolls. About 140 days after planting, or about 45 days after the bolls first appear, the bolls will begin to open. In about 25 weeks after planting, the cotton is ready to be harvested.

Cotton production has been growing steadily for over 100 years on the South Plains. Over the years, the number of acres planted in cotton, the number of acres harvested, the total number of bales produced, and the average yield per acre have all steadily increased. The rise in productivity did not happen by accident. It took years of hard work, problem solving on a vast scale, and dedication to a historic crop and a way of life. The story of cotton-growing on the South Plains is an agricultural success story, which will no doubt continue into the near future.

One

PLANTING

Tremendous advances have taken place on the South Plains in the planting of cotton. At first, since cottonseeds were so cheap, little care was given to their planting. However, as labor and seed costs grew, more care was taken in their planting. Today, with the aid of computers, expensive cottonseed is planted at the exact depth and spacing the farmer desires.

A century ago, most cotton on the South Plains was either sown by hand in rows or by one or two row planters drawn by teams of horses or mules. Cottonseeds were intentionally sown thicker than required since most cotton was hand-hoed at least once. It was easy to thin the cotton to the desired spacing while weeding. Later, team-drawn planters planted faster and more accurately than hand planting, but it was still hard to plant seeds at the proper depth and spacing. During these times, it was not unusual for a farmer to replant his cotton more than once in order to make a stand.

As more-powerful tractors began to appear on the South Plains between world wars, bigger and more accurate planters emerged as well. As the tractors grew bigger, they could pull more and heavier planters through the field. Today, 16-row planters are common, and computers in the tractor cab and electric eyes mounted in the planters keep track of planting, tracking the amount of seed used, the depth it is planted, and its spacing in the row. If something goes wrong, the computer-assisted planter can immediately make adjustments.

With the cottonseed spaced accurately in the row, planted at the desired depth and with fertilizer and possibly herbicide placed nearby, the cottonseed is ready to start its journey to becoming a fully developed cotton plant. All the seed needs are a little moisture and the warmth of the sun to sprout and protection from insects and weeds to grow.

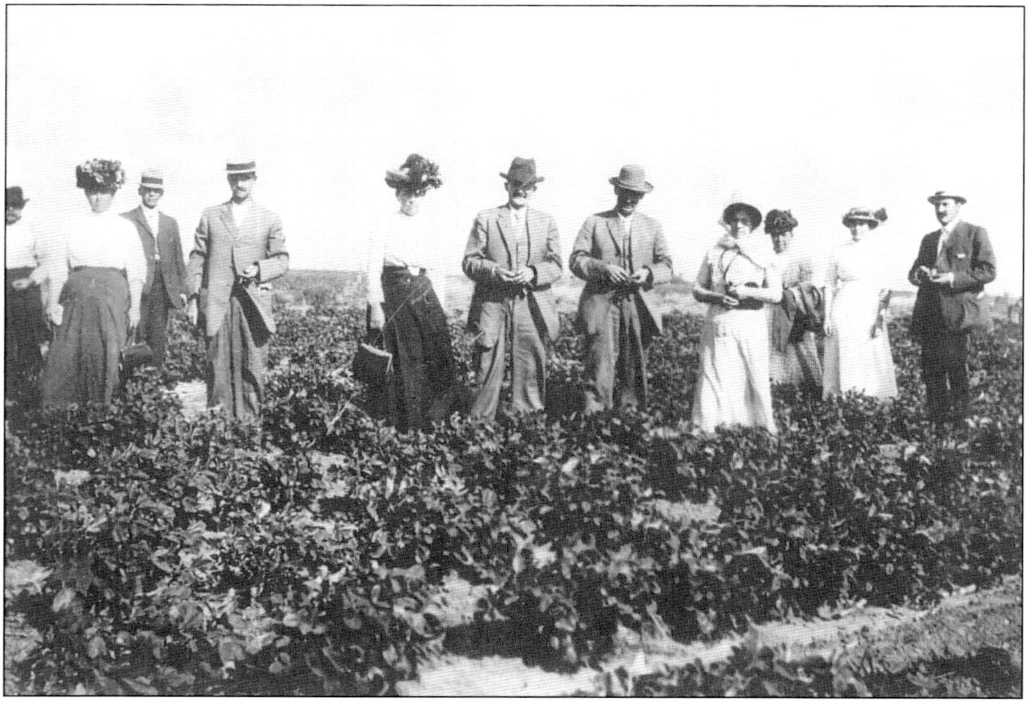

Around 1924, a group of visiting farmers and their wives inspects cotton grown in the Ralls area. Either John R. Ralls, or more likely his brother, Percy, brought this group of prospective residents to Crosby County. The brothers promoted the town of Ralls and Crosby County by bringing farmers to the area in hopes they would stay. The visit allowed for close inspection of the cotton in two different fields (see following page). Field demonstrations like this allowed farmers to inspect new varieties of cotton, new agricultural techniques, and in this case, a possible new site to farm. (Both photographs courtesy of the Ralls Historical Museum.)

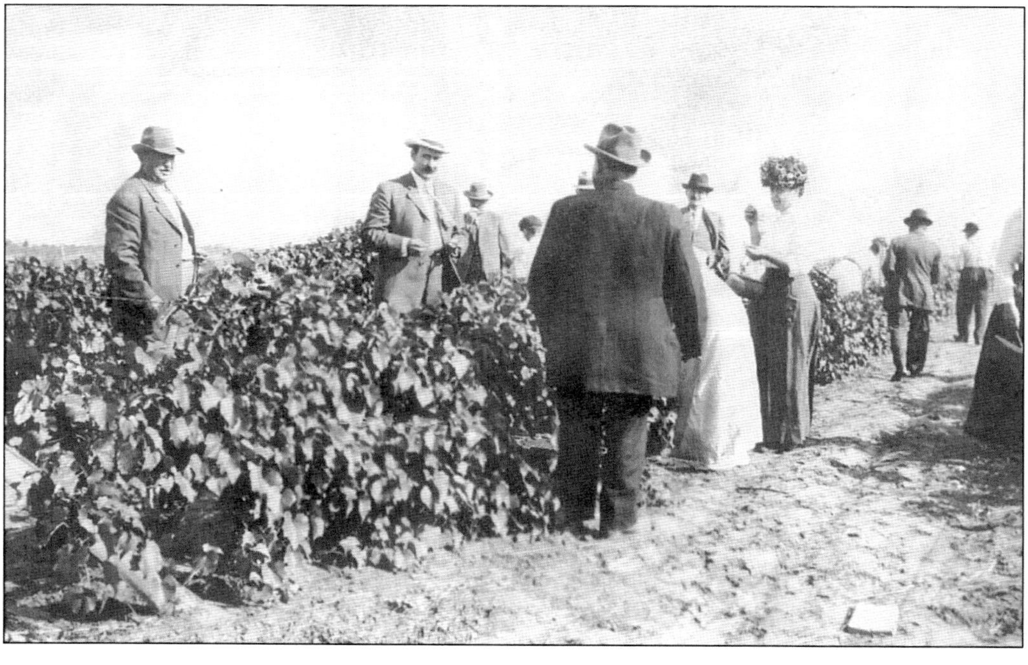

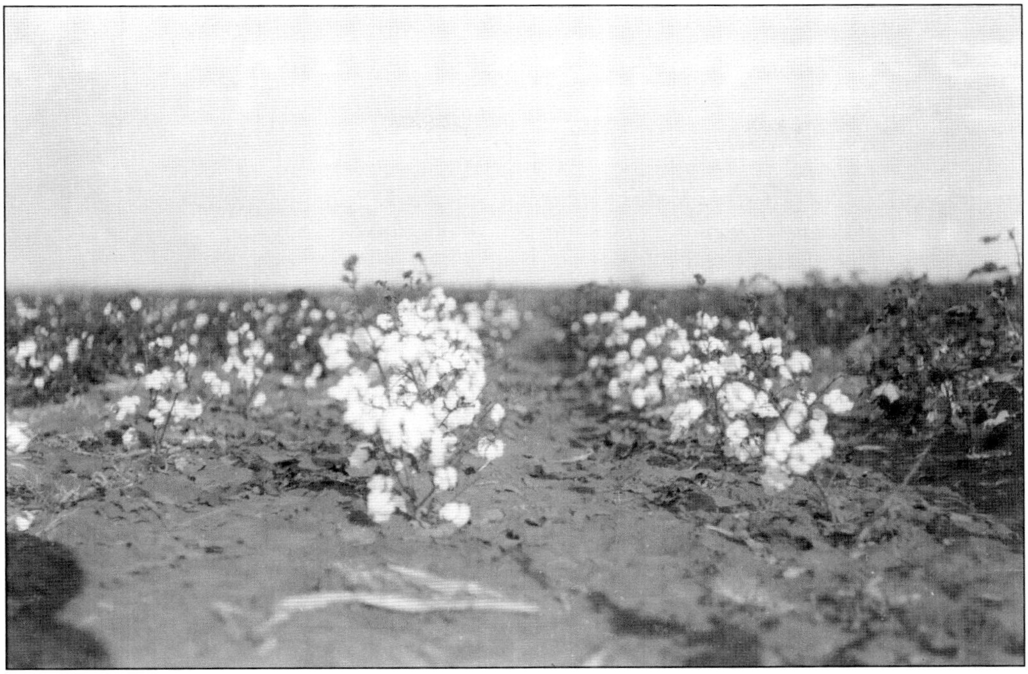

The photograph above, taken on October 10, 1922, shows several varieties of cotton grown side-by-side in rows. Cotton in row nine was considered excellent; row eight, good; but row ten, poor. As depicted in the March 3, 1924, photograph below, a cotton field at the Lubbock County Experiment Station is prepared for planting with a walking lister. The lister prepared the seed bed by building alternating furrows and mounds of soil, where the cotton was actually planted. Cotton research on the South Plains began in early 1922 at the Burnett Agricultural Research Center north of Lubbock, Texas. (Both photographs courtesy of the Texas AgriLife Research and Extension Center – Lubbock, Texas.)

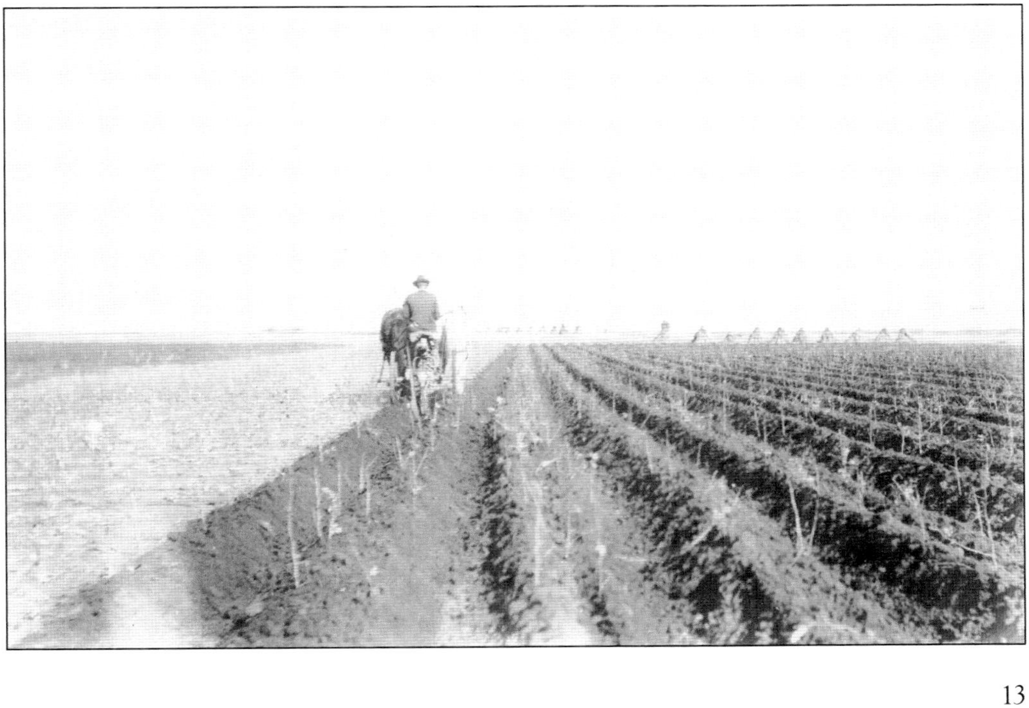

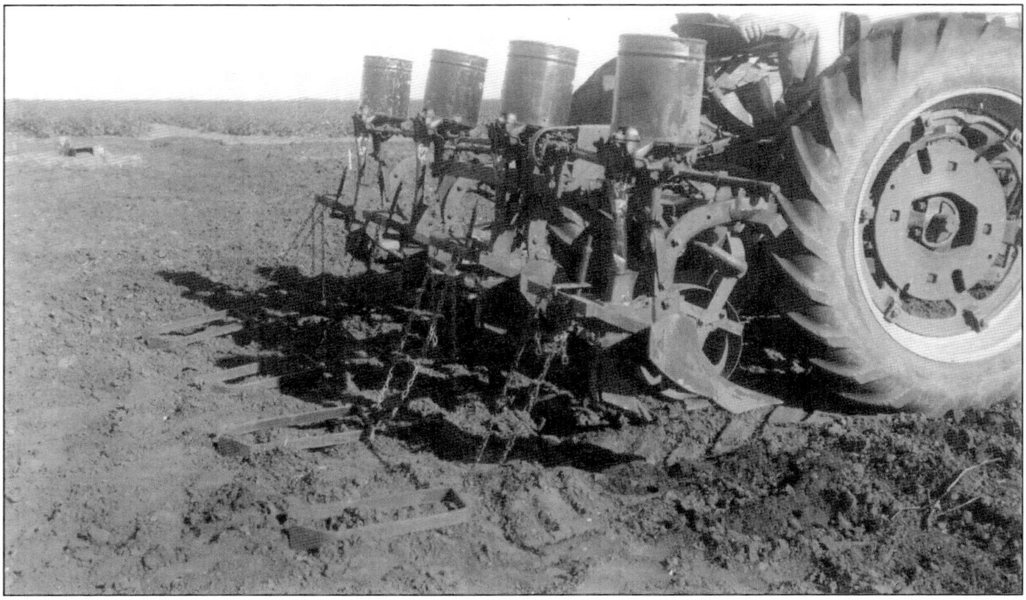

By 1948, when the above photograph was taken, improvements made in agricultural technology had given rise to the use of tractors. The four-row lister planter and homemade chisel-covering units are mounted on the back of this tractor. In one pass, the lister prepared the soil for the seed, the planter planted the seed, and the covering unit covered the seed. Below, a four-row cotton planter with attached lister is in operation. One function of the hollow iron rectangle dragged behind the planter was to cover the tracks of the tractor. (Both photographs Courtesy of the Texas AgriLife Research and Extension Center – Lubbock, Texas.)

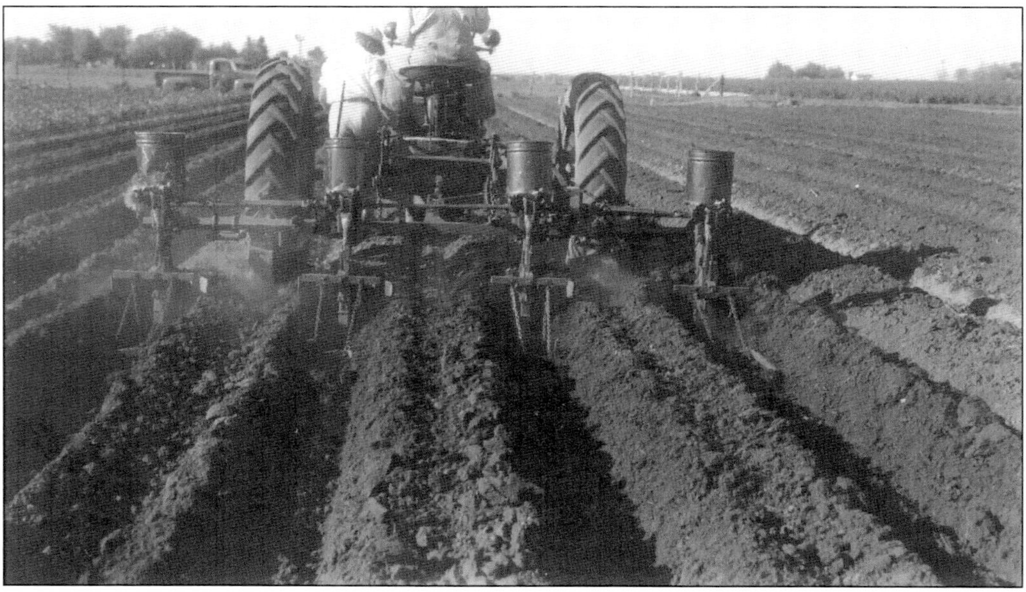

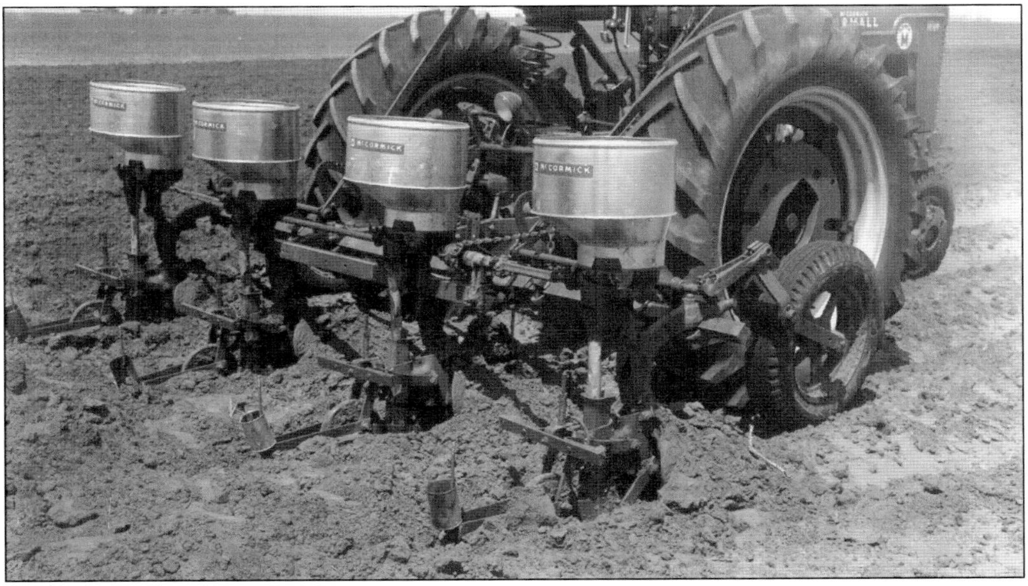

Agricultural mechanization continued to improve, and by 1953, the four-row planter rig with one-inch-by-ten-inch hollow rubber-tire press wheels added to the efficiency of the planter. Adjusted properly, the press wheels aided in the germination of the cottonseed by compressing the soil over the cottonseed at the proper level. (Courtesy of the Texas AgriLife Research and Extension Center – Lubbock, Texas.)

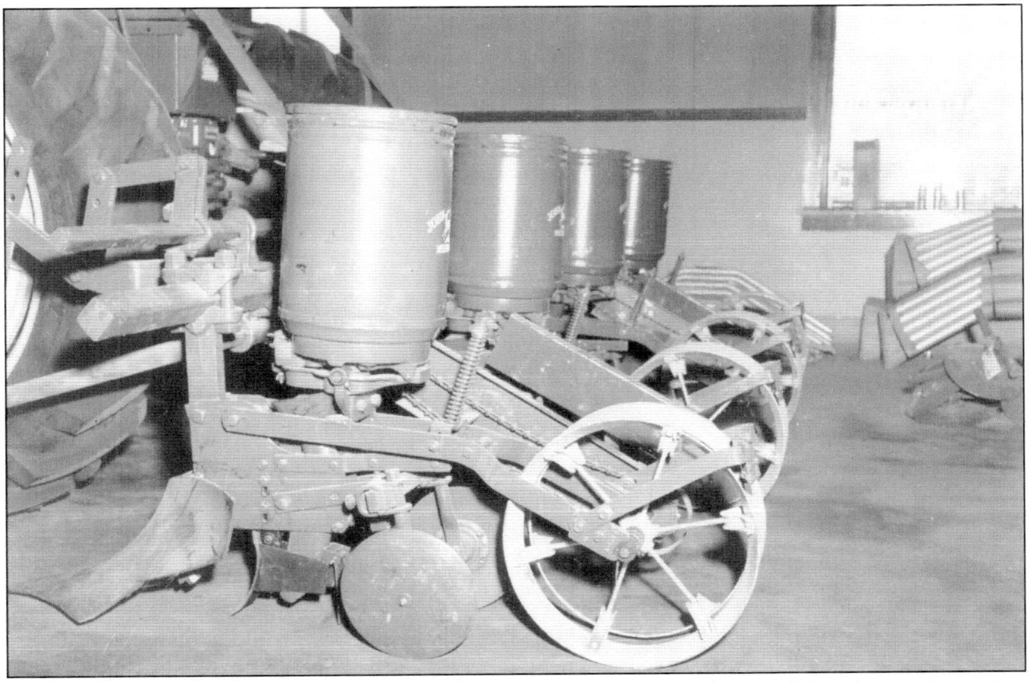

In 1954, John Deere engineers developed a four-row planter with redesigned chisel-covering units, as opposed to the homemade chisel model in 1948. Technological improvements to farm machinery were often helped by more powerful tractors, as seen here. Also, take note of the improved lister blades for planting and covering seeds. (Courtesy of the Texas AgriLife Research and Extension Center – Lubbock, Texas.)

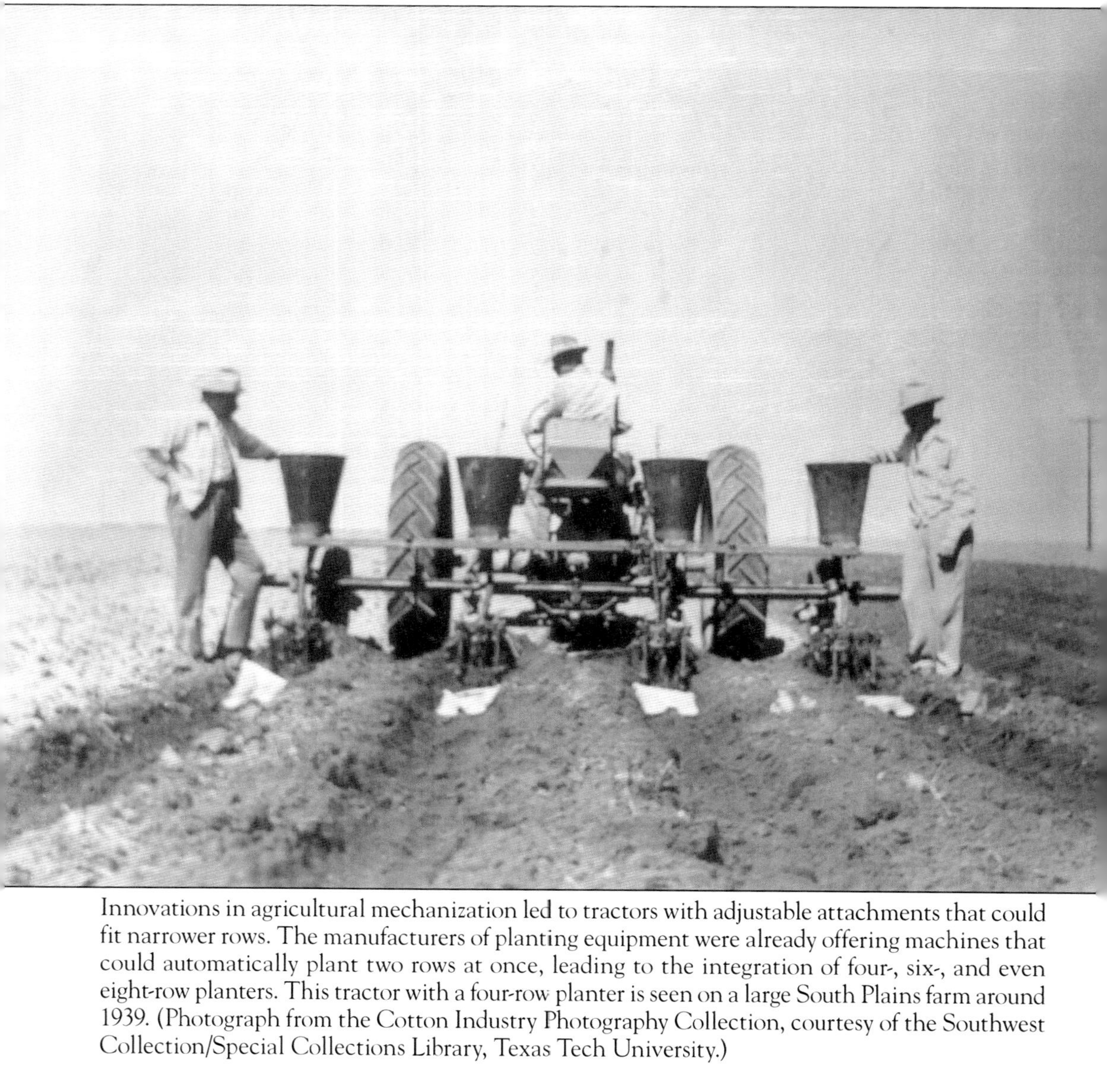

Innovations in agricultural mechanization led to tractors with adjustable attachments that could fit narrower rows. The manufacturers of planting equipment were already offering machines that could automatically plant two rows at once, leading to the integration of four-, six-, and even eight-row planters. This tractor with a four-row planter is seen on a large South Plains farm around 1939. (Photograph from the Cotton Industry Photography Collection, courtesy of the Southwest Collection/Special Collections Library, Texas Tech University.)

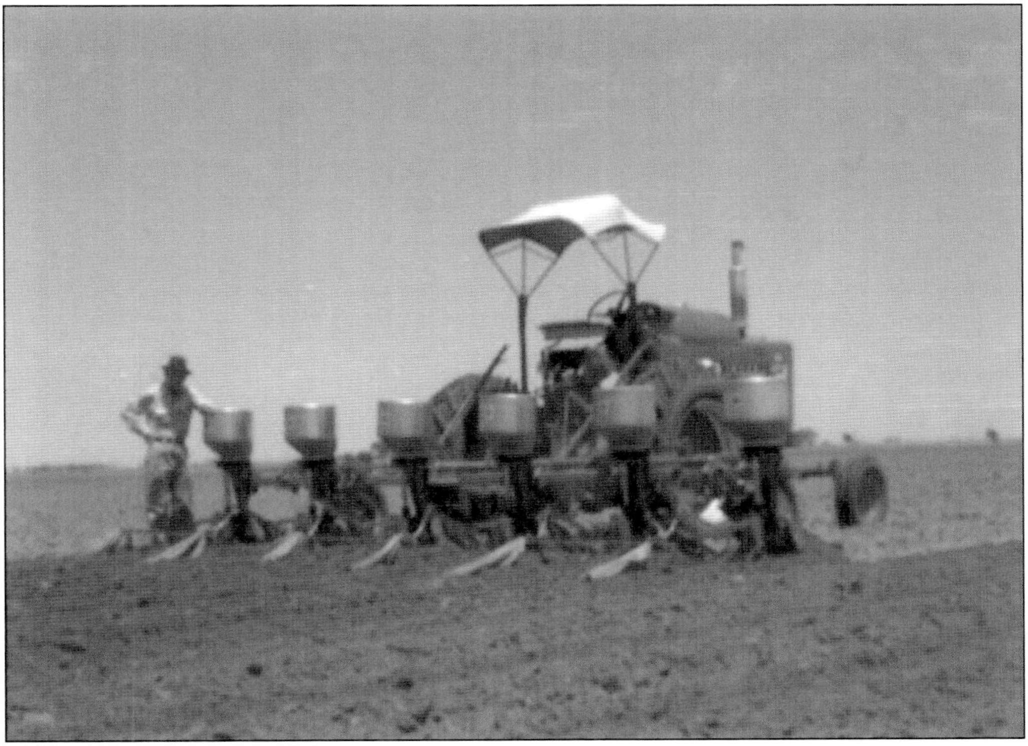

Planting in a conventional manner required the farmer to sow in a field previously plowed and disked. This farmer takes a break from planting in May 1965. He is using a six-row International planter and tractor. As tractors became more powerful, farmers could use bigger equipment like this six-row planter. (Courtesy of Carol and Powell Adams.)

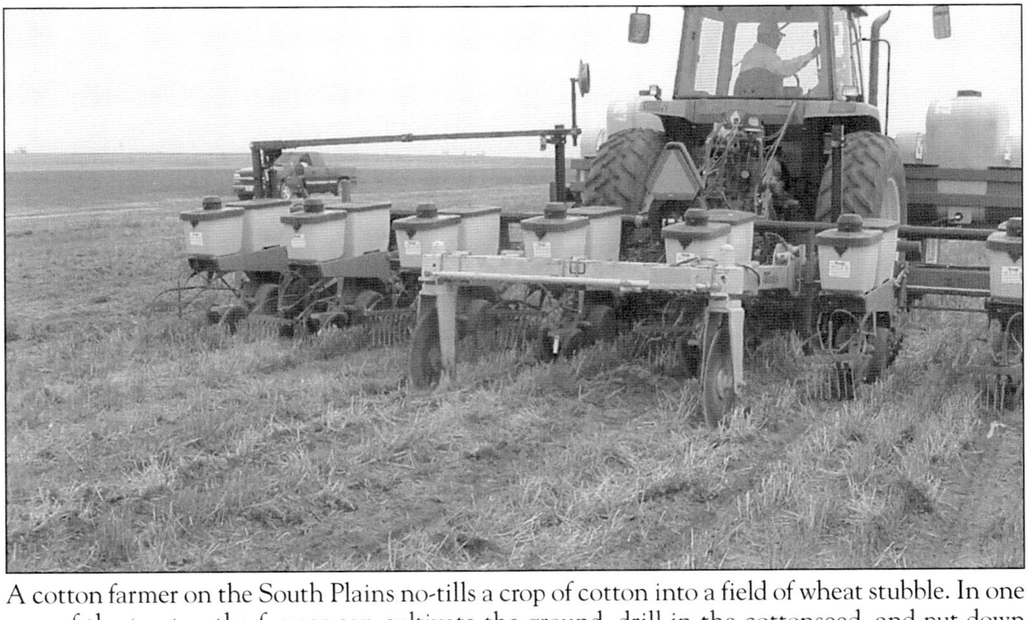

A cotton farmer on the South Plains no-tills a crop of cotton into a field of wheat stubble. In one pass of the tractor, the farmer can cultivate the ground, drill in the cottonseed, and put down herbicide and fertilizer. No-till preserves the topsoil and allows the farmer to rotate his crops without plowing the field. (Courtesy of Dan Taylor.)

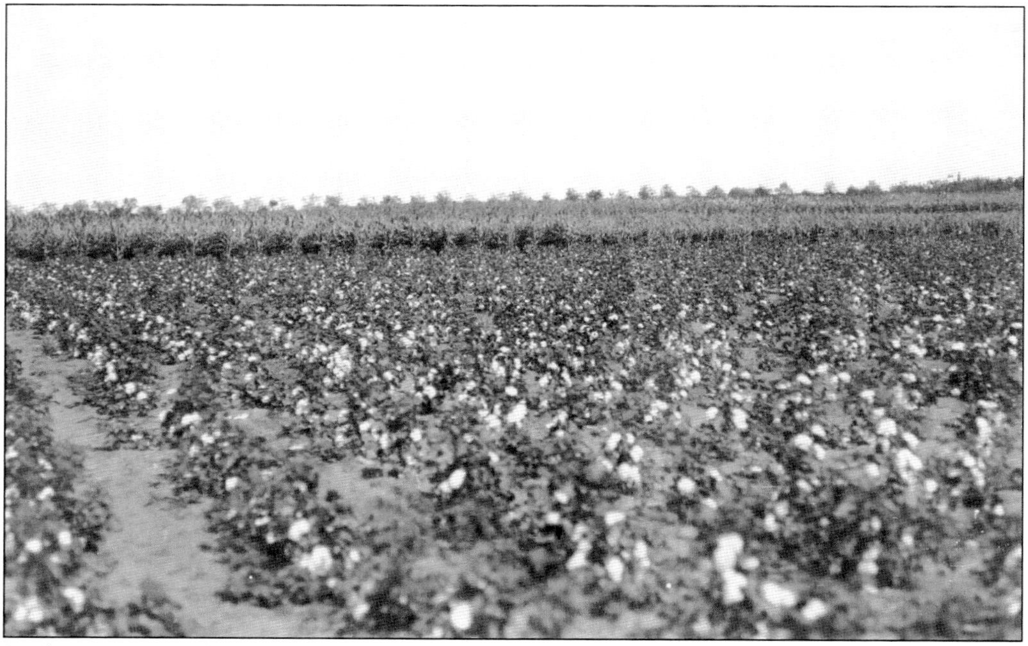

In this 1924 test plot, cotton is blooming 110 days after planting. Grown at the experimental station outside of Lubbock, the cotton seems to be evenly spaced and of good quality but very low to the ground. The quality of the cotton fiber is dependent on how soon it is stripped after opening. (Courtesy of the Texas AgriLife Research and Extension Center – Lubbock, Texas.)

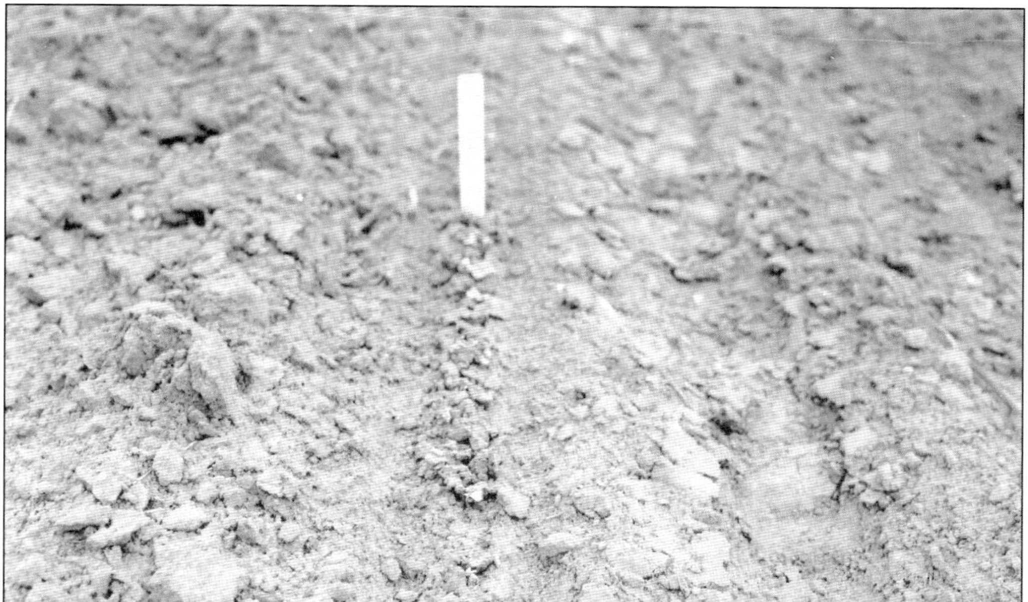

Cotton plants emerge at the Lubbock experimental station after they were planted with a lister planter in 1957. Cotton plants normally emerge nine to fifteen days after planting, depending on soil temperature and moisture. A properly designed and used lister planter will speed the rate of germination. (Courtesy of the Texas AgriLife Research and Extension Center – Lubbock, Texas.)

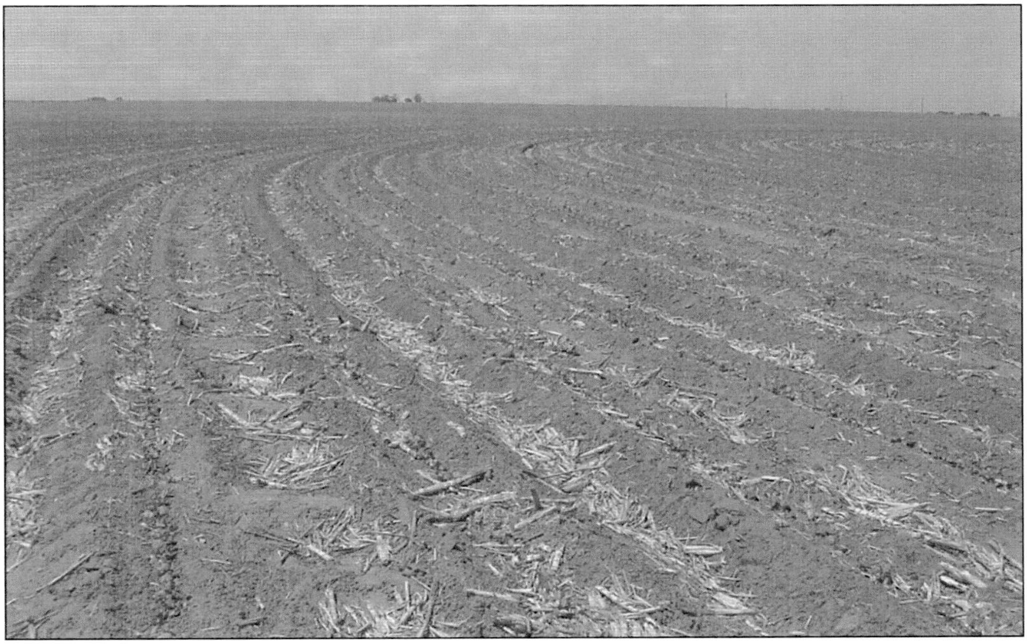

A no-tilled cotton crop, planted into a field that was in milo the previous year, makes a promising start. The milo stubble may help shelter the young, tender cotton plants in their first 40 days of life. Looking closely, one can see dikes, or depressions, dug into every other row, another innovation of the time. (Courtesy of Dan Taylor.)

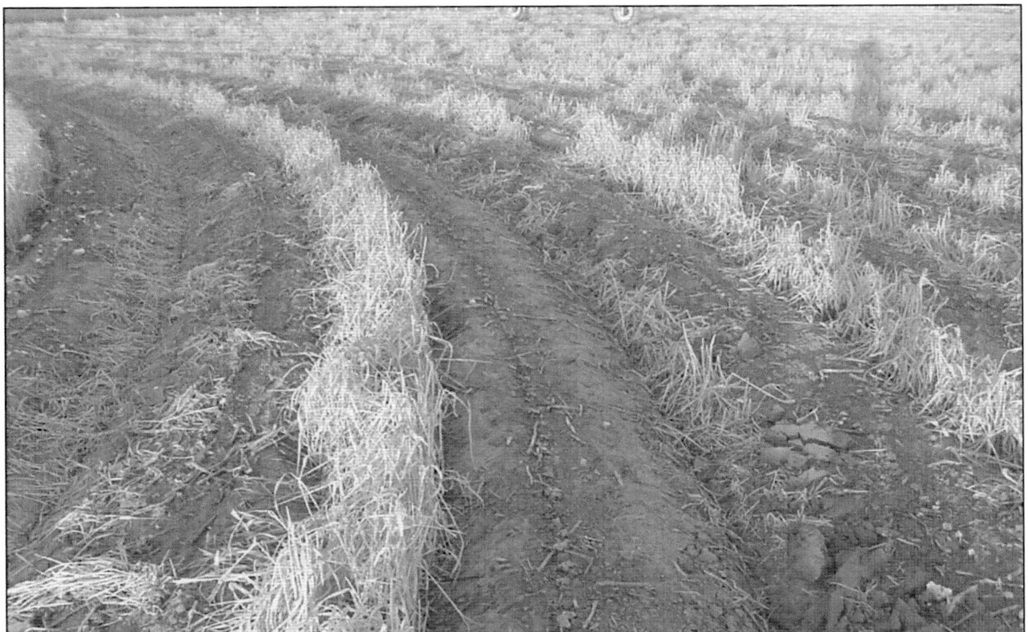

Young cotton plants break ground in a field in Lubbock County. The cotton was drilled—not tilled—into a field of smalls grains. The stubble will protect the young plants from the wind that blows sand and dirt across the field. As the plants grow, the stubble will decompose and return to the soil from which it came. (Courtesy of Dan Taylor.)

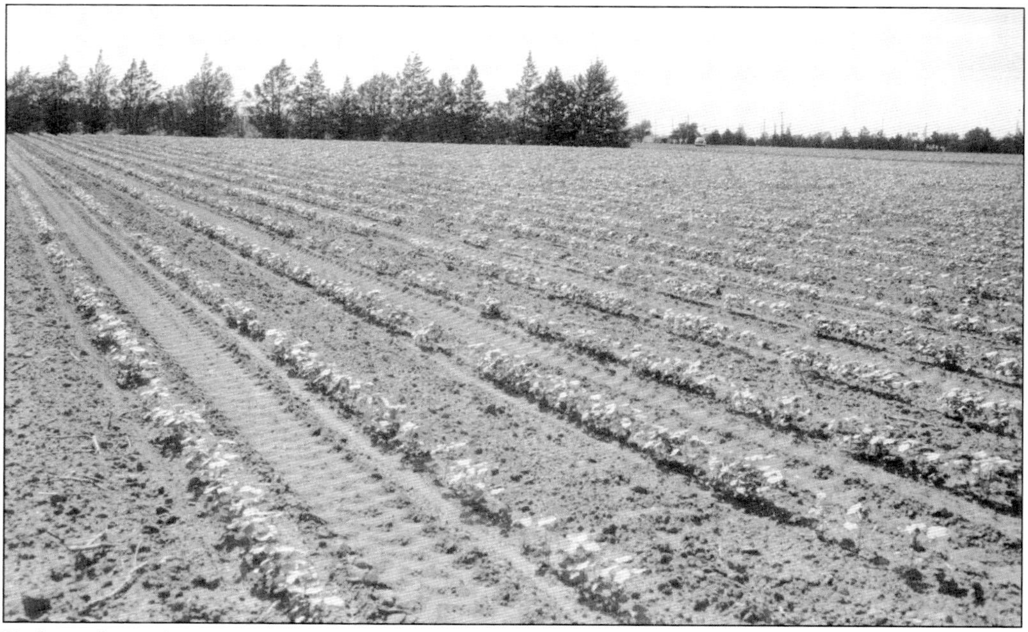

Early in the 1954 growing season, a field of cotton makes a promising start. Although not planted into a field, which was listed and furrowed, the trees at the head of the rows will serve as a windbreak on the blustery South Plains. Furrowed fields on the South Plains helped to reduce wind erosion. (Courtesy of the Texas AgriLife Research and Extension Center – Lubbock, Texas.)

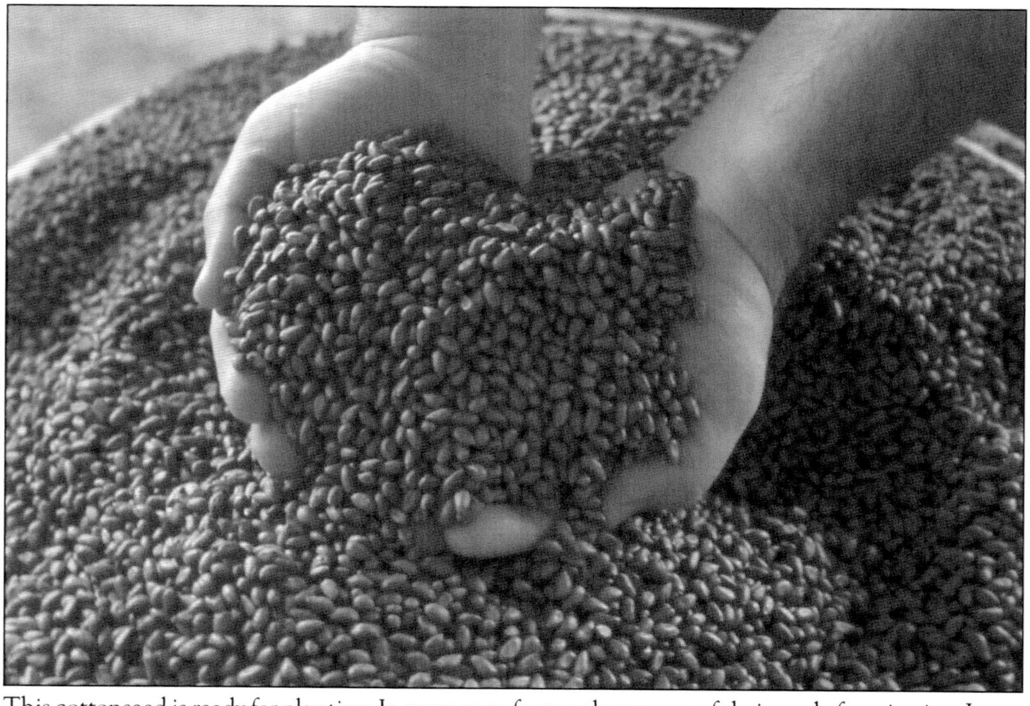

This cottonseed is ready for planting. In years past, farmers kept some of their seed after ginning. Later, seed was purchased as new varieties came to market. Today's high cost of cottonseed is not so much because of the seed itself, but because of the cost of the patent rights to each variety. (Photograph by Lynette Thompson Wilson, courtesy of Plains Cotton Cooperative Association.)

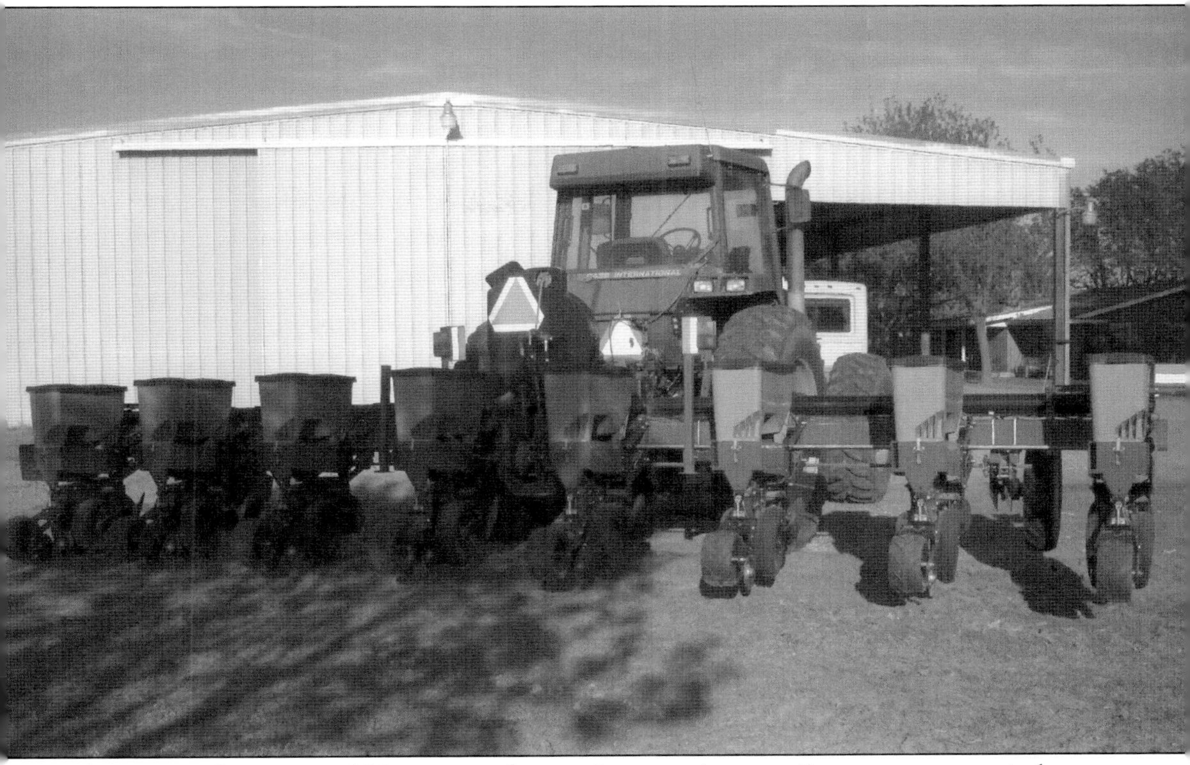

This is a new International Harvester eight-row planter and tractor. For a more economical use while planting, fertilizer was applied in the rows beneath the cottonseed. When the newly sprouted cotton sent roots down into the soil, it would reach the area where the fertilizer was spread, giving an added boost to the young plants. (Courtesy of Carol and Powell Adams.)

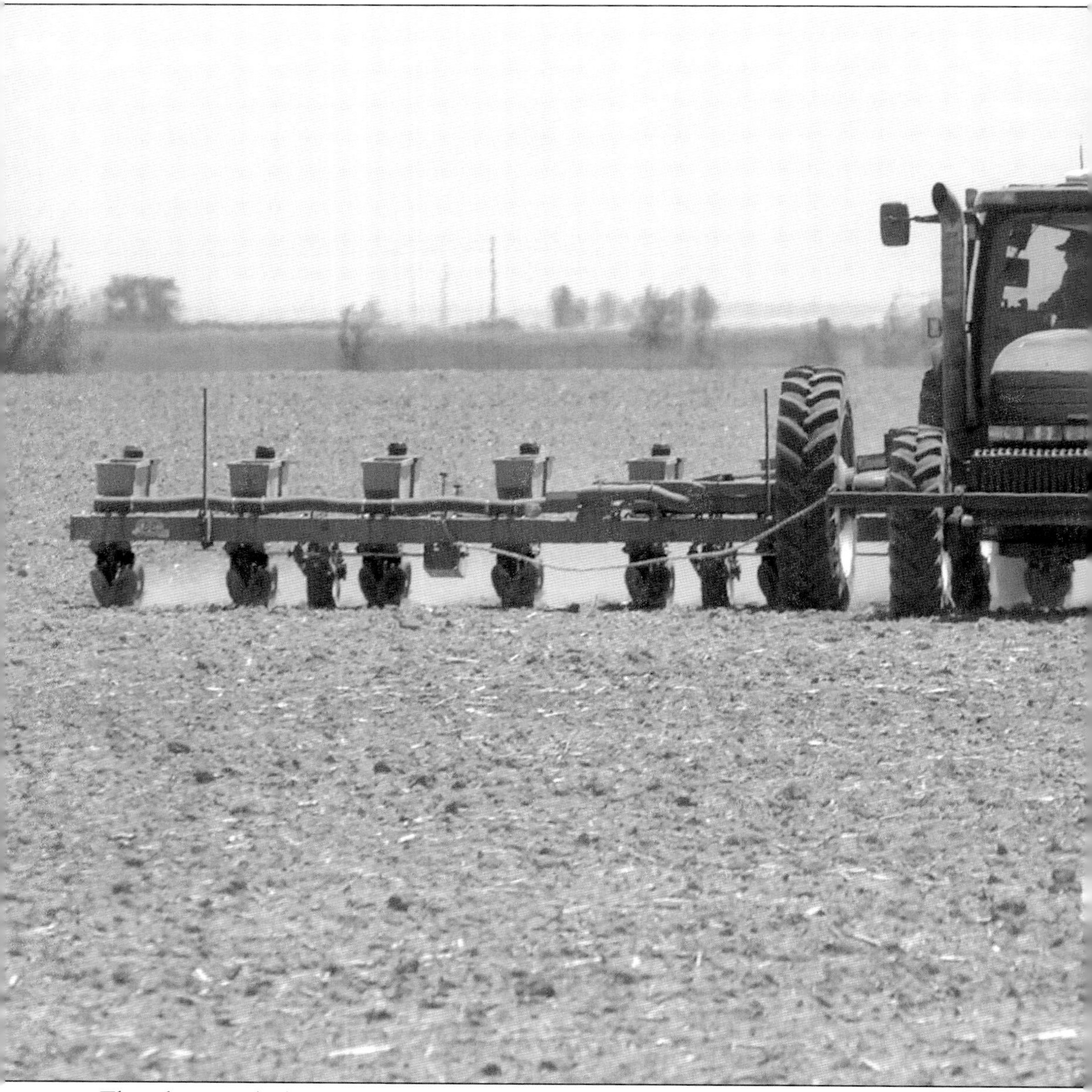

This photograph shows a Case IH MX285 tractor pulling a 16-row planter across the field. It takes a lot of horsepower to pull this much equipment, and this Case tractor has it—285, to be exact. The tandem rear wheels help, as four rear wheels give the tractor added traction. As the

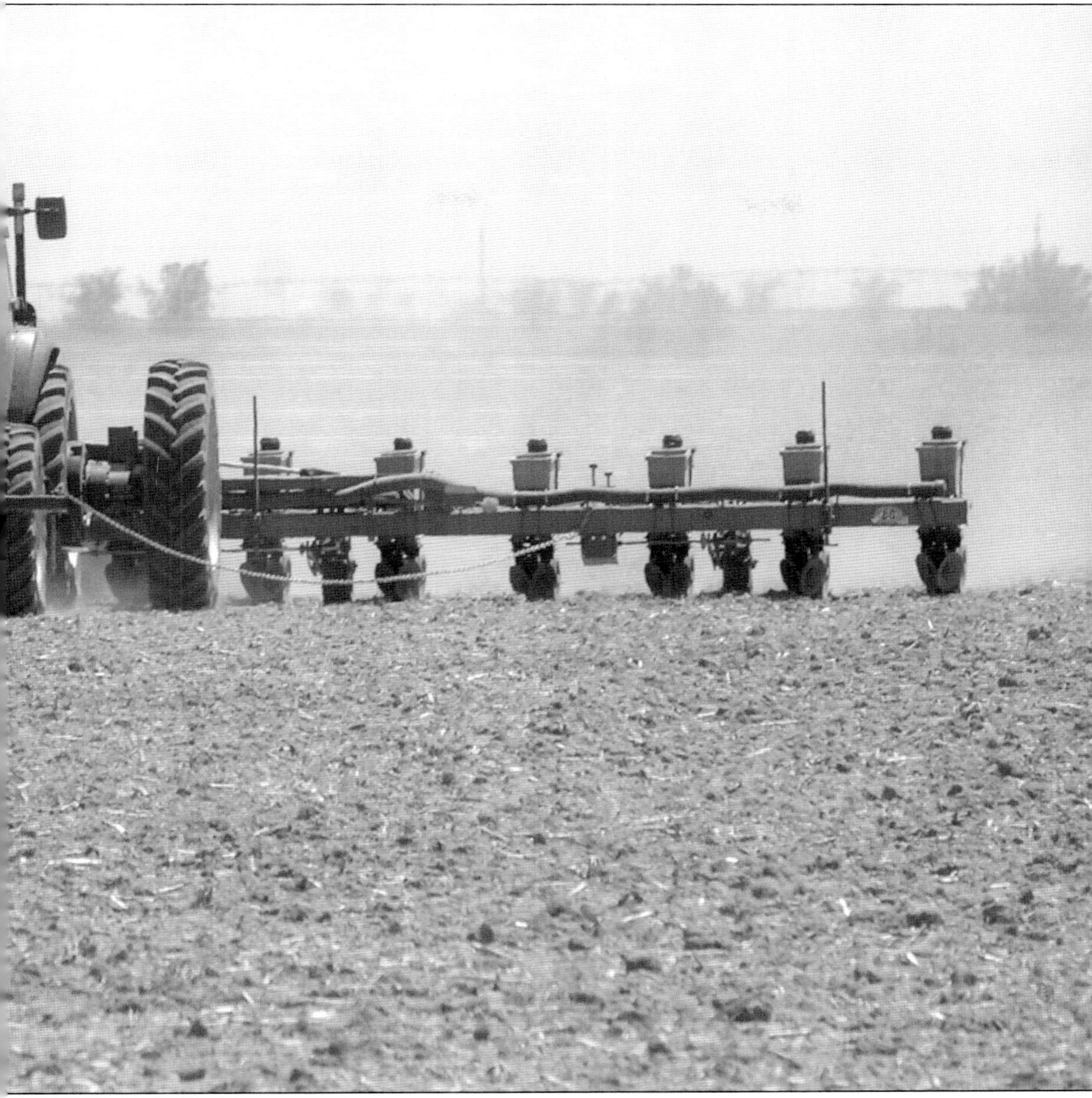

tractor and equipment get heavier, compaction of the soil becomes an issue, but a tractor this big pulling a 16-row planter can plant up to 20 acres per hour. (Photograph by Richard Porter, courtesy *Plainview Daily Herald*.)

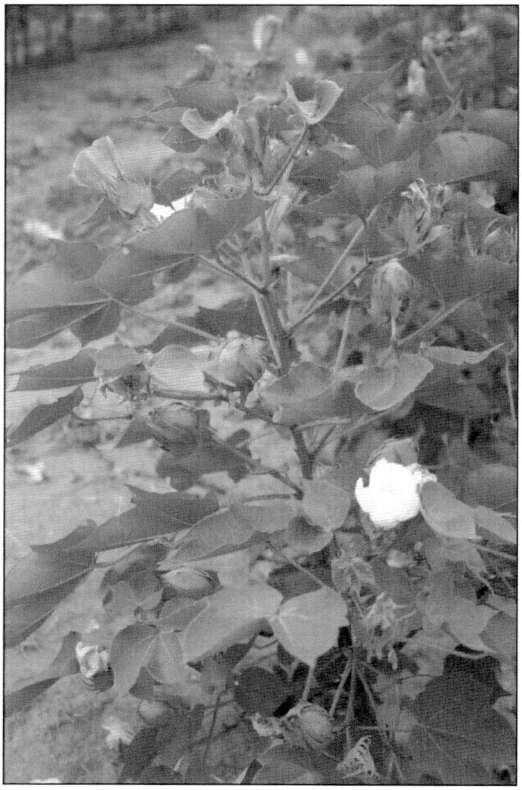

When cotton starts to blossom, its first color is a pale yellow, but it quickly turns a soft pink and ends up a bright dark pink (see top of plant). When the blooms dry up and fall off, they expose a walnut-sized boll underneath (see bottom of plant). (Photograph by Lynette Thompson Wilson, courtesy of Plains Cotton Cooperative Association.)

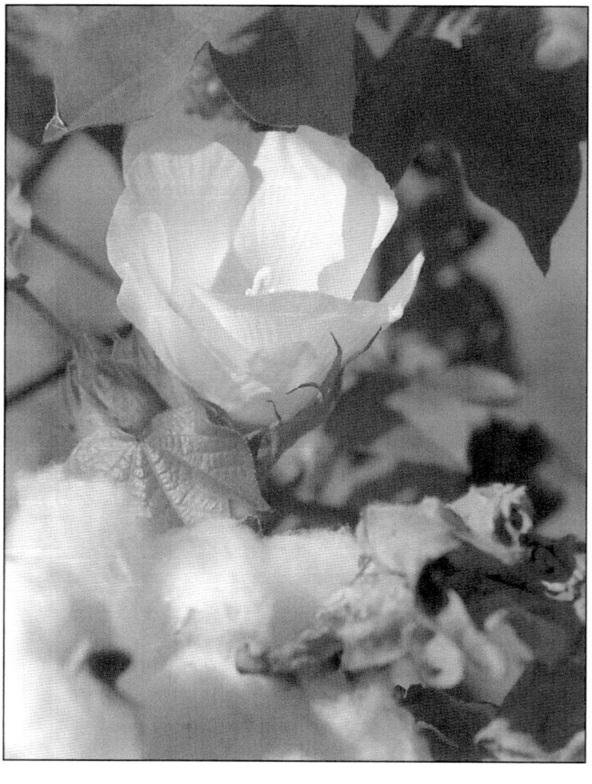

A single cotton plant shows the life cycle of a cotton flower as it turns into a boll. First, the cotton plant produces a flower, which later dries up and falls off, revealing a boll. Finally, the boll ripens, showing the lint within. As seen here, blooming on a cotton plant usually begins at the bottom and works it way up the plant. (Photograph by Richard Porter.)

Two
CULTIVATION

In the past, cultivation of cotton took place before the cotton was planted and continued up until the cotton was too high to get through with a tractor and cultivator. Today, modern herbicides and improved cultivating equipment have lessened the number of trips across a field to prepare it for planting, saving the farmer time and money.

Great care must be taken to ready the field for planting, since cotton is a notoriously finicky plant when it is young. If the ground is not prepared correctly, the young cotton plants will have difficulty breaking through the soil and not live past 40 days. A thin crop or one with gaps in it could be the result of poor preparation of the soil.

After planting, care must be taken to prevent the soil from crusting over, keeping air and water out of the topsoil and increasing the chances the cotton seedlings will be killed by blowing sand. Sand fighters up to 16 rows across break up the topsoil, lessening the chance that blowing sand or dirt will harm the young cotton plants.

With the advent of modern herbicides, irrigation, and insecticides, most cotton today does not see a tractor passing it by regularly. If conditions remain favorable, only one trip through the field may be required.

Traditionally, cotton was thought to require constant cultivation to keep the soil open for air and water and to cover weeds that competed with the cotton for nutrients and sunlight. With modern equipment, agrichemicals, irrigated water, and to a lesser extent, the cotton itself, cotton farmers can produce a crop of cotton with minimum cultivation. In fact, with the advent of no-till cotton and round-up-ready cotton, only one pass through the field may be necessary—when it is planted.

So, if the cotton has been planted on time and at the right depth and spacing, and if it has been tended by the farmer, it is probably getting a great start in its young life. Now, all it needs is time, a little water, and lots of sunlight to make a crop.

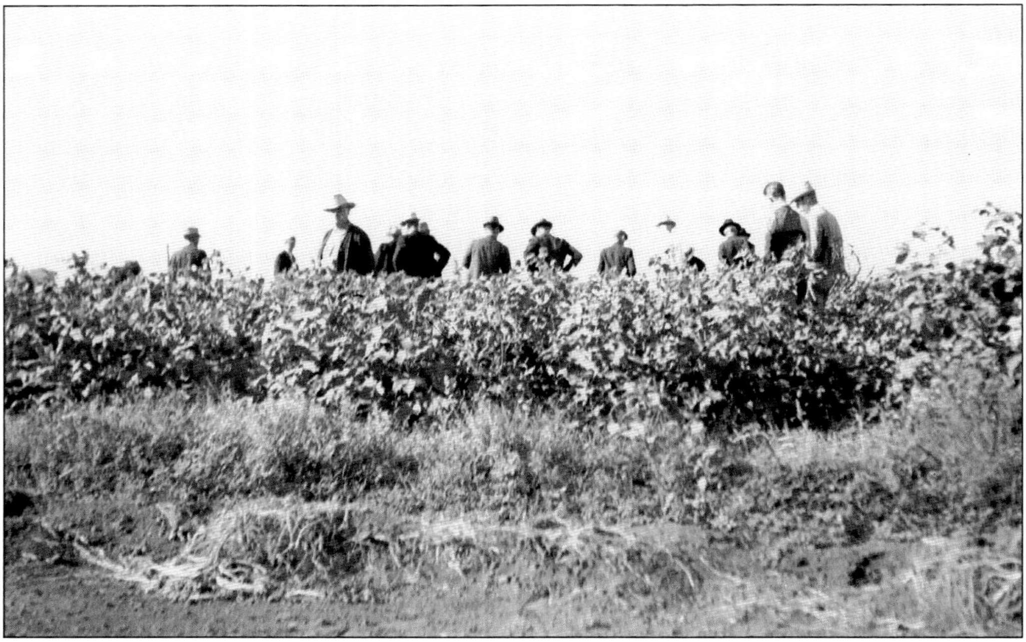

During the Depression years of the 1930s, the federal government helped cotton farmers in numerous ways. In these two images, the Crosby County agricultural extension agent holds a field day in 1938, in which area farmers inspect a new, more productive variety of cotton. Field days also allowed farmers to inspect new techniques, like contour plowing, or new technologies, such as improved irrigation equipment. County agents became a source for new and improved farming techniques, as the federal government not only helped disseminate new ideas but also helped develop them. (Both photographs courtesy of the Floyd County Historical Museum.)

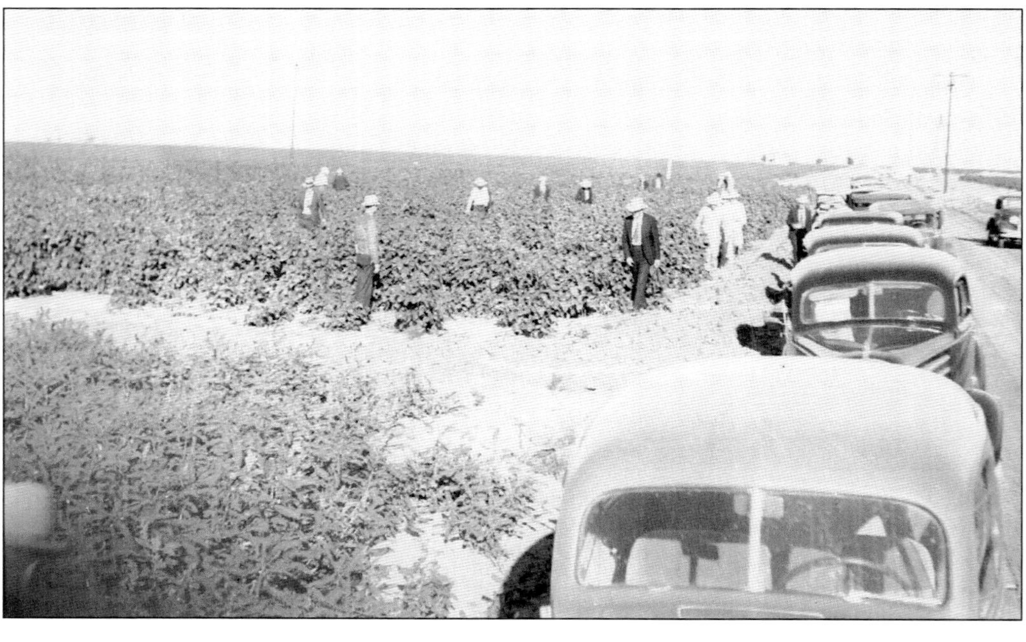

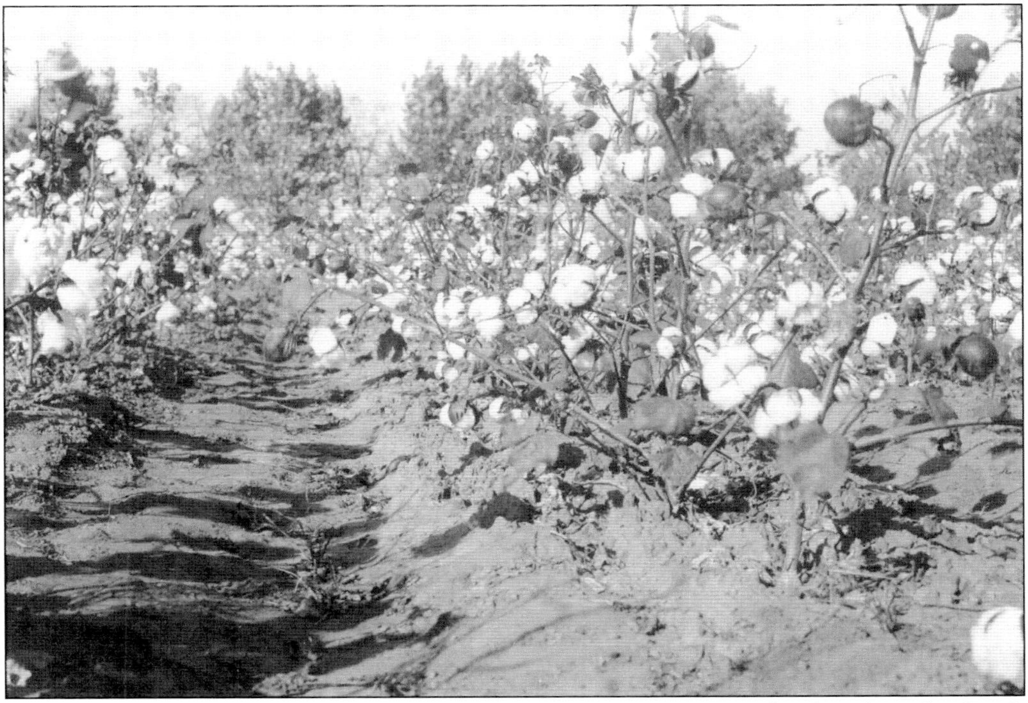

Through careful genetic selection, improved varieties of cotton were developed on the South Plains. Here, a variety of cotton named for its developer, Hynek Macha, a Czechoslovakian immigrant, demonstrates its ability to hold on to its cotton. The bolls of Macha cotton do not open very wide and became known on the South Plains as storm-proof cotton. (Courtesy of the Texas AgriLife Research and Extension Center – Lubbock, Texas.)

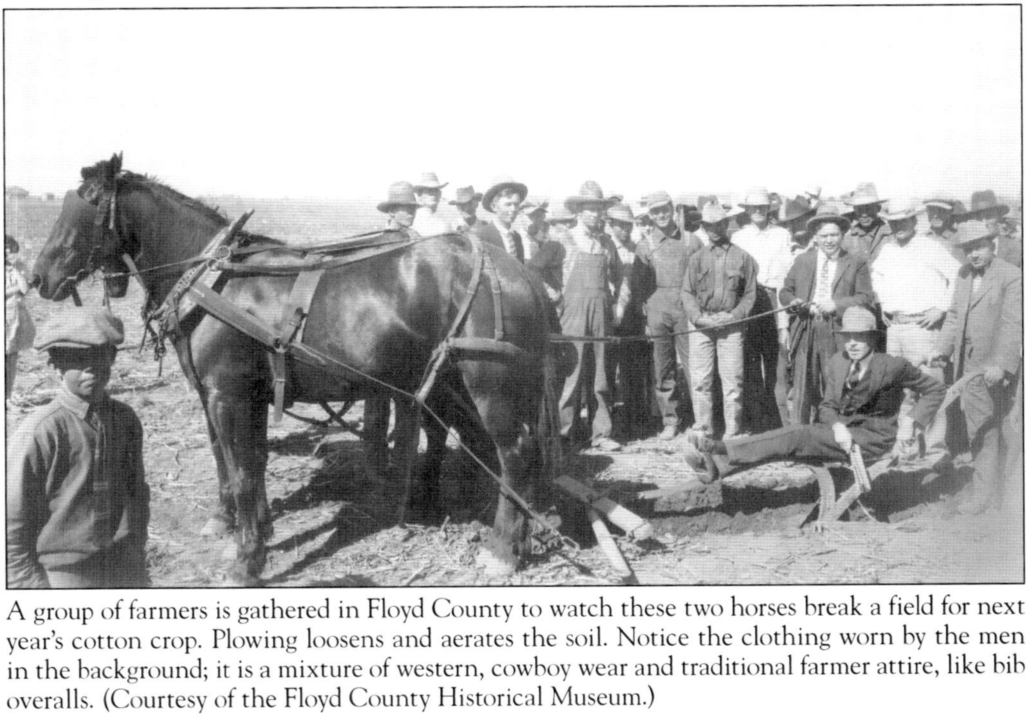

A group of farmers is gathered in Floyd County to watch these two horses break a field for next year's cotton crop. Plowing loosens and aerates the soil. Notice the clothing worn by the men in the background; it is a mixture of western, cowboy wear and traditional farmer attire, like bib overalls. (Courtesy of the Floyd County Historical Museum.)

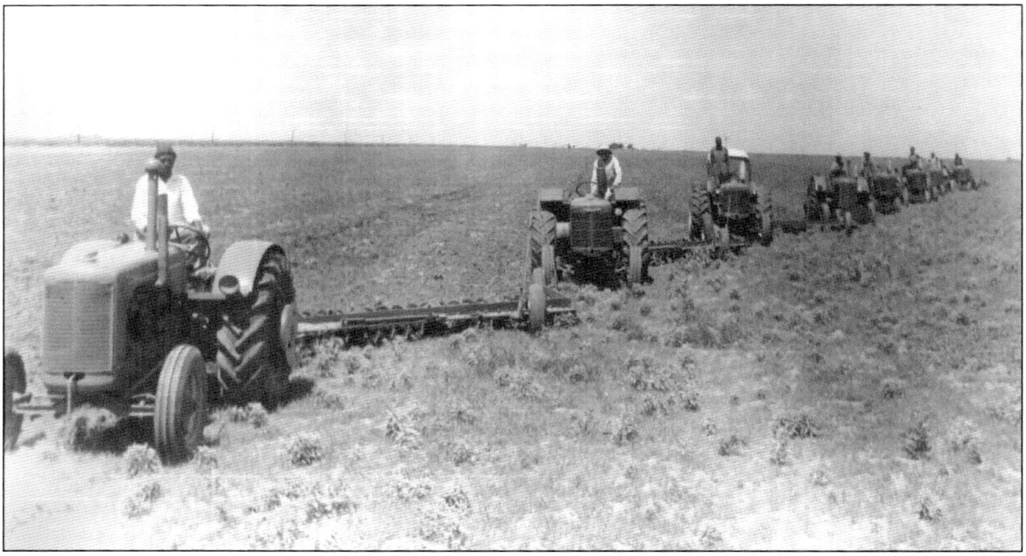

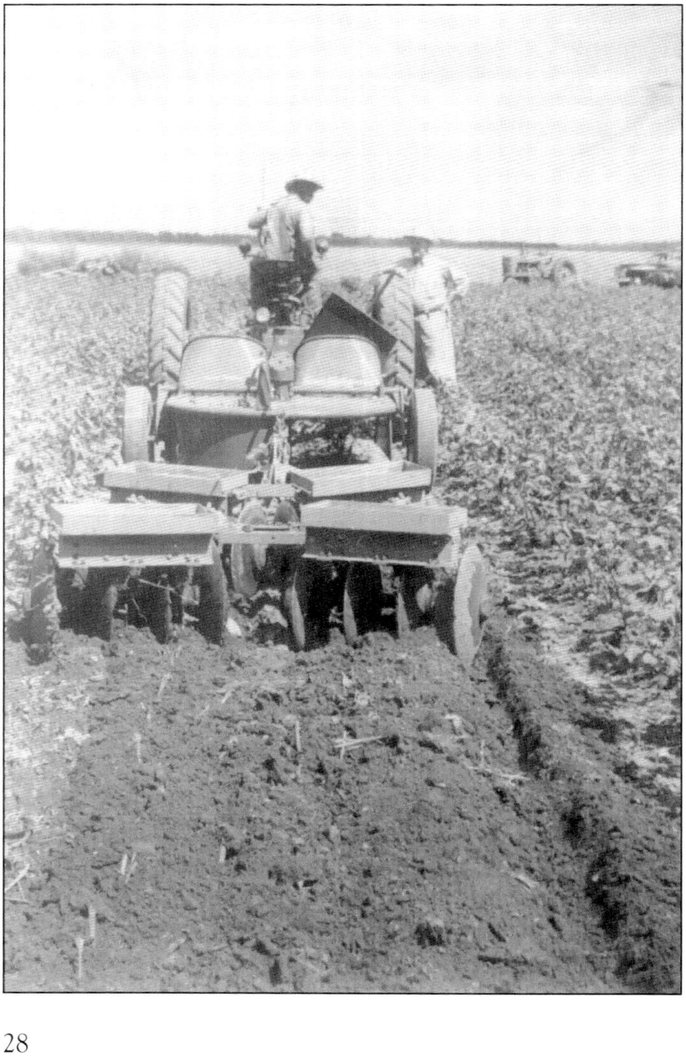

The one-way plow was designed by Henry Krauss in 1916. It was a conservation tillage tool designed to leave crop residue on the soil surface, which helped fight wind erosion. The one-way plow cuts into the ground, throwing the soil in one direction. This image shows eight tractors in one field. (Courtesy of the Floyd County Historical Museum.)

This tractor cuts stalks with a tandem disc as it tears up cotton bolls and other crop residues. Shredding and disking destroys boll weevils and other pests in the standing cotton stalks. Methods such as this are simple and economical and prevent pests from attacking next year's crop. (Photograph from the Cotton Industry Photography Collection, courtesy of the Southwest Collection/Special Collections Library, Texas Tech University.)

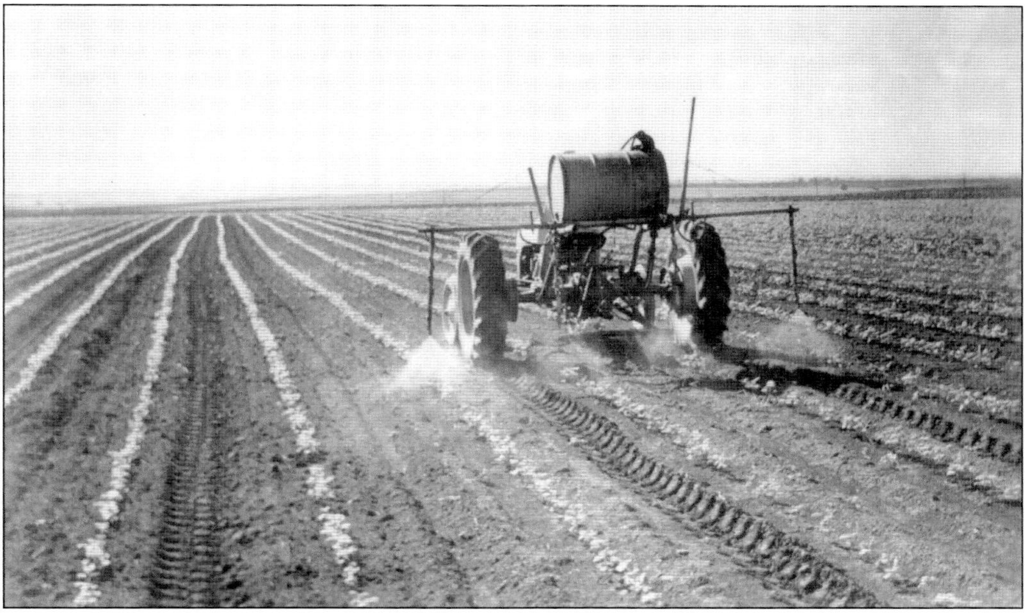

According to experts, the first 40 days are the most critical period in cotton production. The cotton plant needs to be free from stress, diseases, weeds, and insects. Spraying at the appropriate time is crucial. This farmer applies early-season chemicals using rudimentary spraying equipment around 1950. (Photograph from the Cotton Industry Photography Collection, courtesy of the Southwest Collection/Special Collections Library, Texas Tech University.)

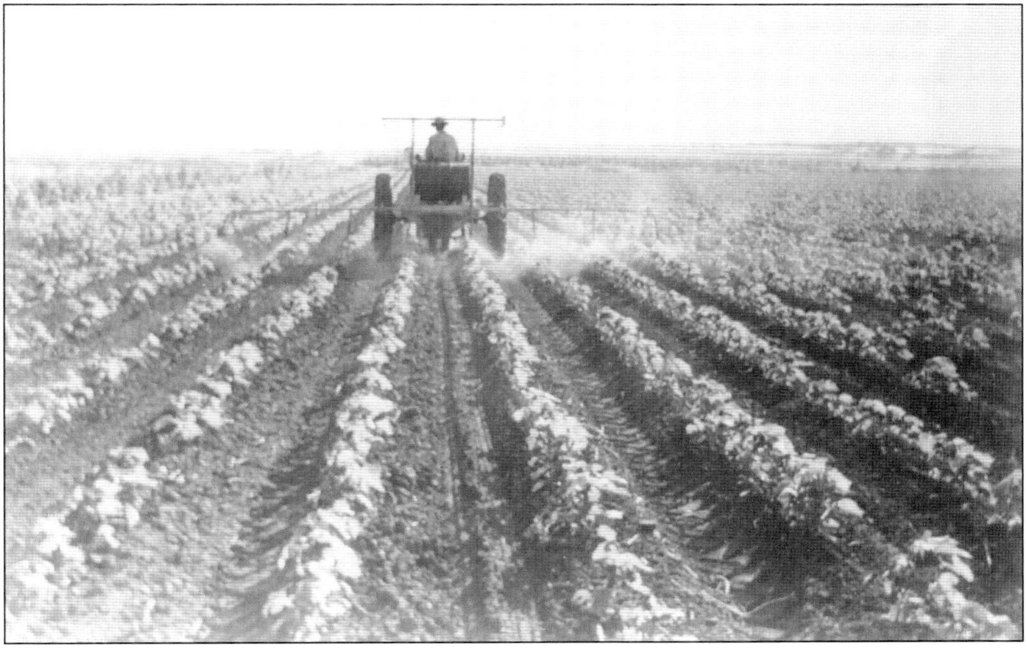

When using chemicals to spray cotton plants for insect control, atmospheric conditions are important. This image shows what happens when spraying or dusting is done when it is too windy. Adjusting the level of the spray boom helps, but the wind speed and direction determine the dispersion pattern of the chemicals. (Photograph from the Cotton Industry Photography Collection, courtesy of the Southwest Collection/Special Collections Library, Texas Tech University.)

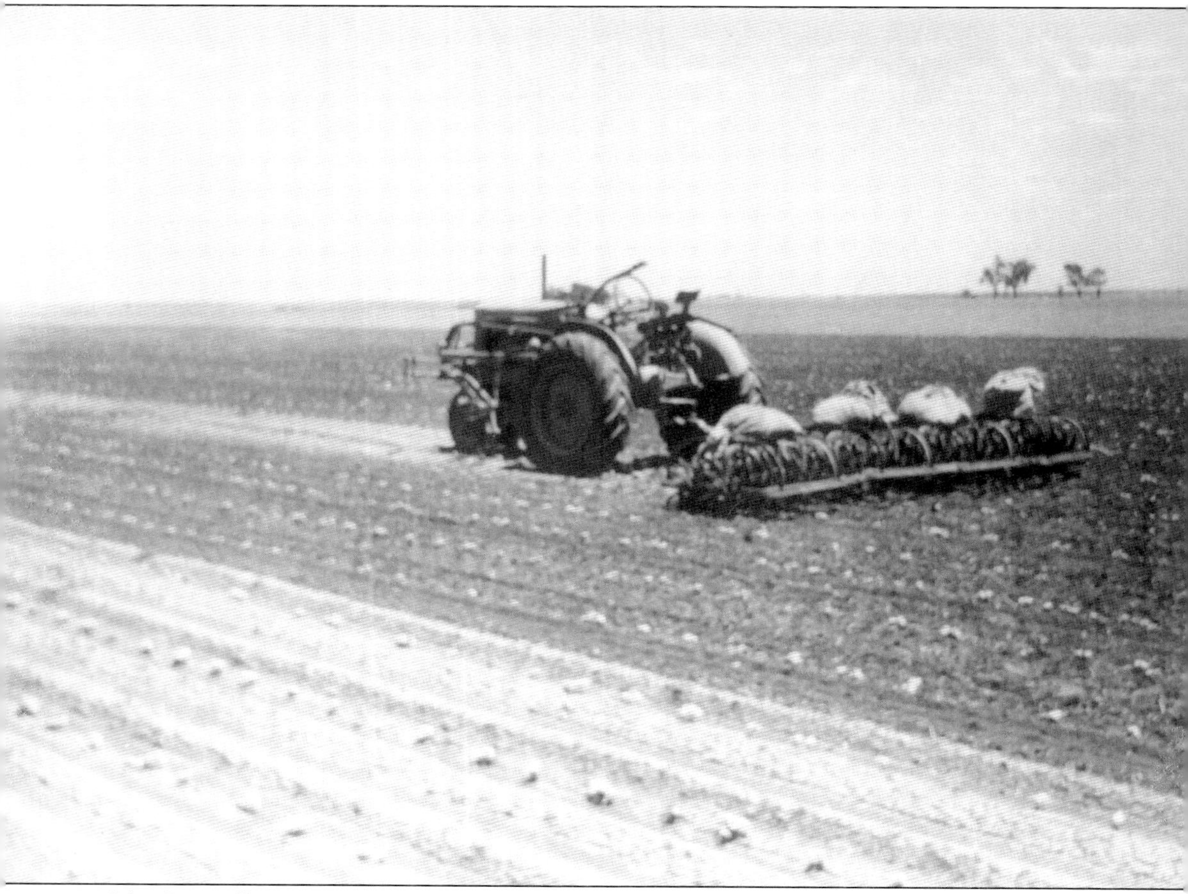

This Farmall tractor is attached to a four-row cultivator that is not only covering weeds but is functioning as a sand fighter as well, by opening the soil to moisture and air. The bags placed evenly along the cultivator probably are there to help hold it down, forcing it deeper into the ground. (Photograph from the Cotton Industry Photography Collection, courtesy of the Southwest Collection/Special Collections Library, Texas Tech University.)

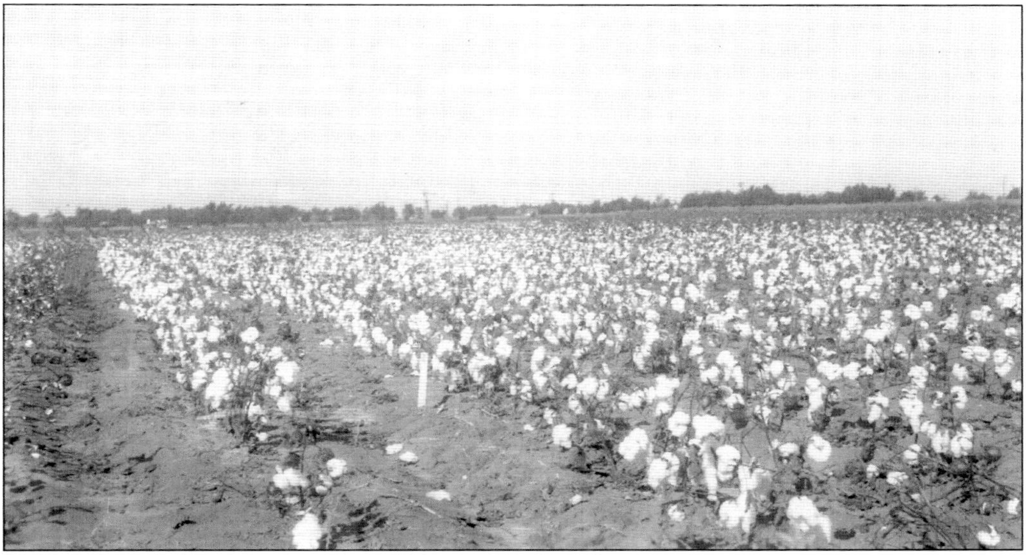

The art and science of defoliation—the removal of leaves—is an important management practice that determines both the quality and quantity of the cotton yield by removing the unwanted leaves before stripping. Various chemicals are used, such as the cyanamide dust in this 1944 image. Defoliants were dusted on before the advent of spraying. (Courtesy of the Texas AgriLife Research and Extension Center – Lubbock, Texas.)

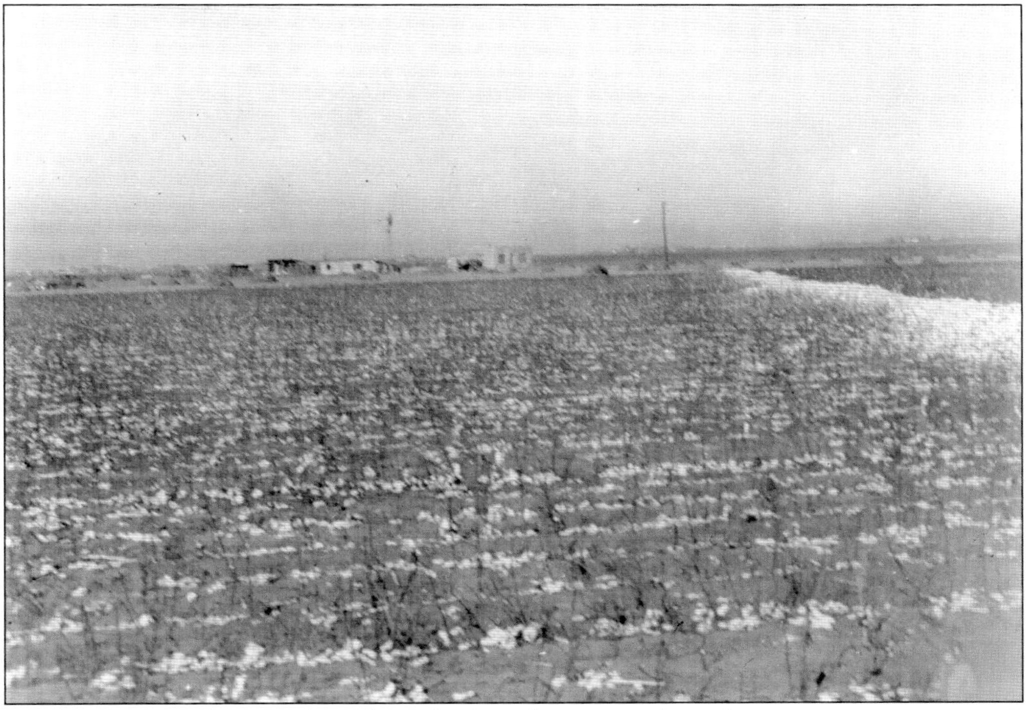

Mother Nature can be unpredictable. In the days when meteorological science was more guesswork than science, cotton farmers had little advance notice of changes in the weather. This 1944 image from near Anton, Texas, shows a field ruined by a hailstorm. Note the damaged cotton plants and the cotton lying on the ground. (Courtesy of the Texas AgriLife Research and Extension Center – Lubbock, Texas.)

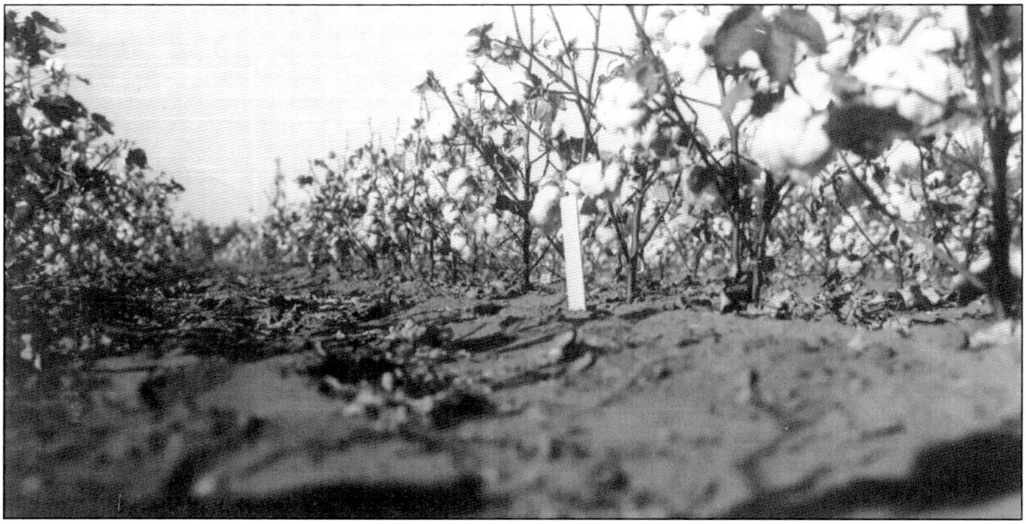

The height of the cotton plant's first boll from the ground (see ruler) begins to draw the attention of plant breeders, as this 1947 image demonstrates. Cotton bolls farther away from the ground stay cleaner, are graded higher, make more money for the farmer, and are easier for harvesting equipment to strip. (Courtesy of the Texas AgriLife Research and Extension Center – Lubbock, Texas.)

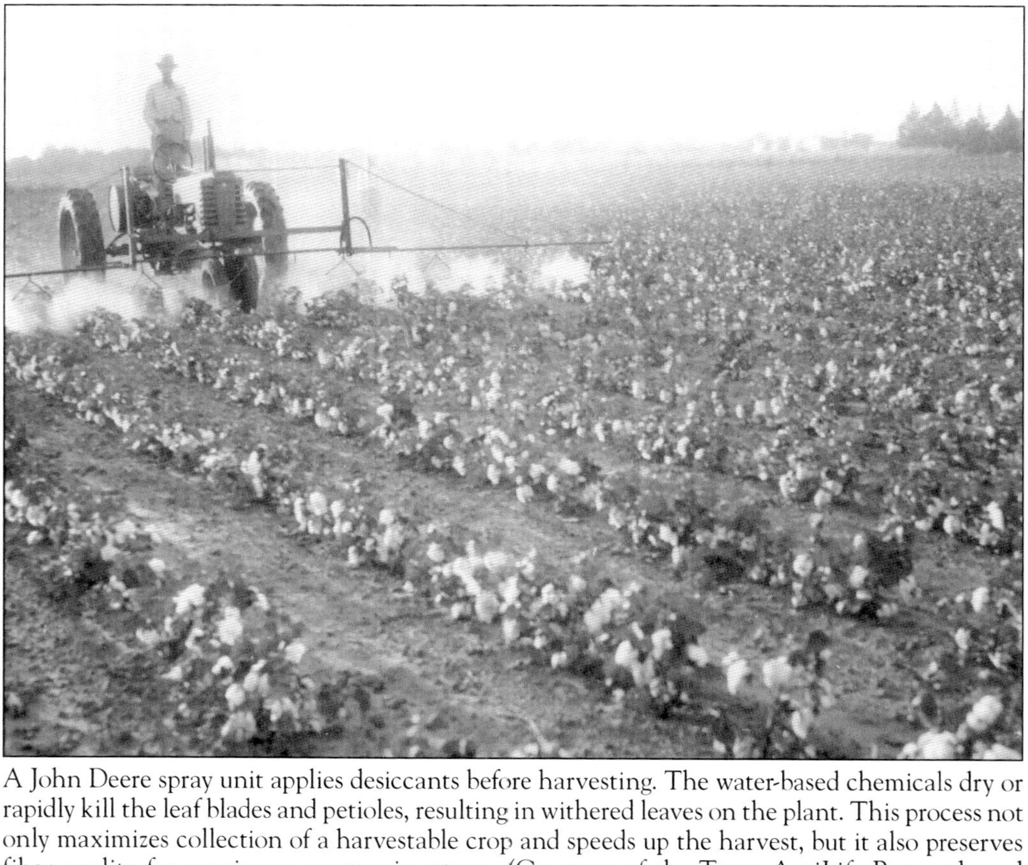

A John Deere spray unit applies desiccants before harvesting. The water-based chemicals dry or rapidly kill the leaf blades and petioles, resulting in withered leaves on the plant. This process not only maximizes collection of a harvestable crop and speeds up the harvest, but it also preserves fiber quality for maximum economic return. (Courtesy of the Texas AgriLife Research and Extension Center – Lubbock, Texas.)

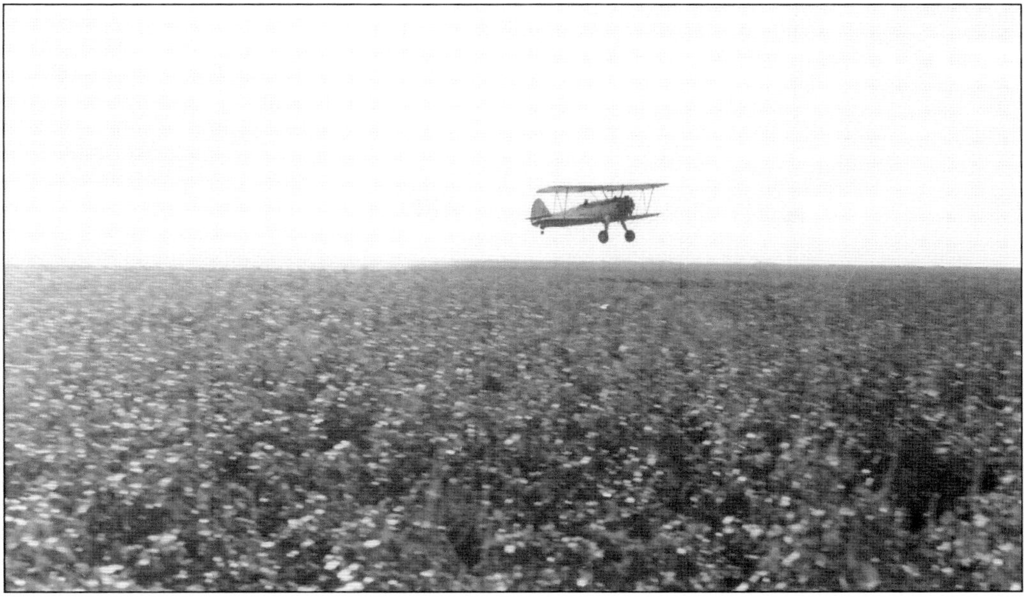

A crop duster flies over a Lubbock County farm around 1950 applying defoliants—note the open cotton bolls in the background. Although an expensive way to apply agricultural chemicals, sometimes crop dusters were the only way a farmer could catch up after extensive weather-related delays, problems with equipment, or the lack of farmworkers. (Courtesy of the Texas AgriLife Research and Extension Center – Lubbock, Texas.)

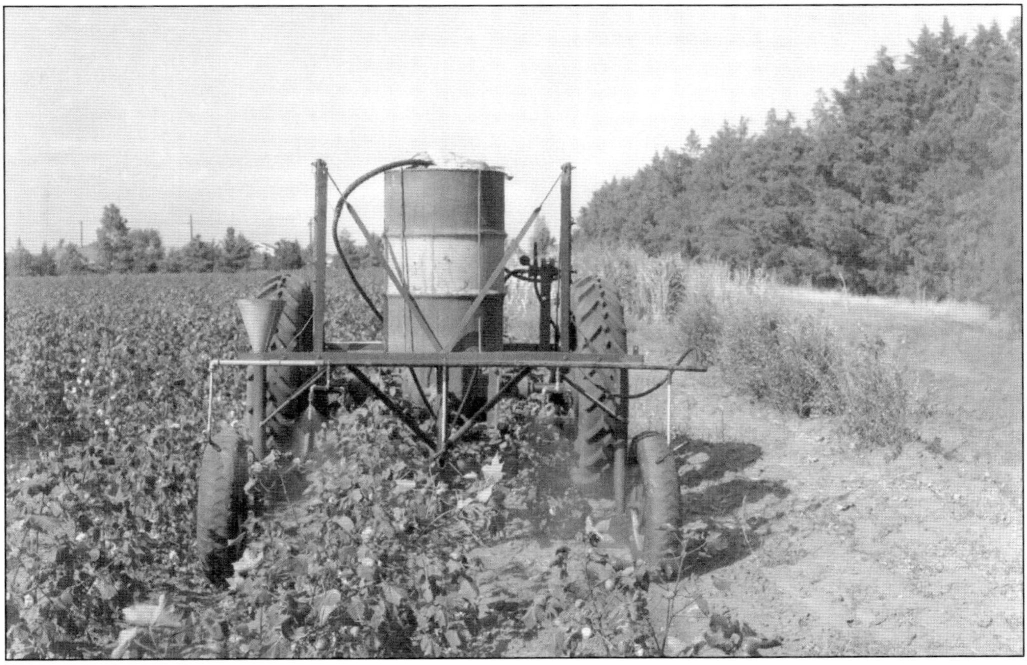

In the early days, ingenuity and improvisation were the rule rather than the exception in cotton farming. This image shows a sprayer made from a used 55-gallon drum fitted with a pump and lines running to three sprayers, which allowed the farmer to spray three rows of cotton in one pass through the field. (Courtesy of the Texas AgriLife Research and Extension Center – Lubbock, Texas.)

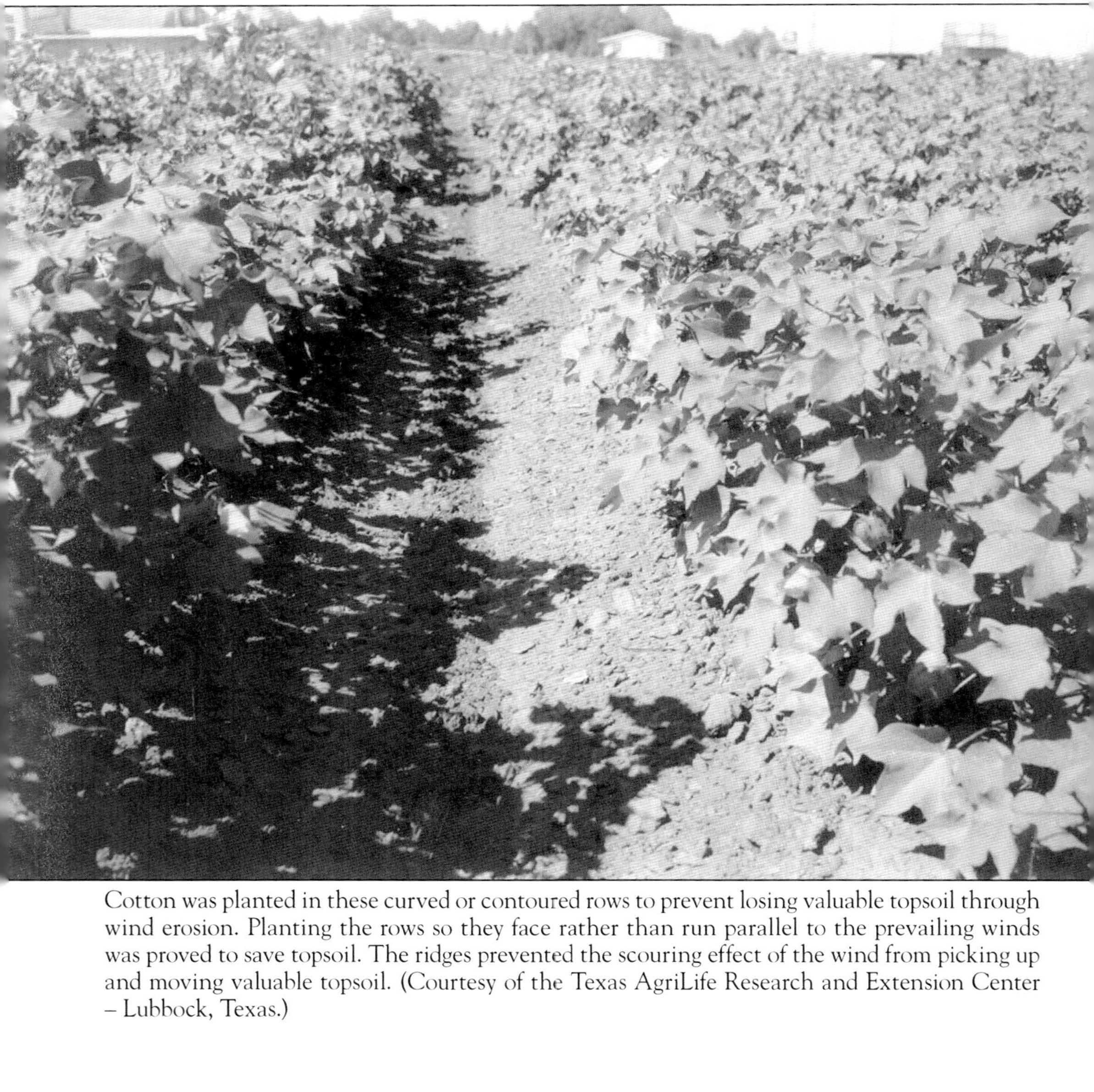

Cotton was planted in these curved or contoured rows to prevent losing valuable topsoil through wind erosion. Planting the rows so they face rather than run parallel to the prevailing winds was proved to save topsoil. The ridges prevented the scouring effect of the wind from picking up and moving valuable topsoil. (Courtesy of the Texas AgriLife Research and Extension Center – Lubbock, Texas.)

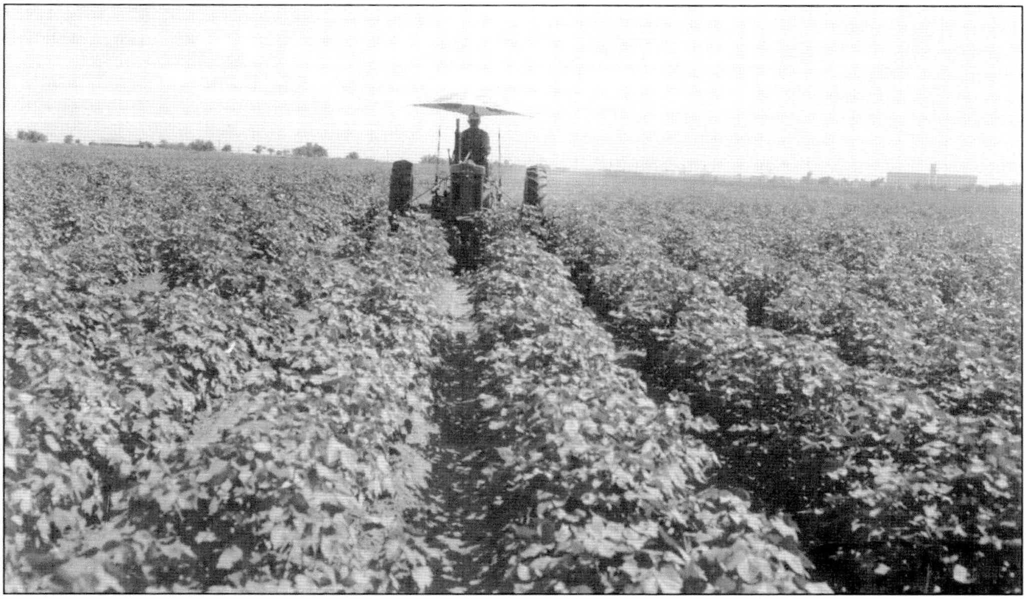

A farmer cultivates his cotton crop for the first time (above) and the last time (below). Notice the height of the cotton in the field. He must drive very slowly so as not to damage the high cotton. Cultivation aerates the soil, covers weeds, and allows water to move easily down to the roots of the cotton plants. He is pulling a 22-inch sweep, or cultivator, which allows him to use only one sweep per row, so that he can cultivate deeper if he so desires. (Both photographs courtesy of the Texas AgriLife Research and Extension Center – Lubbock, Texas.)

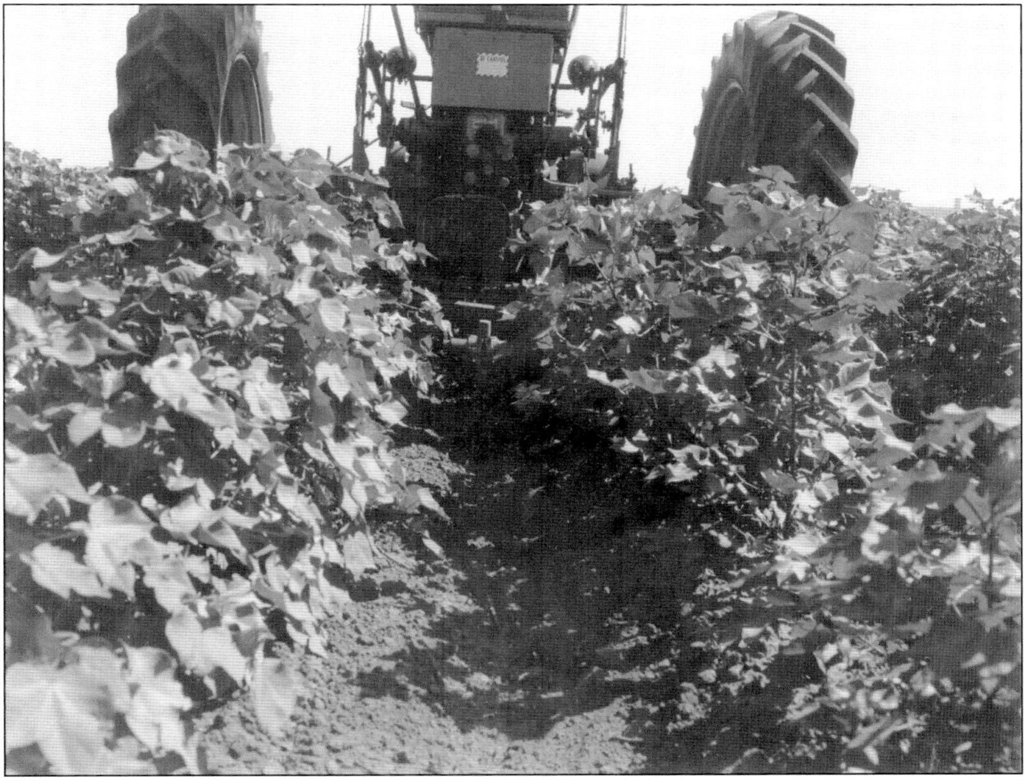

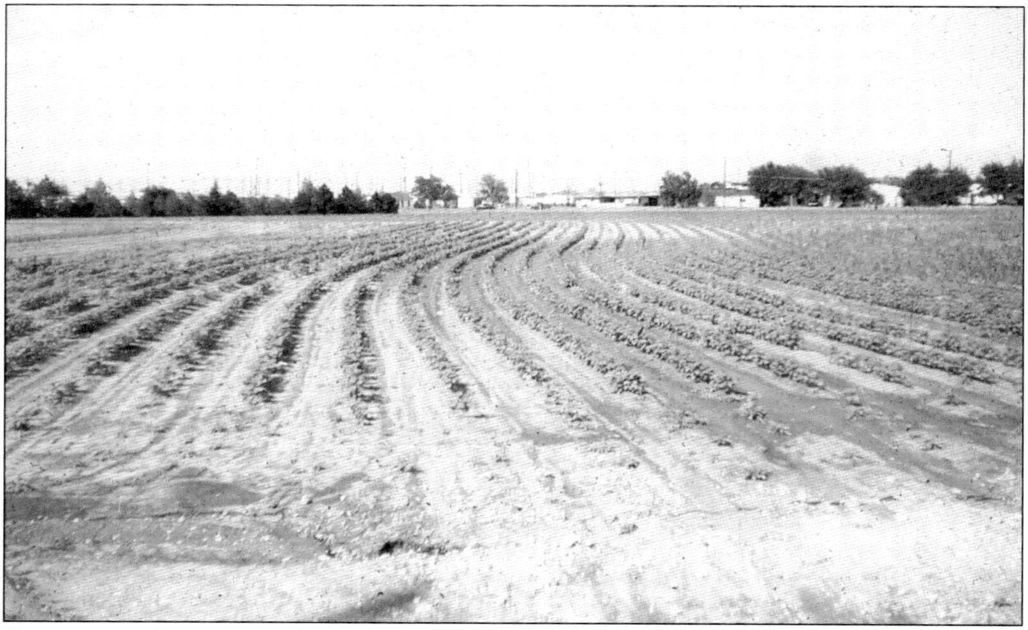

Contour row plowing is a soil conservation method where plowing follows the contours of the land or the direction of the prevailing wind. Cotton is seen here planted in contour rows in Lubbock around 1955. The contours slow down runoff, giving water time to infiltrate the soil. They also prevent topsoil loss during high winds. (Courtesy of the Texas AgriLife Research and Extension Center – Lubbock, Texas.)

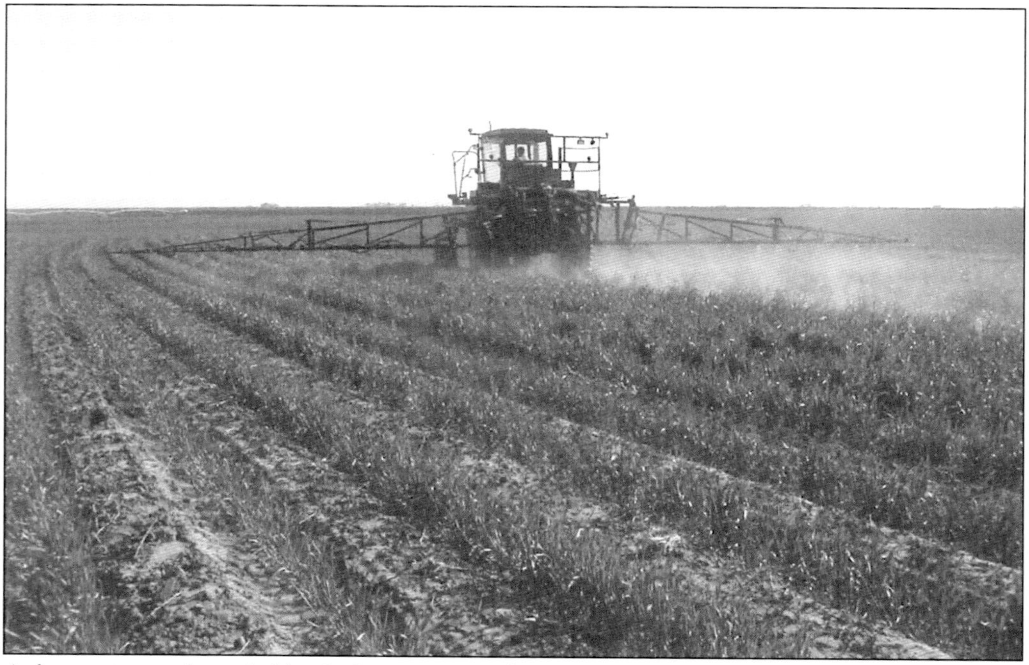

A farmer in southern Lubbock County sprays his cotton using a John Deere 4930 tractor and a 16-row sprayer. He is spraying insecticide on the cotton to protect it from pests. South Plains farmers were instrumental in developing equipment such as this, which both cut down on time in the field and increased profits. (Courtesy of Dan Taylor.)

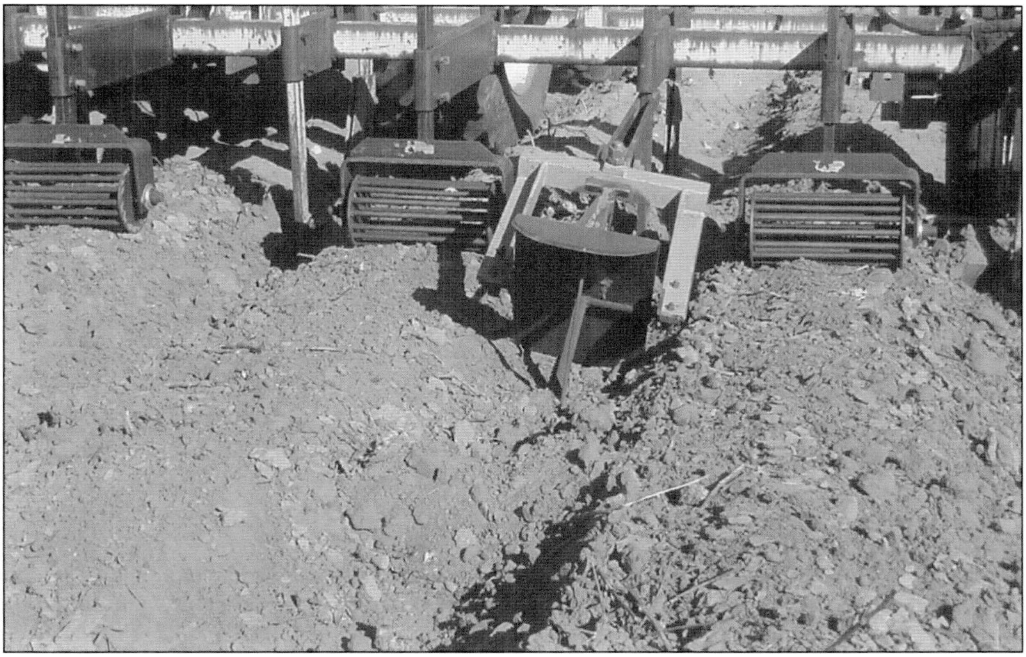

A diker is in action in the field. During the cultivation of the field, a diker prepares the ground to capture rainwater. The equipment makes small depressions in the ground, which are especially useful in dryland cotton. Major storm events on the South Plains can cause sudden flooding and erosion, which the diker helps to prevent. (Courtesy of Dan Taylor.)

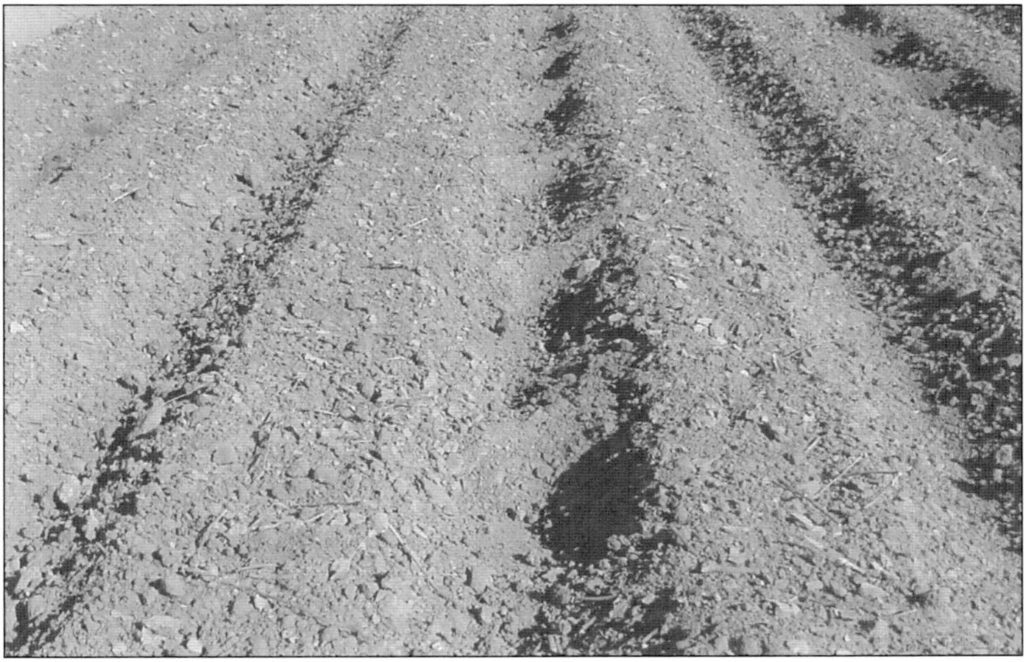

A cotton field is ready for planting. Notice that every other row has been diked. Skipping a row still allows every cotton plant to benefit from any rainwater that the dikes catch. Plants are on the tops of the furrows so water can run freely along the rows without harming the cotton. (Courtesy of Dan Taylor.)

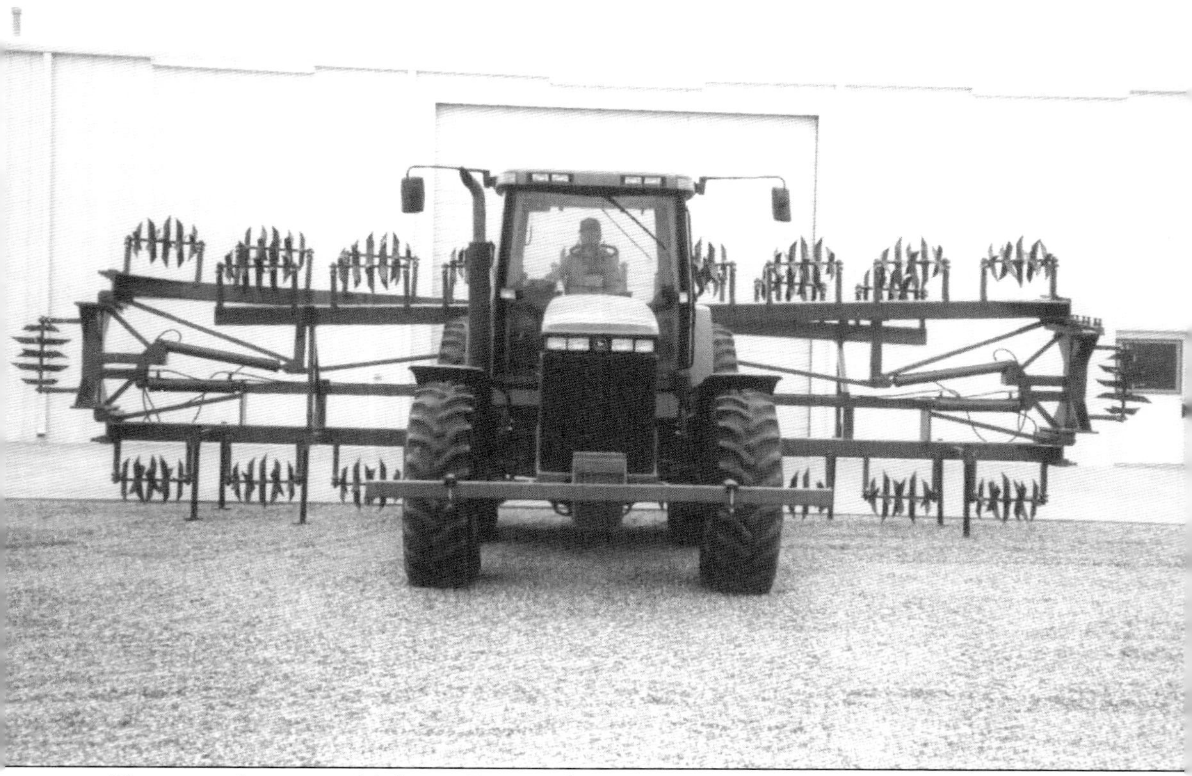

This image shows a sand fighter at Buzz Vardeman's Farm around 1990. This sand fighter is so wide that it has to be folded up on itself (as shown). Folding the equipment allowed for safer transportation and more convenient storage. (Photograph by and courtesy of Vardeman Farms.)

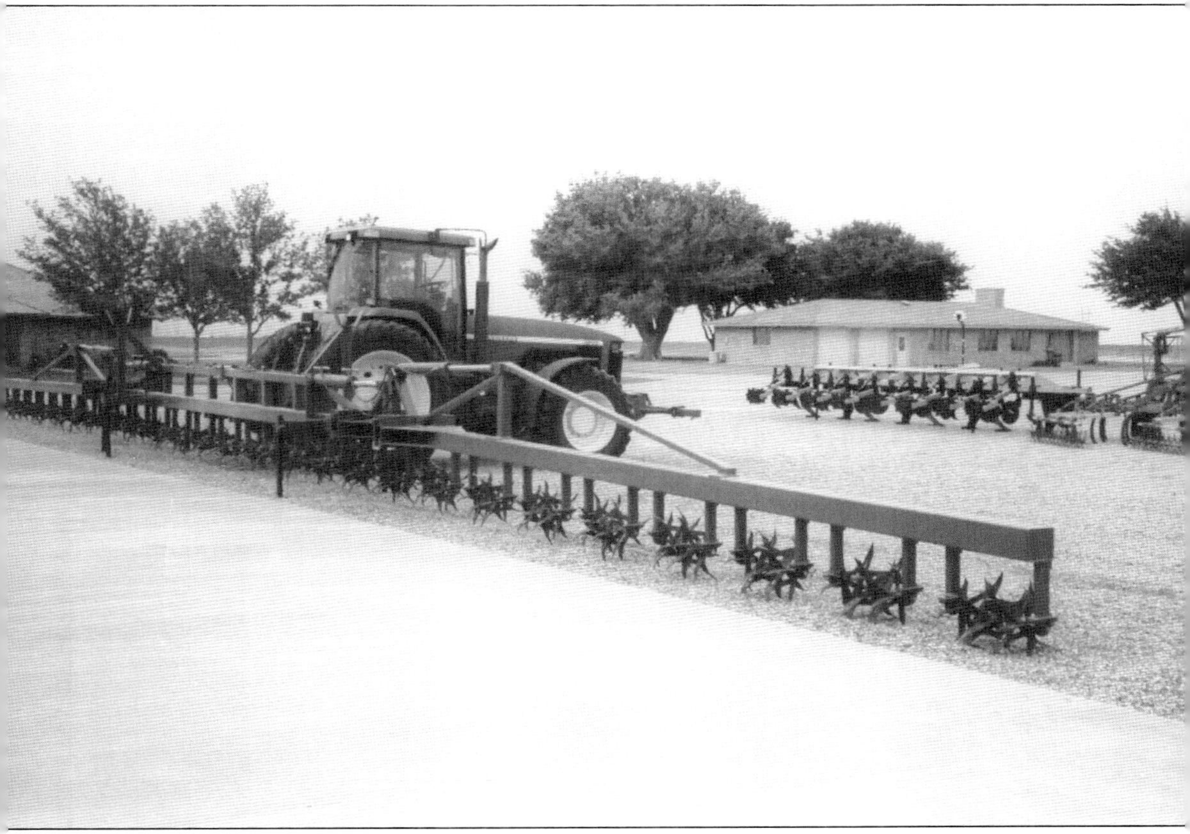

Unpredictable climatic conditions on the South Plains demand constant care of the land and crops. After a rain, the soil often forms a hard crust, which becomes covered with a sheet of fine sand. The sand fighter breaks the crust on top of the soil, which will help protect the young plants. This photograph shows how it would be used in the field. (Photograph by and courtesy of Vardeman Farms.)

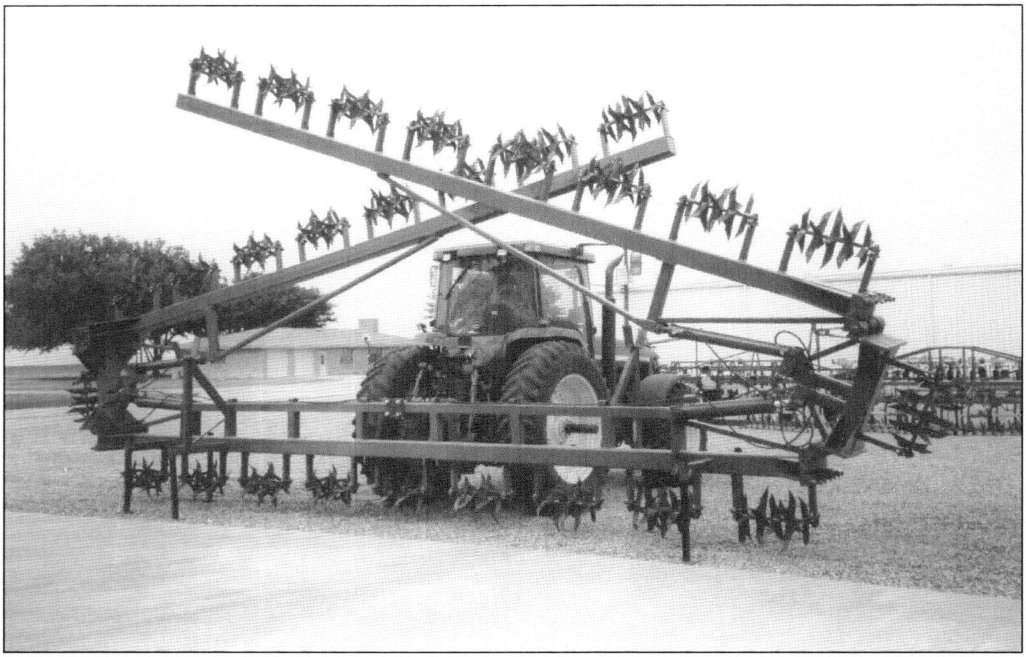

This sand fighter is in the process of being folded up. Buzz Vardeman, the cotton farmer who helped design this machine, had to figure out how to engineer the arms to fold up and across themselves, but also be able to lie out straight in the field. Notice that there are two joints on each arm. (Photograph by and courtesy of Vardeman Farms.)

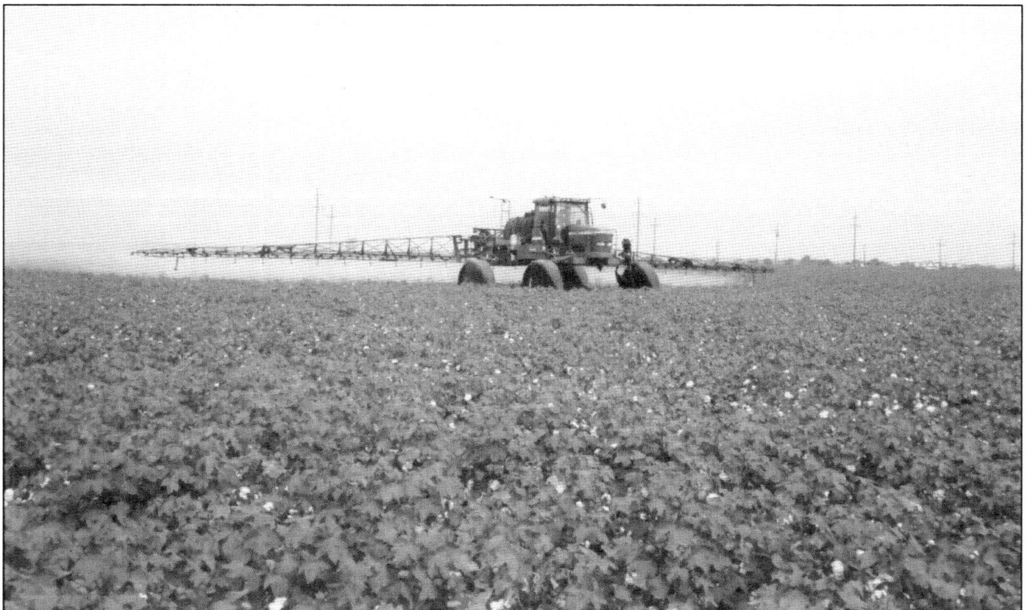

Defoliants cause the leaves to fall off the cotton plant in preparation for harvesting. A combination of crop management techniques, environmental conditions, timing, and chemical use determines the quality of the harvest. In the past, killing frosts determined the harvest date. This image shows defoliation using chemicals at Buzz Vardeman's Lubbock County farm in 2002. (Photograph by and courtesy of Vardeman Farms.)

Three
Irrigation and Cotton Machinery

Nothing on the South Plains was more vital to the growth of the cotton industry than the ability of farmers to tap into the Ogallala Aquifer and irrigate their crops. The ability to "flip a switch and make it rain" has turned the semiarid South Plains into one of the most productive agricultural regions in the world.

By today's standards, the first attempts to irrigate cotton seem primitive and not very efficient. Wells were dug, and pumps set on top of the ground simply flooded the fields with water. As the use of irrigation spread, the level of the Ogallala Aquifer lowered and farmers were forced to conserve water. Irrigation has developed through three phases.

At first, ditches and then pipes carried the irrigated water to where it could run down the rows to water the cotton. Although more effective than simply allowing water to run freely, problems remained, and the plants farthest away from the origin of the water received much less than the plants nearer the source.

Center-pivot irrigation systems solved the problem of distributing water evenly across a field but had issues of their own. These systems were expensive to own and easily damaged by wind. South Plains wind could wreak havoc with the water sprayed from a center-pivot system. On windy days, drift from water could be a serious problem. To combat water drifting, South Plains farmers and engineers developed a system of dropped nozzles, which conserved water. Dropped nozzles, which look something like a garden hose, carried the water down closer to the plants. Some nozzles were within six inches of the ground, while others dragged the ground.

The development of the third phase in irrigation technology continues today as farmers turn to inground drip irrigation systems. The inground system helps the farmer conserve water and lower irrigation costs while producing bumper crops of cotton. In an inground irrigation system, the drip hoses are placed evenly throughout the field at the exact spacing of cotton rows and at a depth young where plants can find them. The Global Positioning Systems (GPS) in many tractors position the seed exactly over the inground drip system.

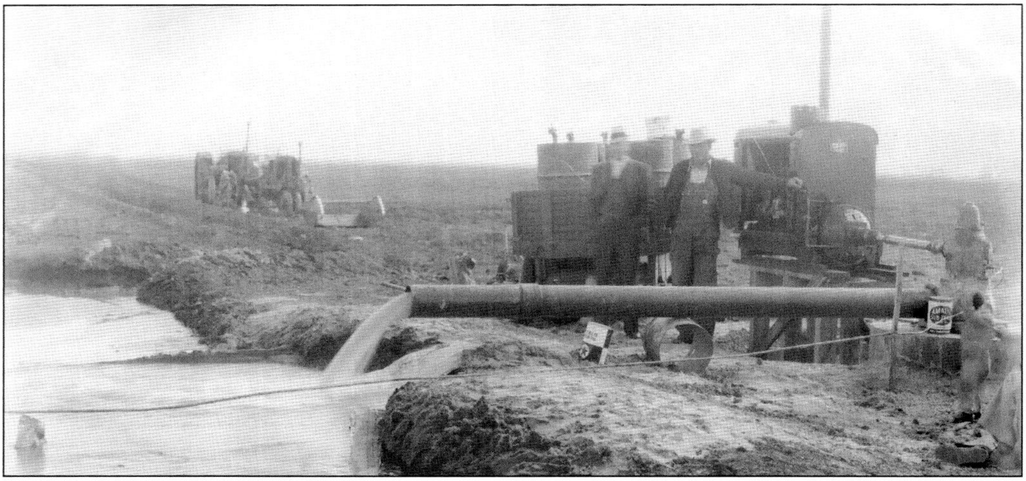

Lovell Jones looks over his Floydada County irrigation well in the 1930s. It was a simple operation, but effective for its time. The motor pumped water up from the aquifer, and the water ran across the field, although it appears some effort was taken to control its flow. Note the tractor and the ditch in background. (Courtesy of the Floyd County Historical Museum.)

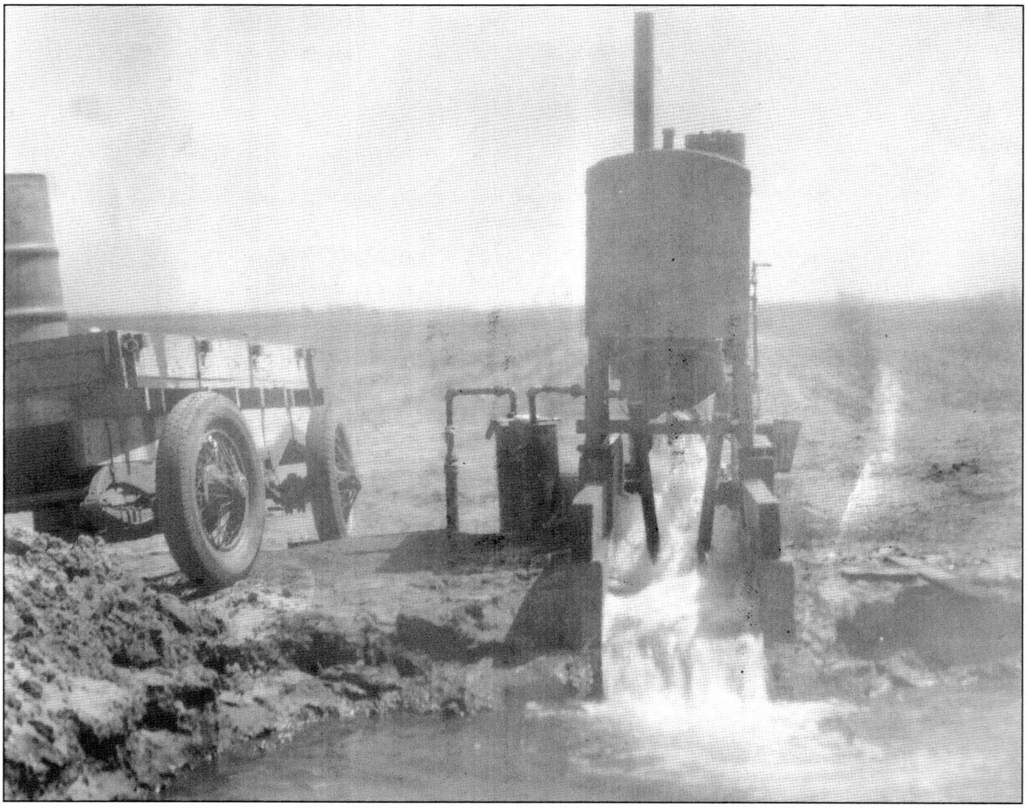

Lovell Jones's irrigation well is seen again here. It has been modified somewhat, as a wooden trough and a retention pond have been built. Both these innovations helped control the flow of the water and limit erosion. The vast and easily accessible Ogallala Aquifer, more than anything else, made the production on the South Plains profitable. (Courtesy of the Floyd County Historical Museum.)

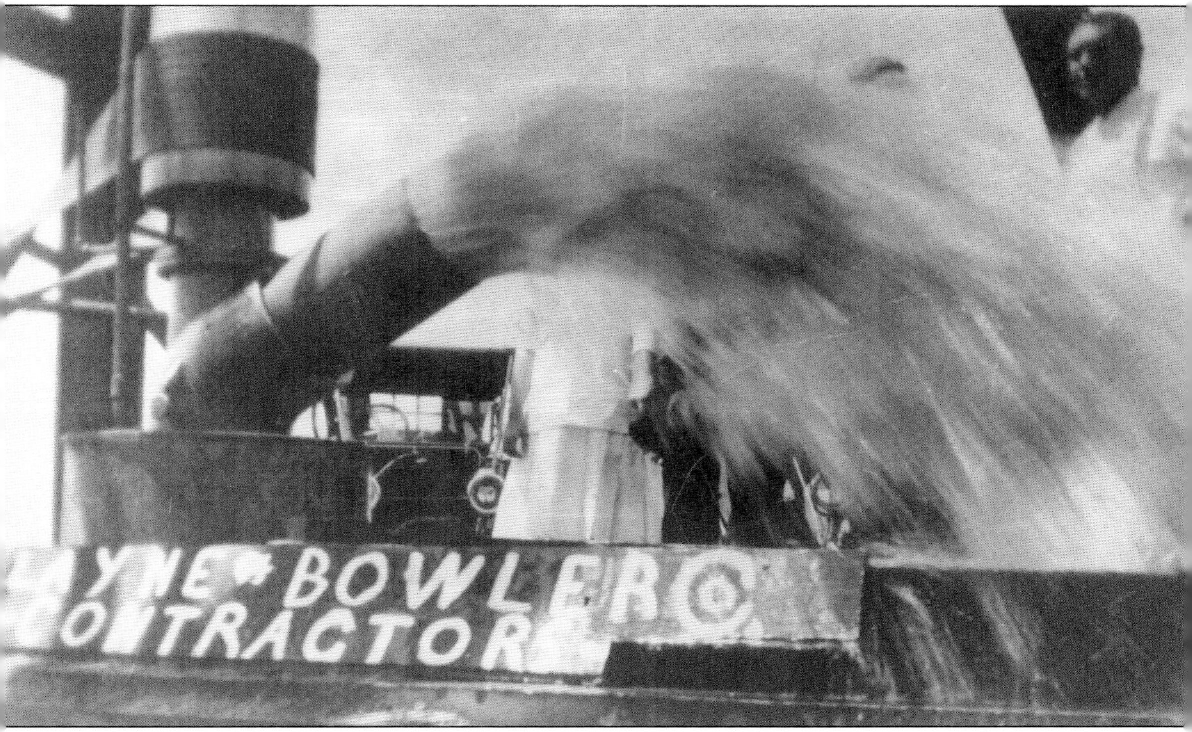

Because of the semiarid nature of the South Plains, irrigation was important for improved crop yields. This image shows a 1913 irrigation scheme. The water flowing out of the aquifer was pumped by a gasoline-powered motor and allowed to flow into the cotton with little or no control over the area covered. (Photograph from the Lubbock Agriculture Collection, courtesy of the Southwest Collection/Special Collections Library, Texas Tech University.)

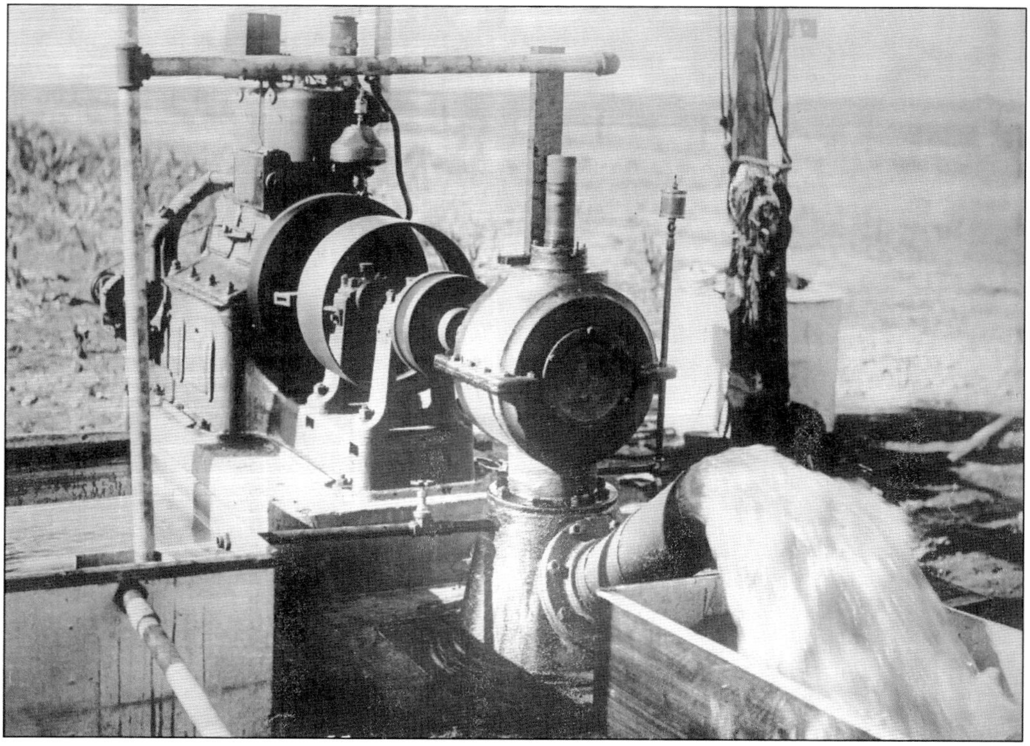

One of the first irrigation pumps was built in Hale Center in 1915 by the Green Machine Company. The engine, with its new heavy-duty gearhead, was made specifically for use in irrigation, as opposed to earlier engines that were simply automobile or truck engines. This pump operated successfully for several years. (Courtesy of Hale County Farm and Ranch Museum.)

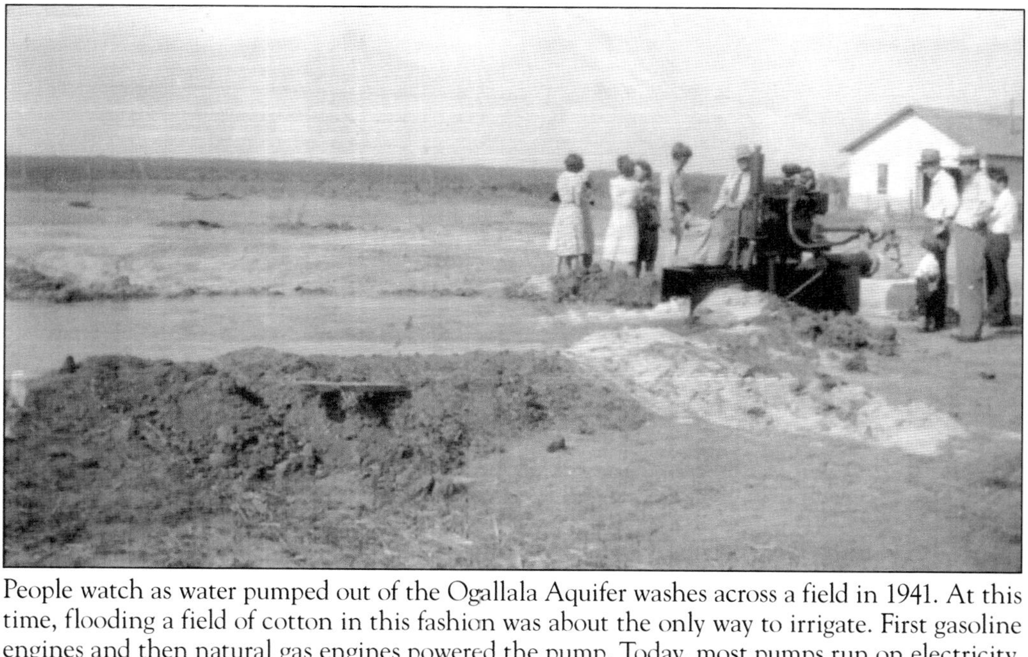

People watch as water pumped out of the Ogallala Aquifer washes across a field in 1941. At this time, flooding a field of cotton in this fashion was about the only way to irrigate. First gasoline engines and then natural gas engines powered the pump. Today, most pumps run on electricity. (Courtesy of Carol and Powell Adams.)

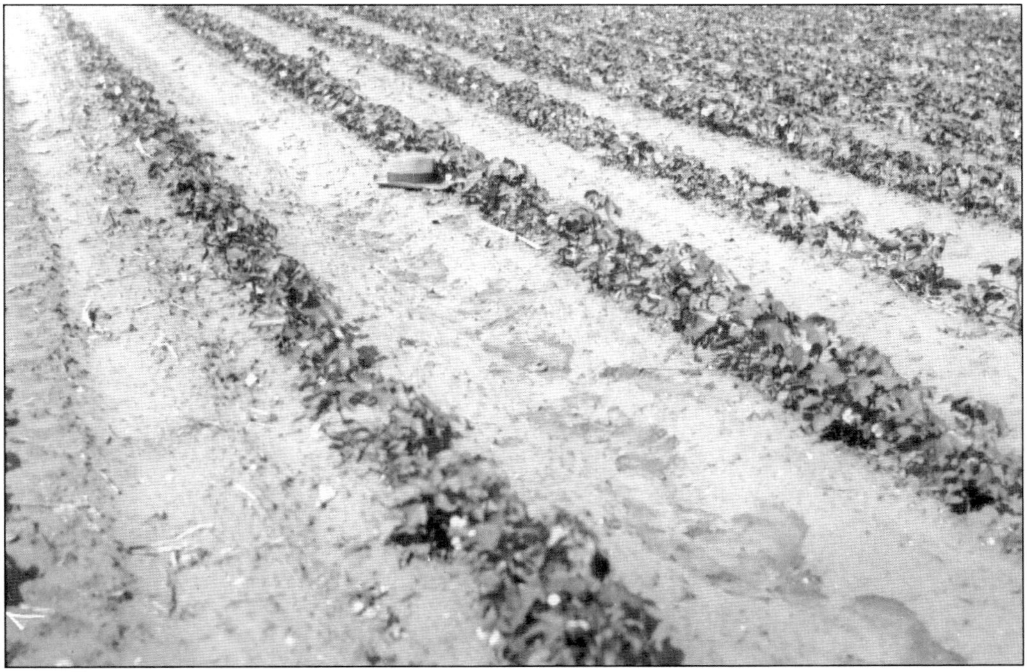

A field of dryland cotton in Lubbock County is seen here in 1948. Compare this cotton to the irrigated cotton below and notice how small this cotton is compared to the cotton that was only watered once. As of 2011, about half of all the cotton grown on the South Plains was irrigated. (Courtesy of the Texas AgriLife Research and Extension Center – Lubbock, Texas.)

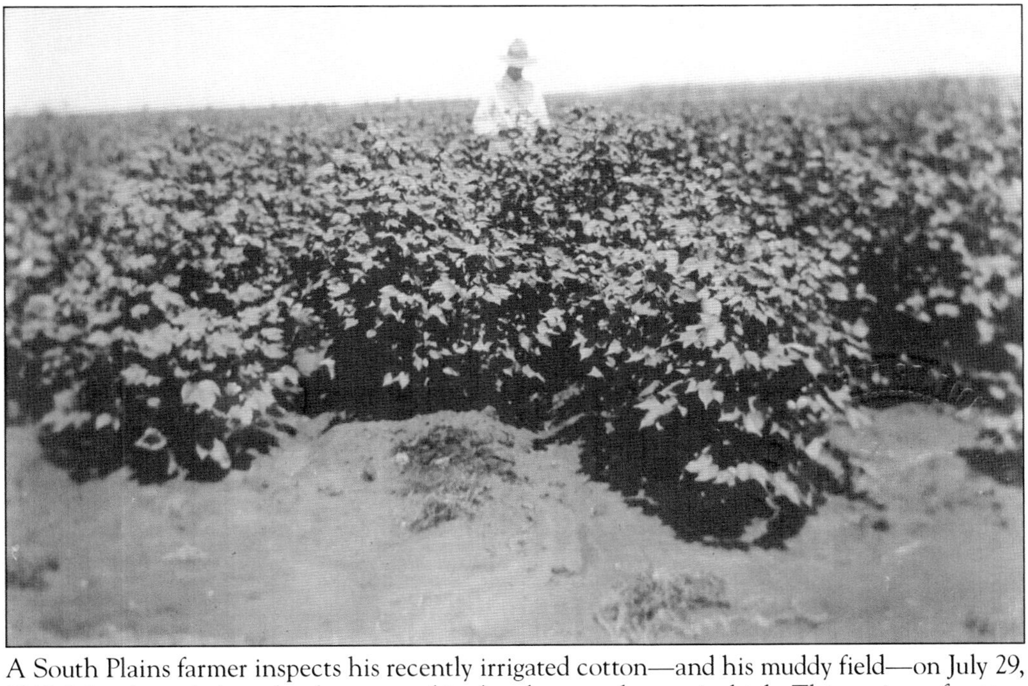

A South Plains farmer inspects his recently irrigated cotton—and his muddy field—on July 29, 1919. It has been irrigated only once and is already more than waist-high. This variety of cotton is called Durango. Today, Durango cotton is mostly grown in Arizona and California. (Courtesy of the Texas AgriLife Research and Extension Center – Lubbock, Texas.)

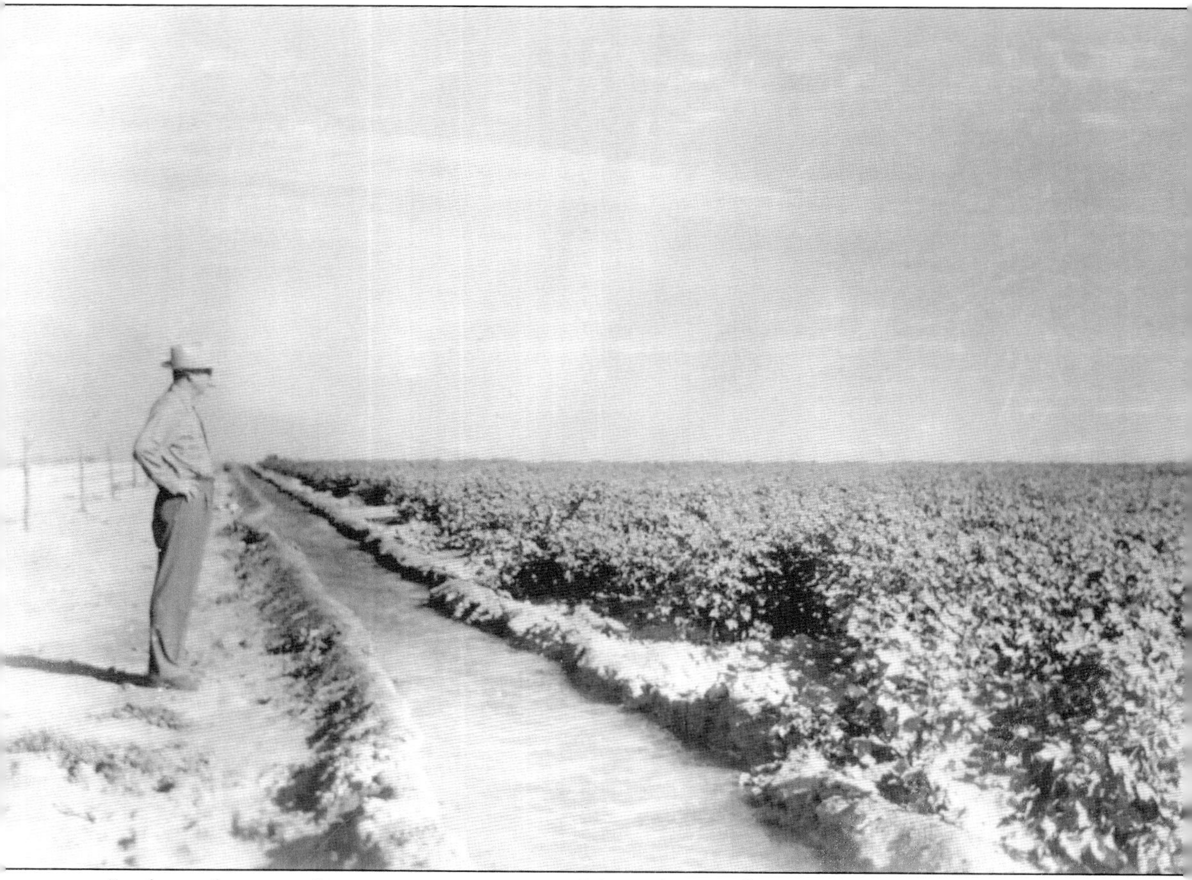

In the early years of irrigating, water pumped from the aquifer was allowed to flow to the cotton via rows and miniature dams constructed to direct the water. This farmer stands observing the water as it erodes part of his field, all in an effort to irrigate the farthest reaches of his cotton. (Photograph from the Cotton Industry Photography Collection, courtesy of the Southwest Collection/Special Collections Library, Texas Tech University.)

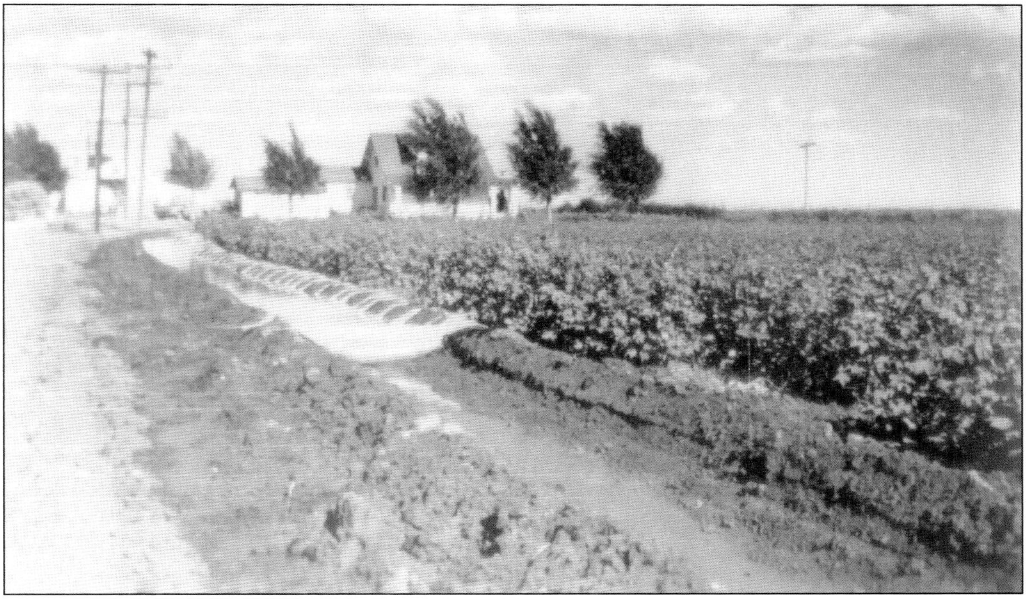

A small step forward in irrigation technology was the use of plastic pipes to direct the flow so farmers could better control the water used to irrigate their fields. From a central, or "mother ditch," farmers siphoned water into the rows that needed it. Often, every other row was irrigated, but problems still remained, as the cotton plants farthest down the row often did not get enough water and plants close to the mother ditch got too much. As seen below, erosion still remained a problem. (Both photographs from the Cotton Industry Photography Collection, courtesy of the Southwest Collection/Special Collections Library, Texas Tech University.)

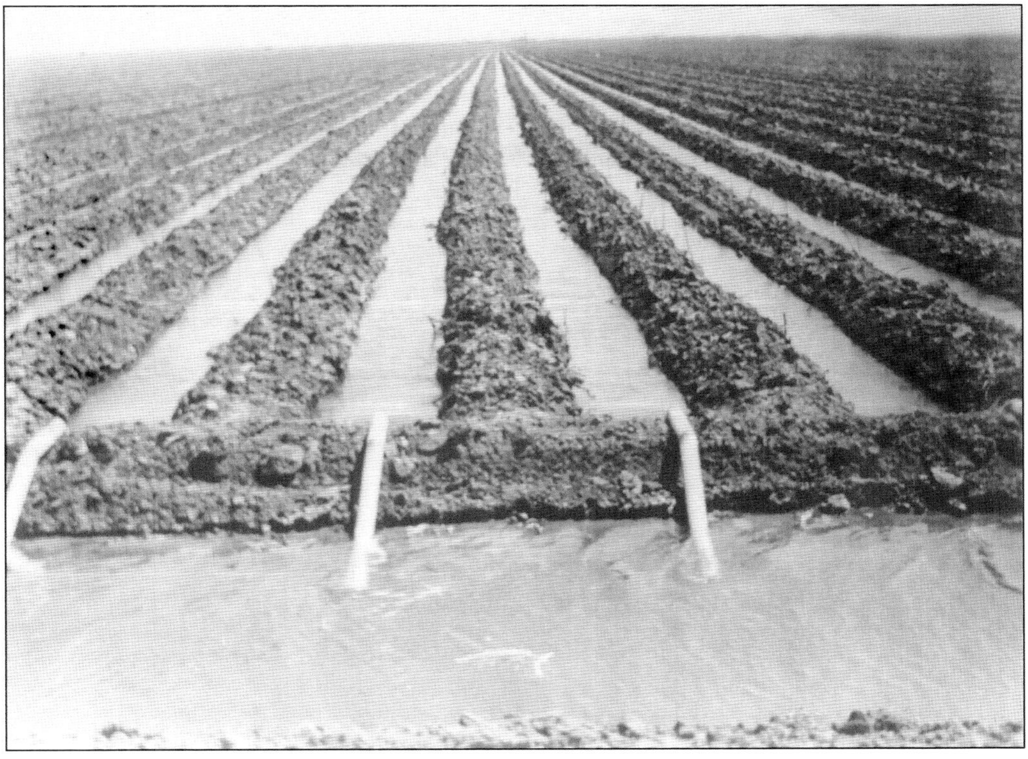

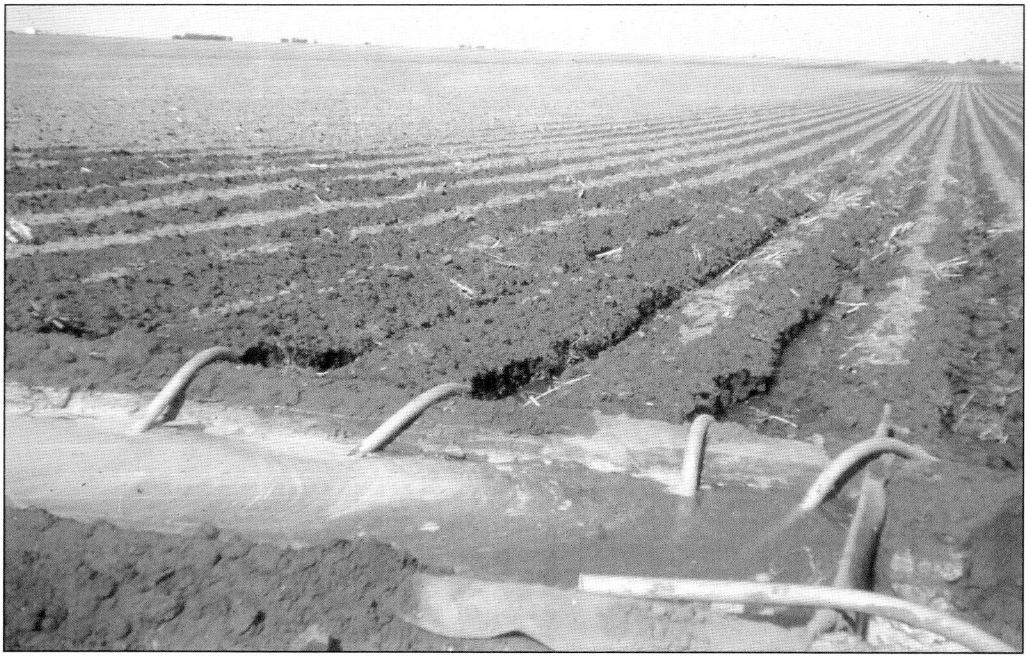

Plastic tubes siphon water from a ditch into rows of cotton. Although not a very efficient method of irrigation, it was a step ahead of simply allowing the water to flow across the field. Looking down the lines of cotton, one can see how far the water ran down the rows. (Courtesy of the Texas AgriLife Research and Extension Center – Lubbock, Texas.)

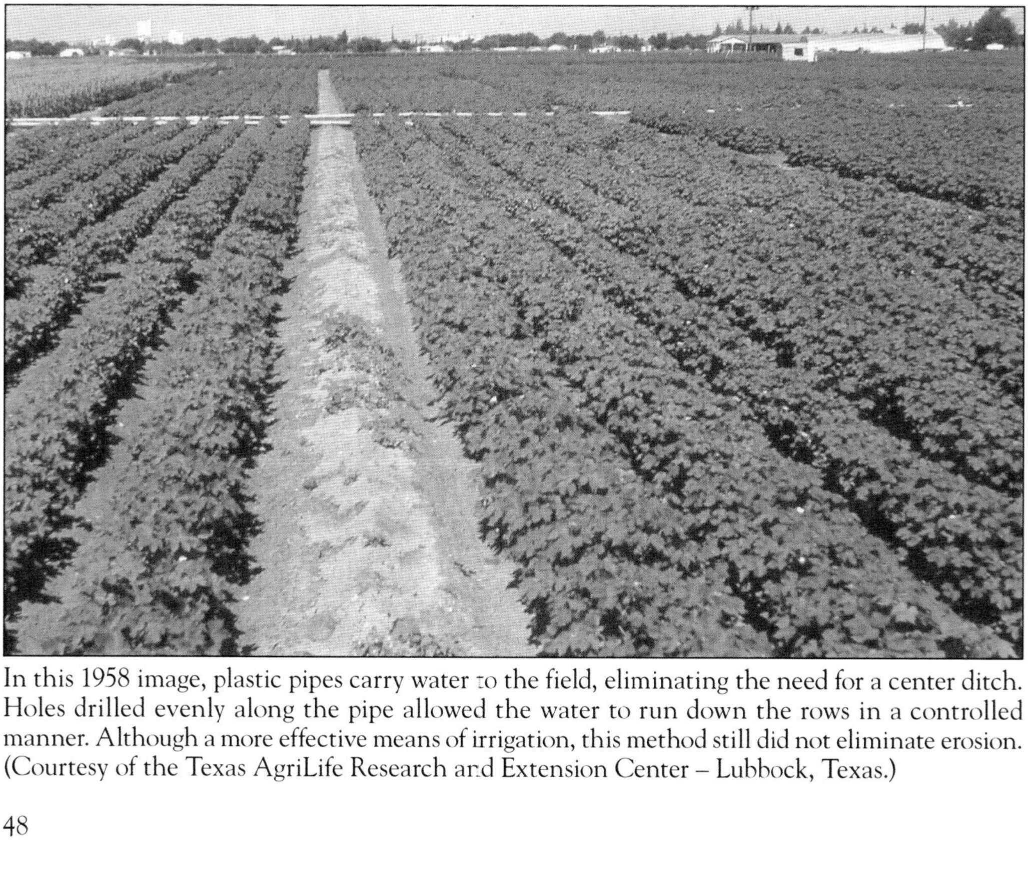

In this 1958 image, plastic pipes carry water to the field, eliminating the need for a center ditch. Holes drilled evenly along the pipe allowed the water to run down the rows in a controlled manner. Although a more effective means of irrigation, this method still did not eliminate erosion. (Courtesy of the Texas AgriLife Research and Extension Center – Lubbock, Texas.)

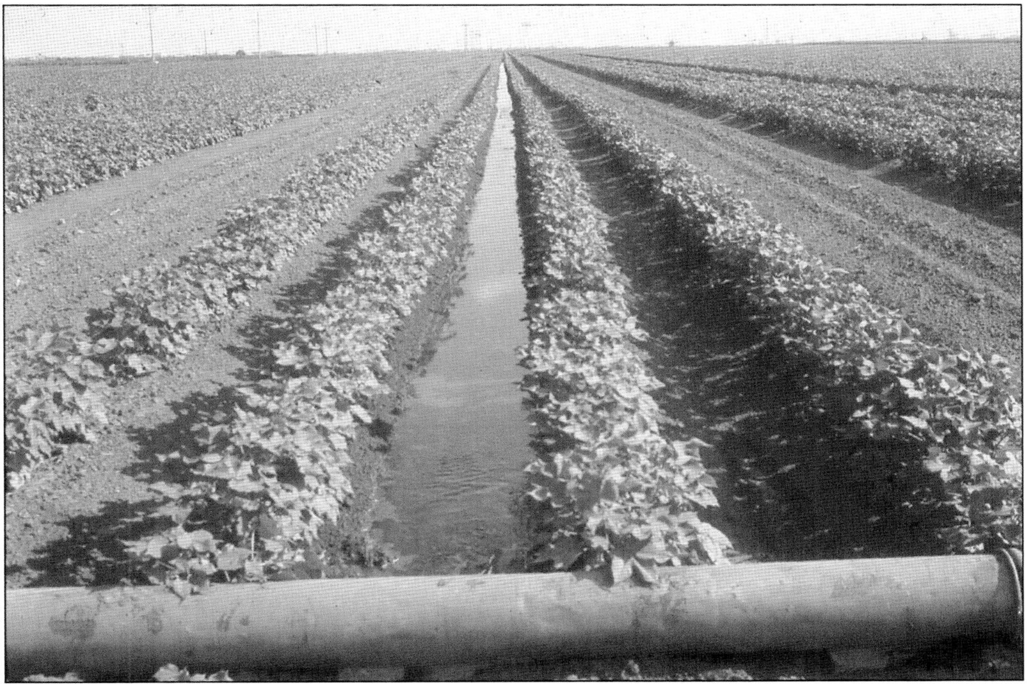

The same field of cotton is seen in both of these images. Above, the cotton gets irrigated water from a pipe that delivers the water only between the second and third rows, which seemingly benefits those two rows. Later in the growing season (below), the cotton looks uniform in height despite two of the four rows not getting any irrigated water. This is because the first and fourth rows were able to capture water that soaked into the ground between rows two and three. (Both photographs courtesy of the Texas AgriLife Research and Extension Center – Lubbock, Texas.)

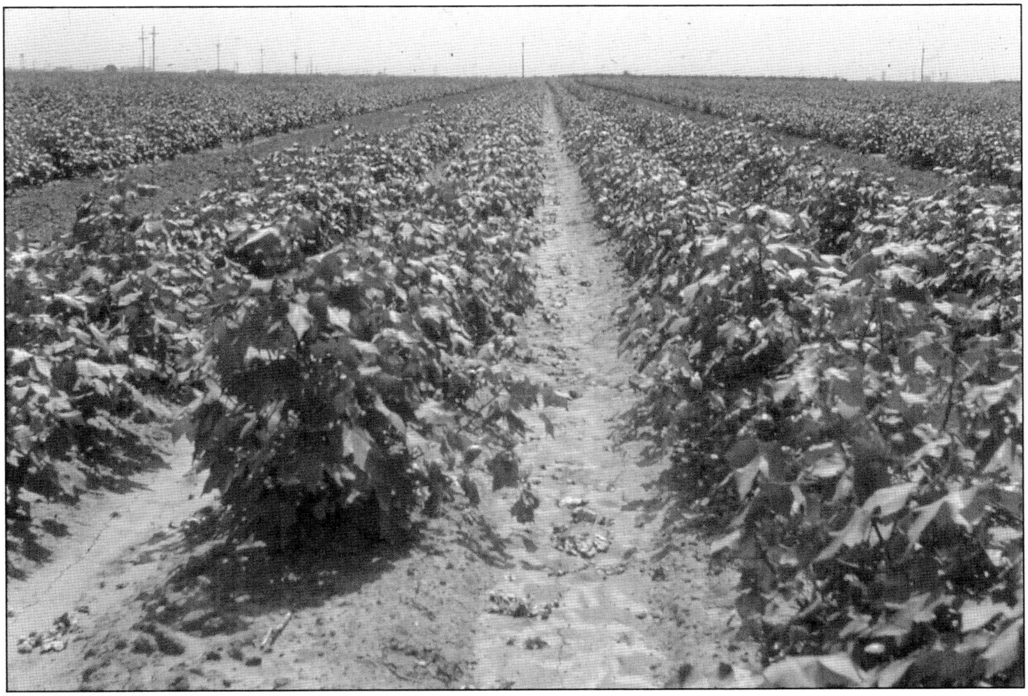

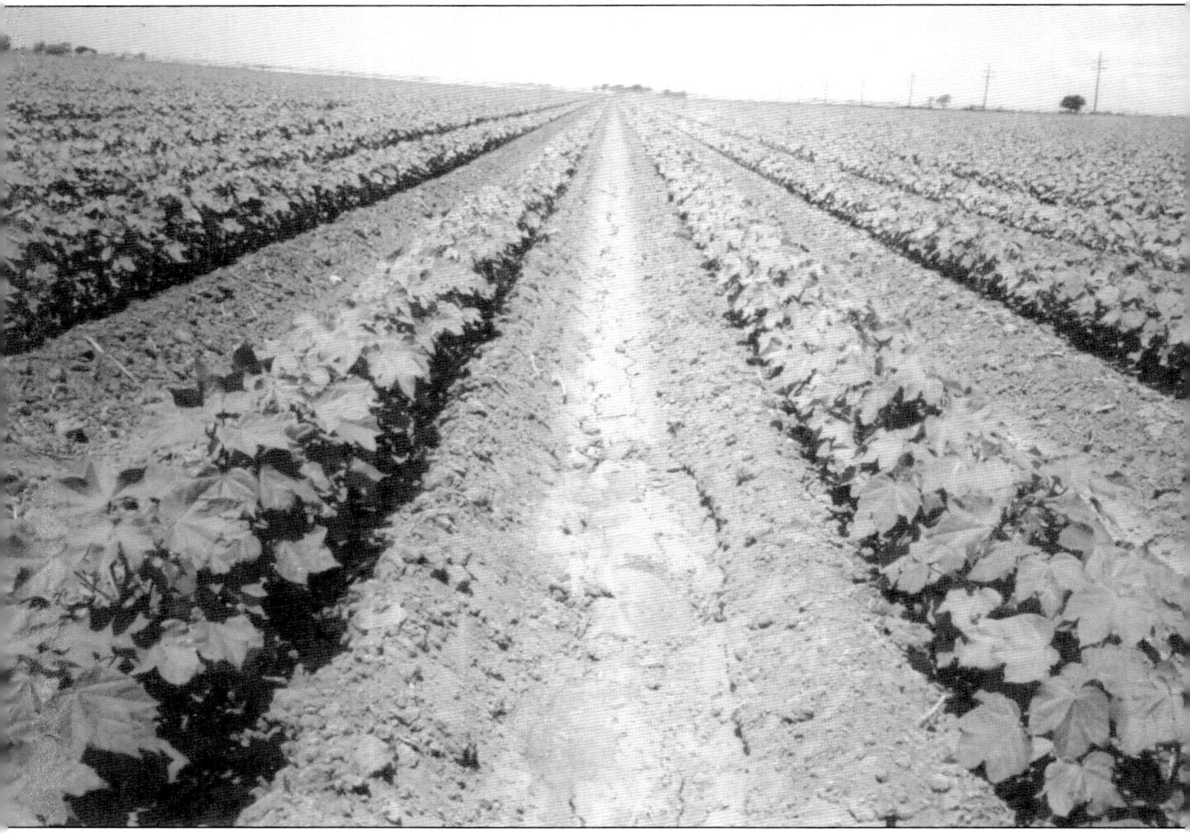

Cotton rows were irrigated by allowing water to flow down the rows freely at speeds determined by the gradient of the land and velocity of the water coming from the pump. This sometimes caused erosion. This image shows irrigation on the Buzz Vardeman cotton farm in 1995. Drip irrigation has pretty much put an end to this practice. (Photograph by and courtesy of Vardeman Farms.)

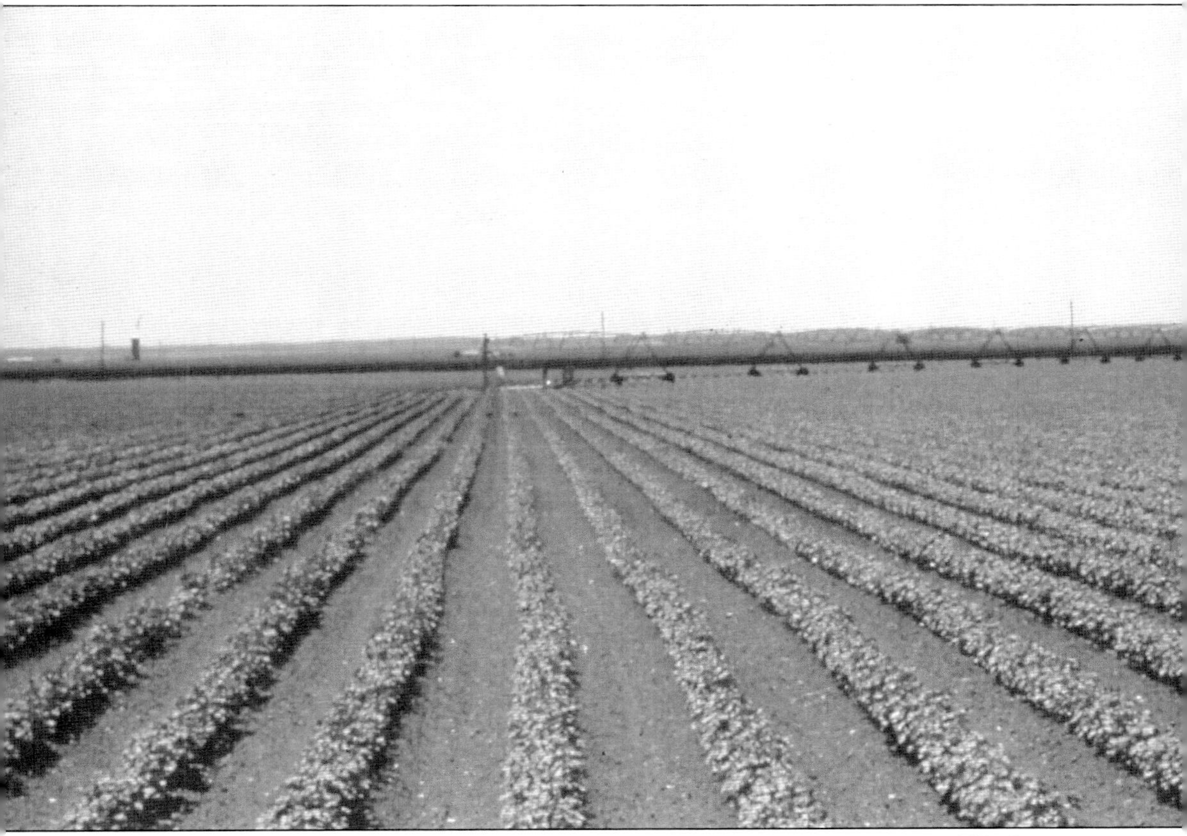

A field of cotton in Bailey County is irrigated by a center-pivot irrigation system in 1978. Center-pivots systems allowed the water to spread evenly over the entire field, which reduced erosion, and could spread chemicals and fertilizer to the cotton as needed during the growing season. (Courtesy of the Texas AgriLife Research and Extension Center – Lubbock, Texas.)

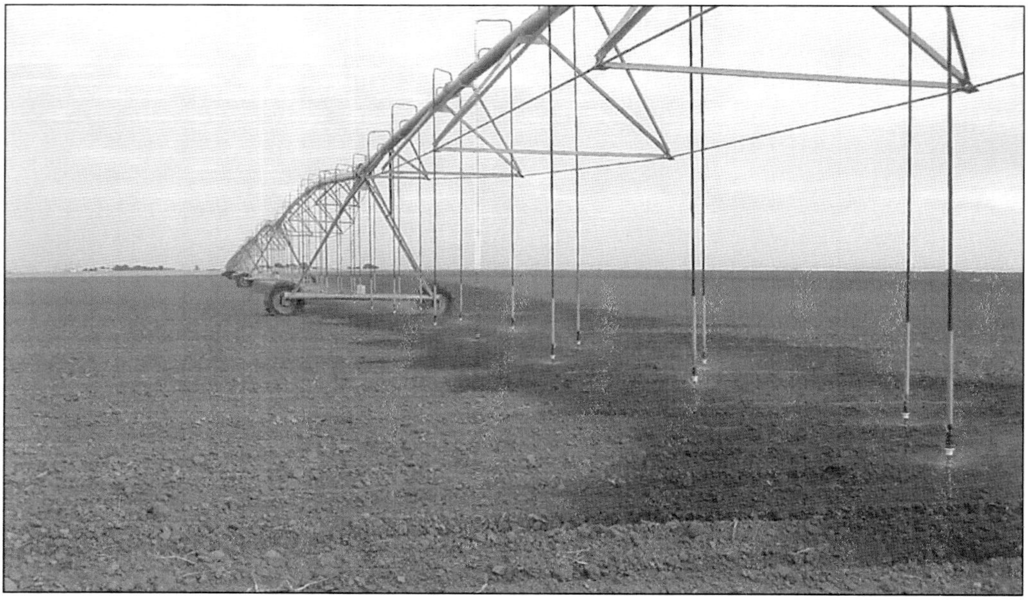

A recently planted cotton field near Ropesville is irrigated for the first time by a center-pivot drop nozzle system. This system saves water by placing the water on or near the ground, preventing the loss of water through wind effect. In most years, the cost of irrigation is the cotton farmer's largest expense. (Courtesy of Dan Taylor.)

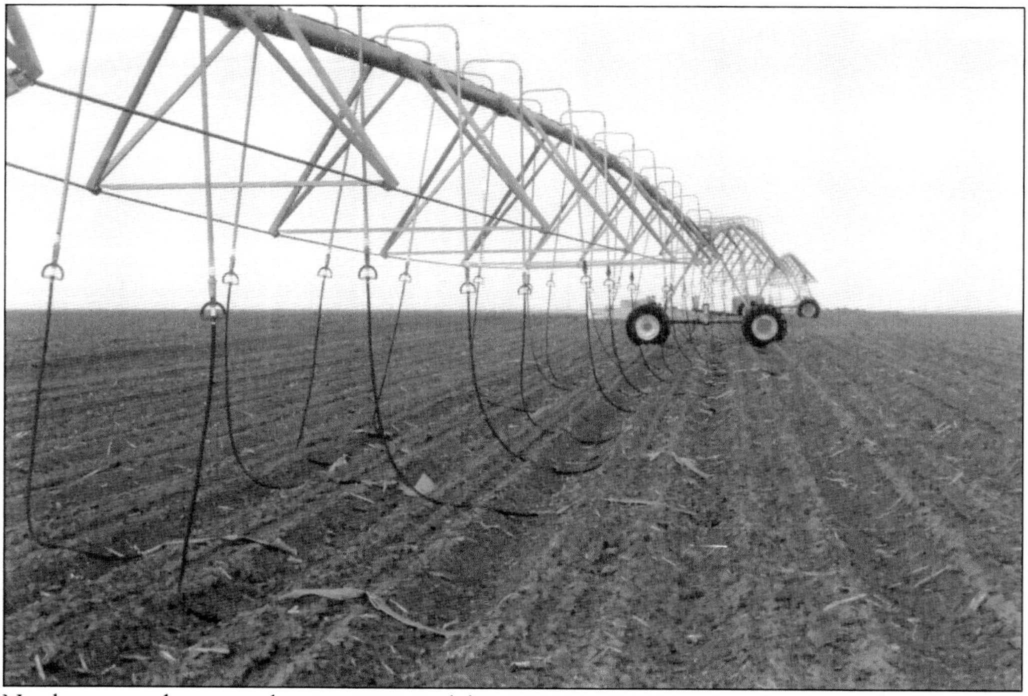

Newly sprouted cotton plants are watered from a center-pivot irrigated system. The advantage of this precision irrigation allows farms to feed fertilizer and herbicides in a targeted manner by spreading the chemicals through the center-pivot system. This type of irrigation system has increased profitability and reduced the environmental damage associated with nitrogen fertilizer by keeping it out of the Ogallala Aquifer. (Courtesy of Dan Taylor.)

This cotton plant is suffering from the effects of the drought on the South Plains during the hot summer of 2011. It is clear that the leaves are wrinkled and fold inwards, hindering photosynthesis and slowing the growth of the plant. Droughts can cause significant losses in yield and quality due to premature defoliation. (Photograph by Richard Porter, courtesy *Plainview Daily Herald*.)

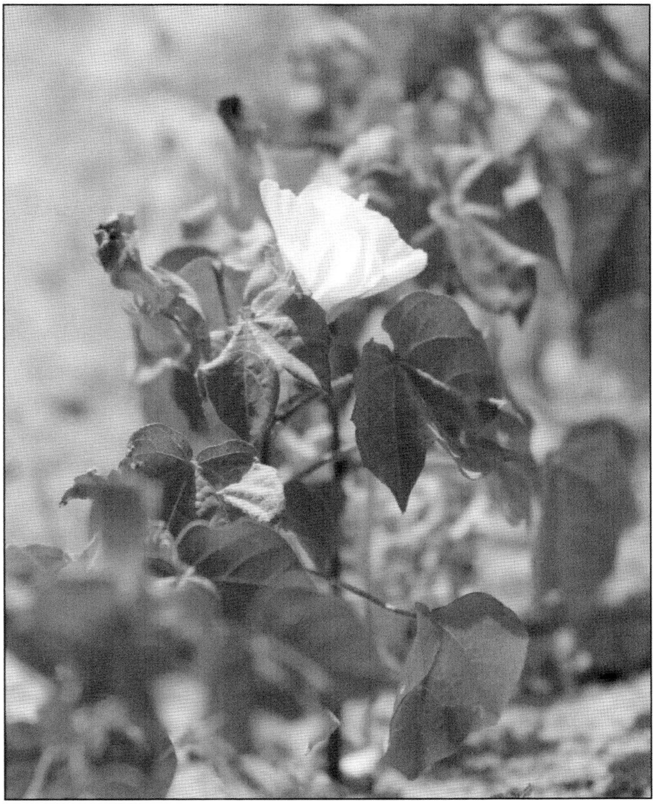

Dan Taylor, a Hockley County cotton farmer, works on his drip irrigation system. He is adjusting the amount of liquid fertilizer going into the drip irrigation lines. Taylor has been a cotton farmer and gin operator for more than 40 years and is an innovator in the use of cotton technology. (Courtesy of Dan Taylor.)

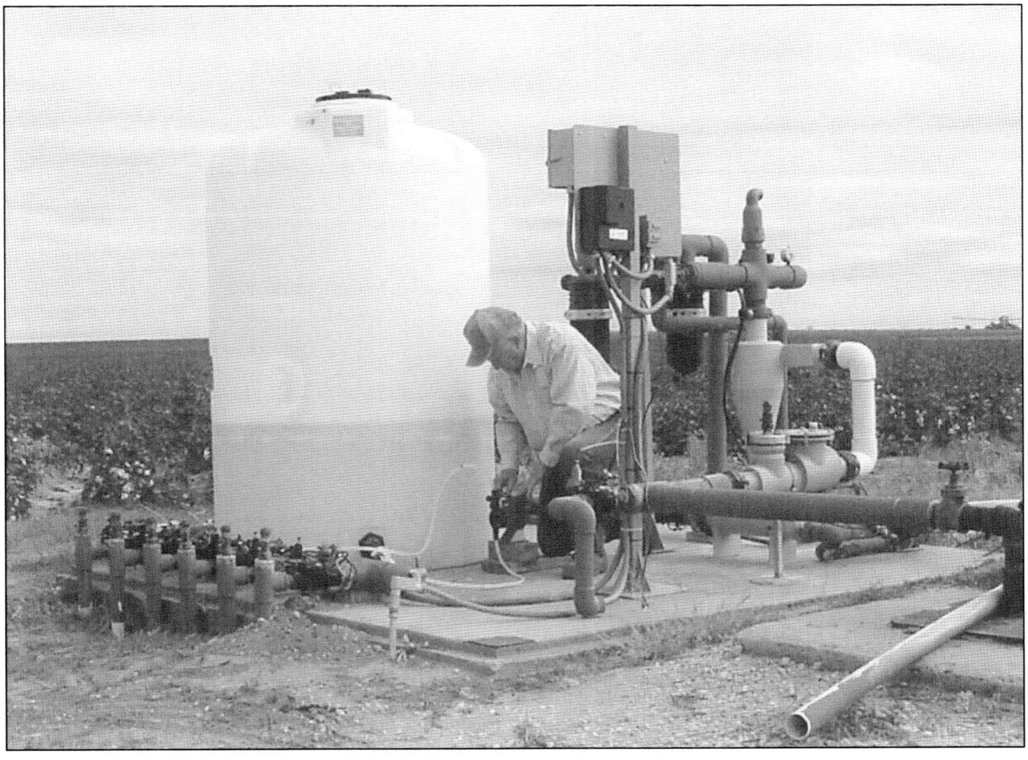

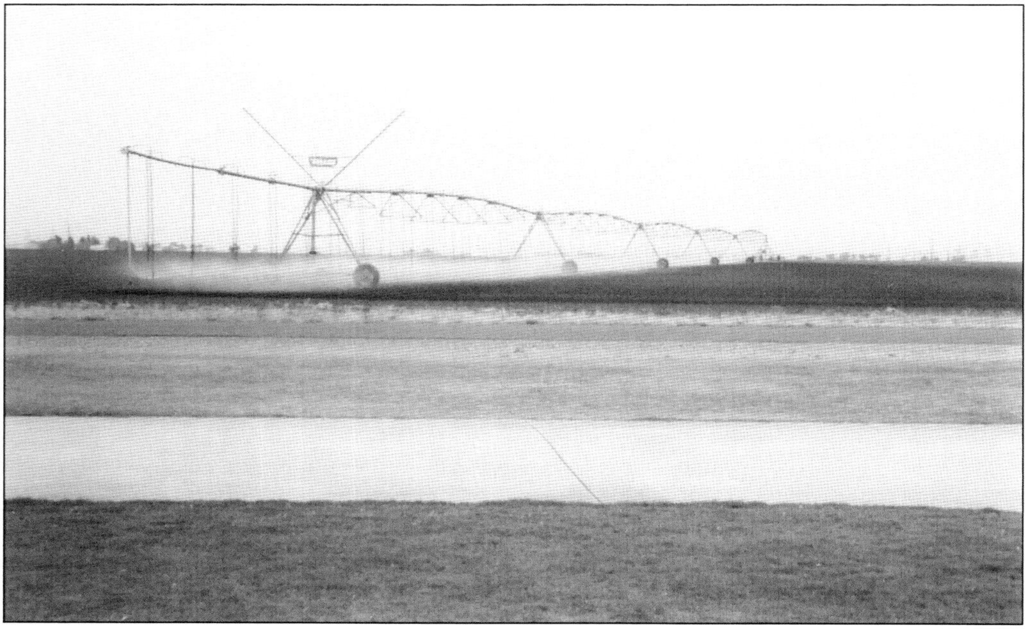

The center-pivot with drop sprinklers is a type of sprinkler irrigation system that moves on wheels in a circular pattern. The drop nozzles suspended from the center pivot hang just above the ground or are dragged along the top. The sprinkler system is fed water from a main pumping source. Many irrigation systems feature a GPS and can be operated automatically by a computer or other mobile devices from a home, office, or truck. (Both photograph by and courtesy of Vardeman Farms.)

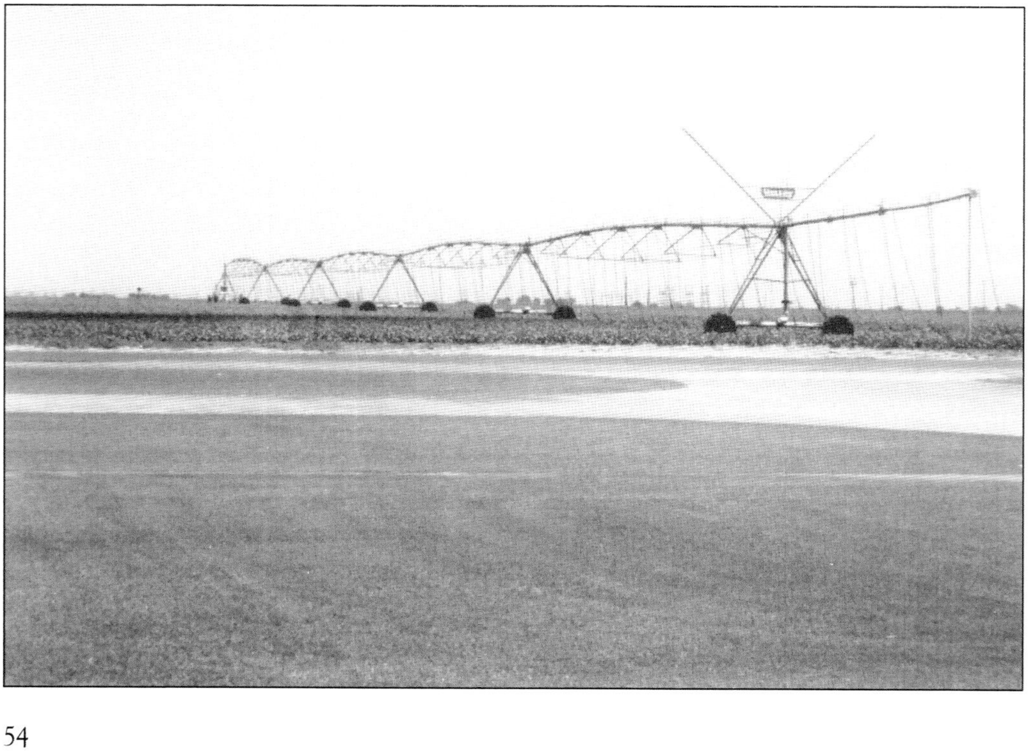

Four
HARVESTING

At one time, large groups of people journeyed to the South Plains to take part in the area's annual cotton harvest. These migrant workers played an important part in making cotton profitable. Workers would start arriving in September and pull cotton until the year's first killing frost put an end to it for another year. Pulling cotton was hard, hot, dirty work, but conditions improved as mechanization increased. Unfortunately, as mechanization increased, available work for unskilled laborers decreased. Presently, there is little seasonal work available during the cotton harvest.

Many of the improvements in harvesting cotton on the South Plains were *made* on the South Plains, by cotton farmers living in the area. In a concerted effort to raise the quality and quantity of the cotton and to increase its profitability, area farmers developed machinery and methods to improve the efficiency of the cotton harvest, increasing the caliber of the crop while improving the living conditions of those harvesting the cotton.

Area farmers helped develop mechanical cotton strippers, which not only harvested cotton more economically but also improved the grade of the cotton grown on the South Plains. In every stage of the development of cotton strippers—from one-row strippers pulled by teams of mules to the latest eight-row cotton strippers—area cotton farmers played an important role in improving the machinery that stripped the area's cotton.

The development of cotton module building technology by South Plains farmers helped them overcome one of the last hurdles in harvesting cotton in an efficient and timely manner. Modules allow cotton farmers to pick their crops without waiting on a gin to empty their cotton trailers, thus allowing farmers to continuously harvest, saving them time and money and producing a higher-quality crop.

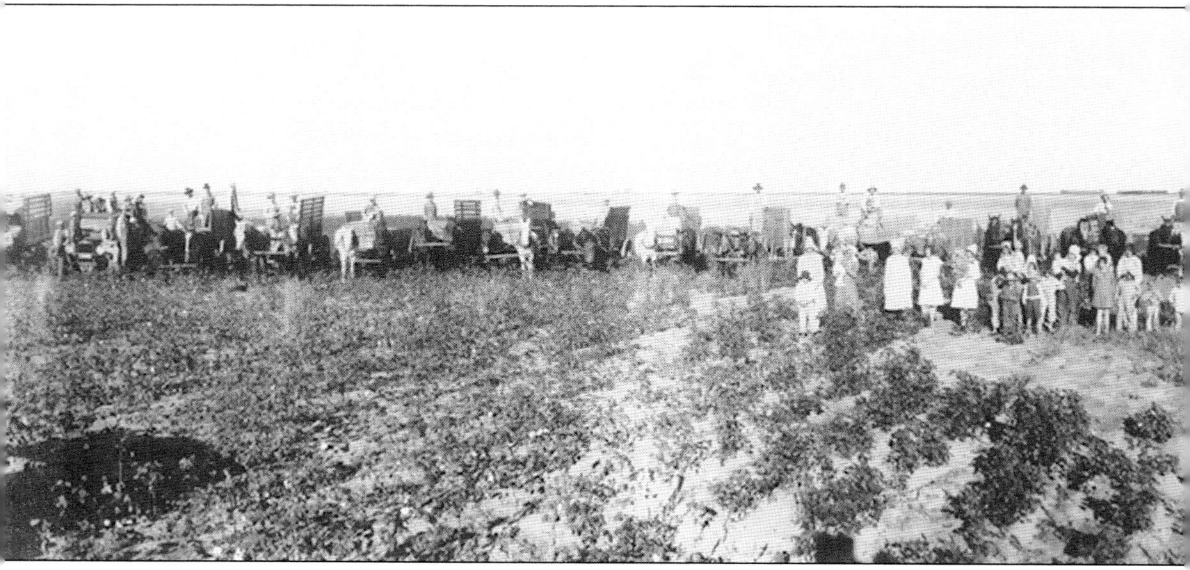

On October 19, 1928, friends and neighbors of the late cotton farmer Mike Smith have gathered on his farm near Floydada to pull his cotton crop for his widow. Smith had died suddenly from an attack of appendicitis before he could harvest his crop. South Plains farmers have a long history

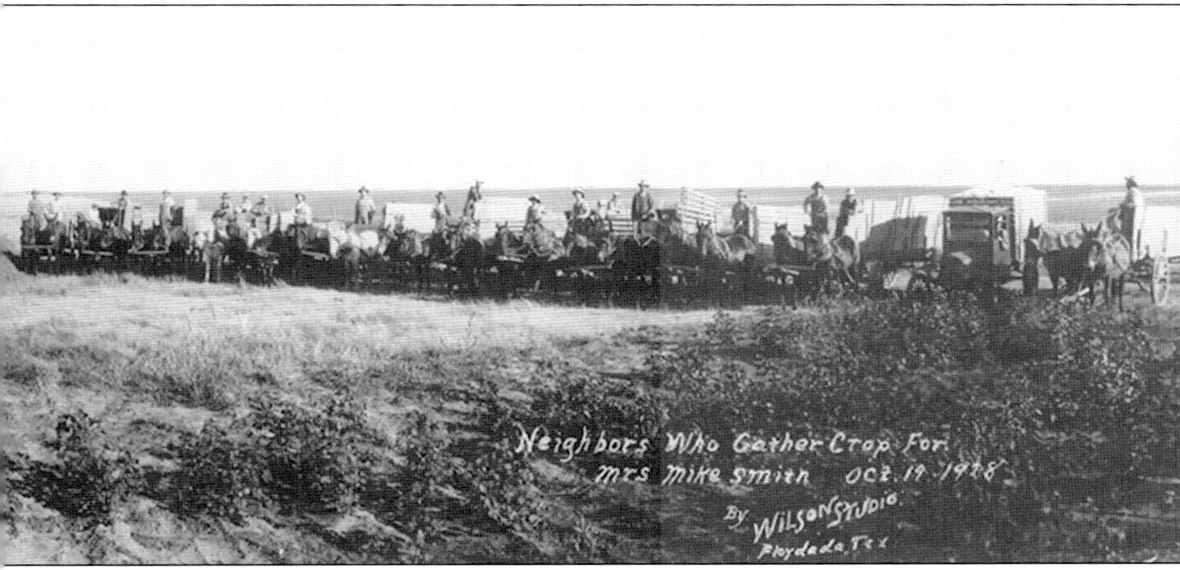

of helping each other out in times of need. Without the aid of friends and neighbors, there was no way Mrs. Smith could have harvested the crop at all. Judging from the image and the date, the cotton was not irrigated. (Courtesy of the Floyd County Historical Museum.)

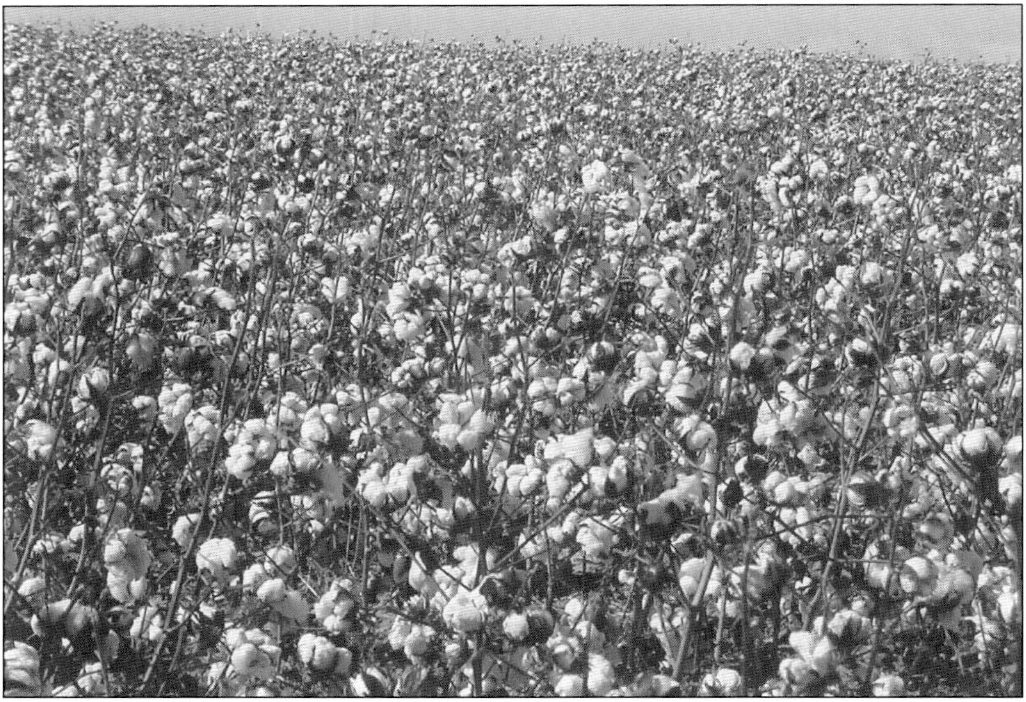

A beautiful site on the South Plains of Texas is a cotton field ready to be stripped. Cotton bolls normally open between 50 and 60 days after the pod ripens and enlarges. After the bolls open, the fibers begin to dry in the arid South Plains climate. This field of cotton seems to be holding up well. (Courtesy of Dan Taylor.)

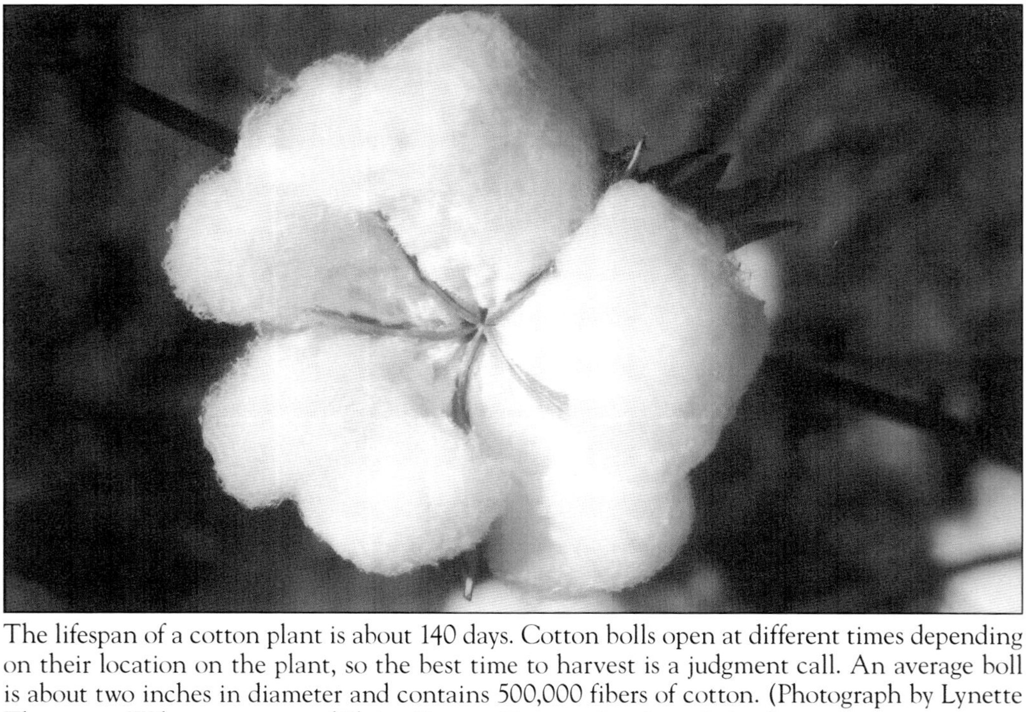

The lifespan of a cotton plant is about 140 days. Cotton bolls open at different times depending on their location on the plant, so the best time to harvest is a judgment call. An average boll is about two inches in diameter and contains 500,000 fibers of cotton. (Photograph by Lynette Thompson Wilson, courtesy of Plains Cotton Cooperative Association.)

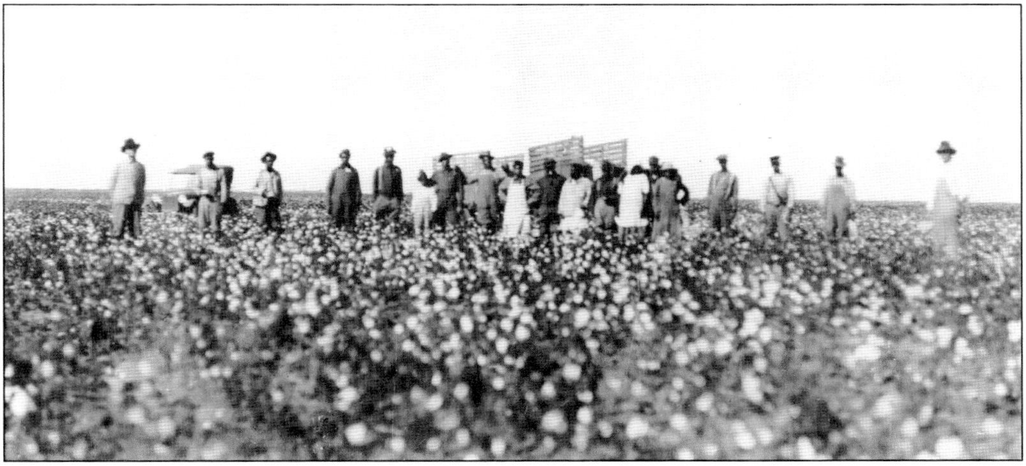

Pat Nix, a cotton farmer from Lubbock County, stands with the workers he has hired to pull his cotton in November 1923. These African American workers came from either East Texas or another Southern cotton-growing state. Most workers picked cotton in East Texas or the valley before moving to the South Plains. (Courtesy of the Texas AgriLife Research and Extension Center – Lubbock, Texas.)

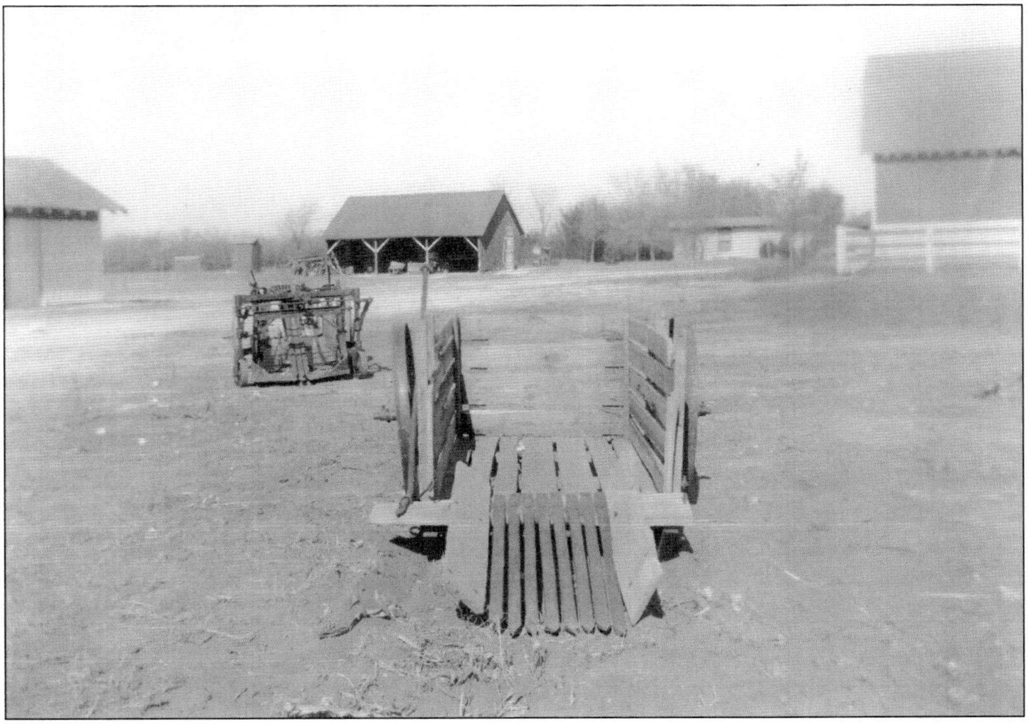

This finger type of cotton stripper was one step above a cotton-stripping sled, which was previously used with some success on the South Plains. Placing the sled on two wheels made it easier to pull down the rows of cotton. One man drove the team while another managed the cotton in the sled. (Courtesy of the Texas AgriLife Research and Extension Center – Lubbock, Texas.)

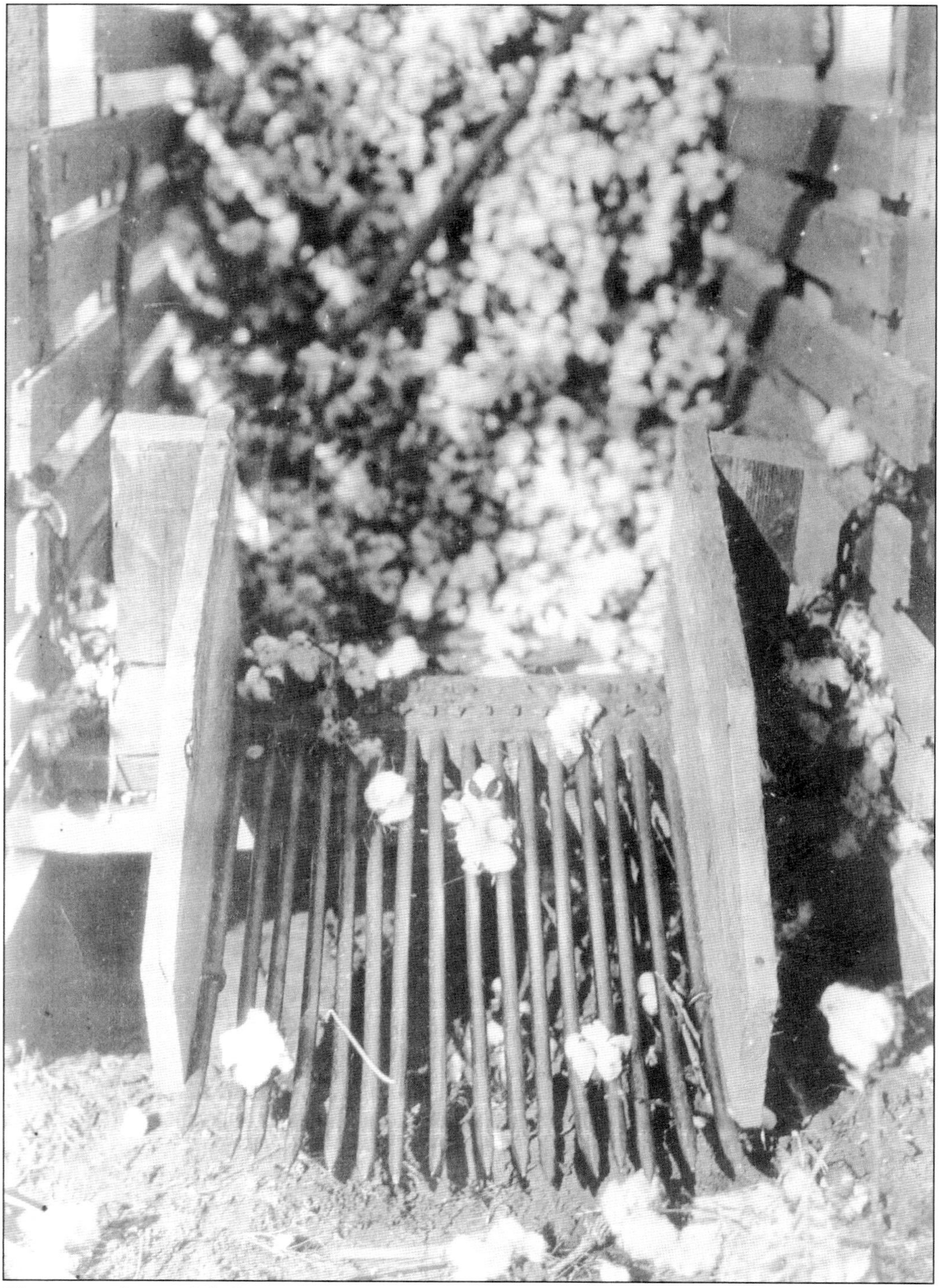

The square-fingered sled was another type of team-pulled cotton stripper. It is a modification and improvement of the round-finger type of sled on the previous page. Here, a square-fingered sled is used on a Lubbock farm in 1927. The square shape allowed more cotton to be pulled between the fingers into the container. (Courtesy of the Texas AgriLife Research and Extension Center – Lubbock, Texas.)

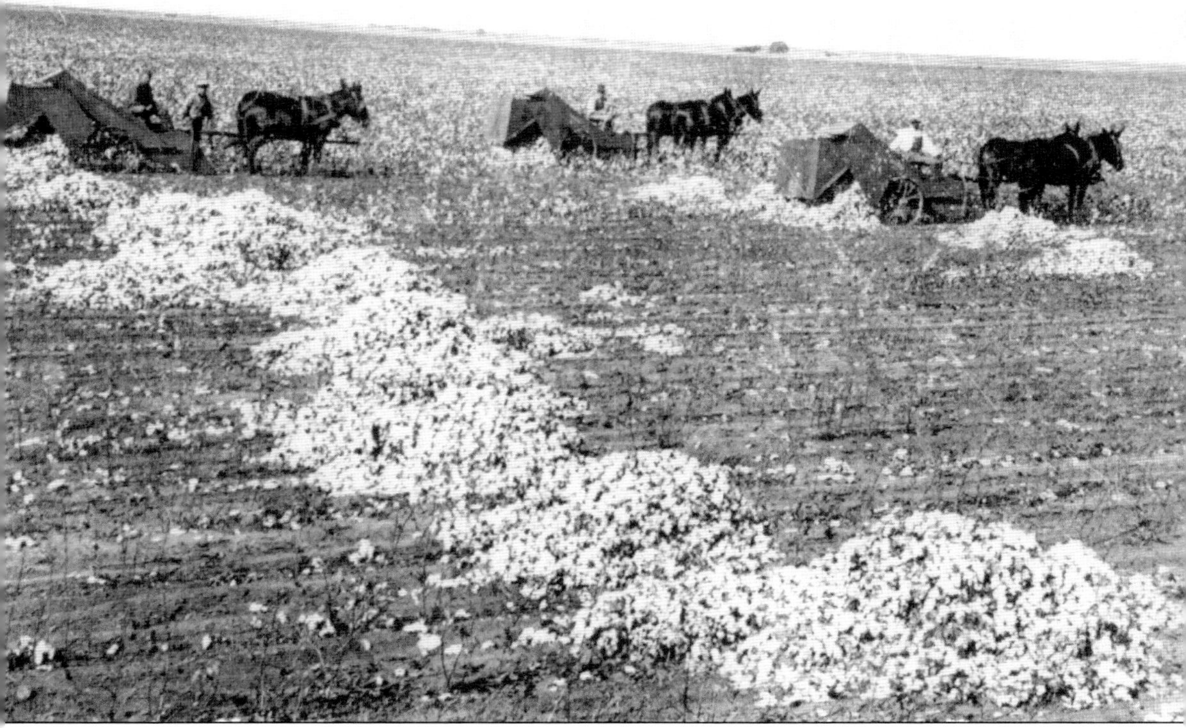

John Deere cotton strippers harvest a field of cotton in Lubbock County in 1932. These mule-drawn strippers took two men to operate and stripped every boll off the plant, ripe or not. A conveyer moved the stripped cotton from the head of the stripper to the back. The moving parts of the stripper operated from the movement of the wheels. (Photograph from the Cotton Industry Photography Collection, courtesy of the Southwest Collection/Special Collections Library, Texas Tech University.)

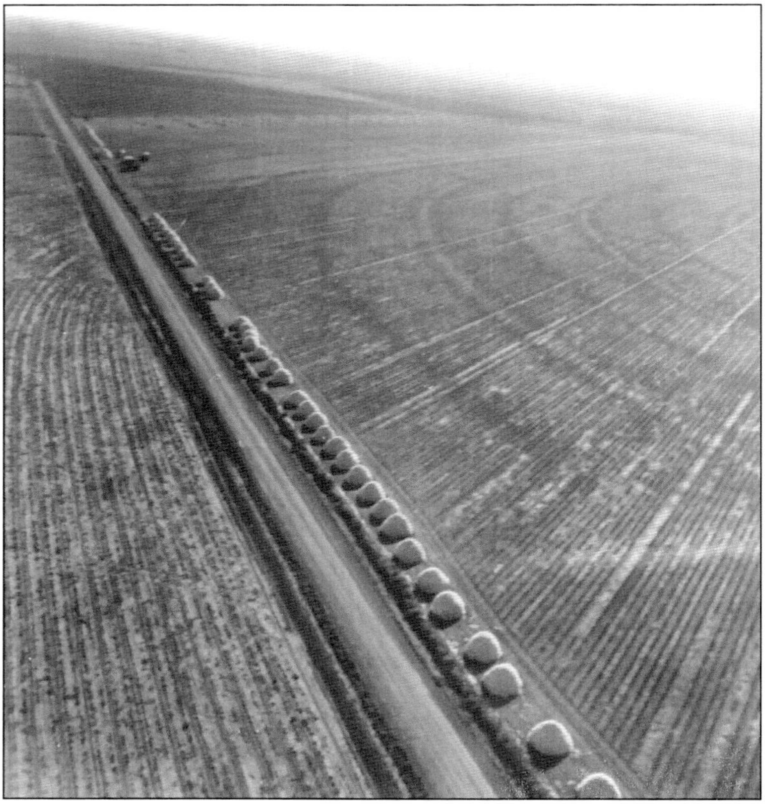

A cotton farmer in Floyd County has dumped cotton from his stripper directly onto the ground. It appears that six rows of stripped cotton went into making one pile of cotton. It is interesting to wonder what happened. Perhaps all the cotton wagons were full and at the gin. No matter the reason, these nicely arranged piles of cotton will not last long if the famous West Texas wind blows. (Courtesy of the Floyd County Historical Museum.)

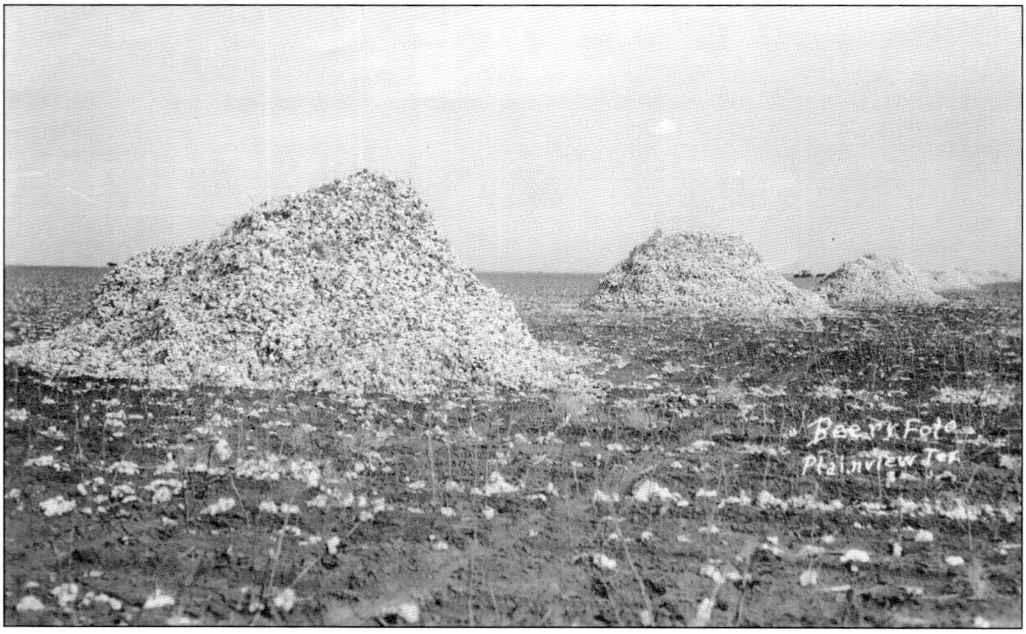

In 1926, R.C. Malone of Plainview harvested his cotton using a sled with a V-shaped opening in the front. The sled was drawn over the cotton plants, pulling the bolls off the plants. When the sled was full, it was dumped into piles. One of these piles equaled 125 sleds full of cotton. (Courtesy of the Texas AgriLife Research and Extension Center – Lubbock, Texas.)

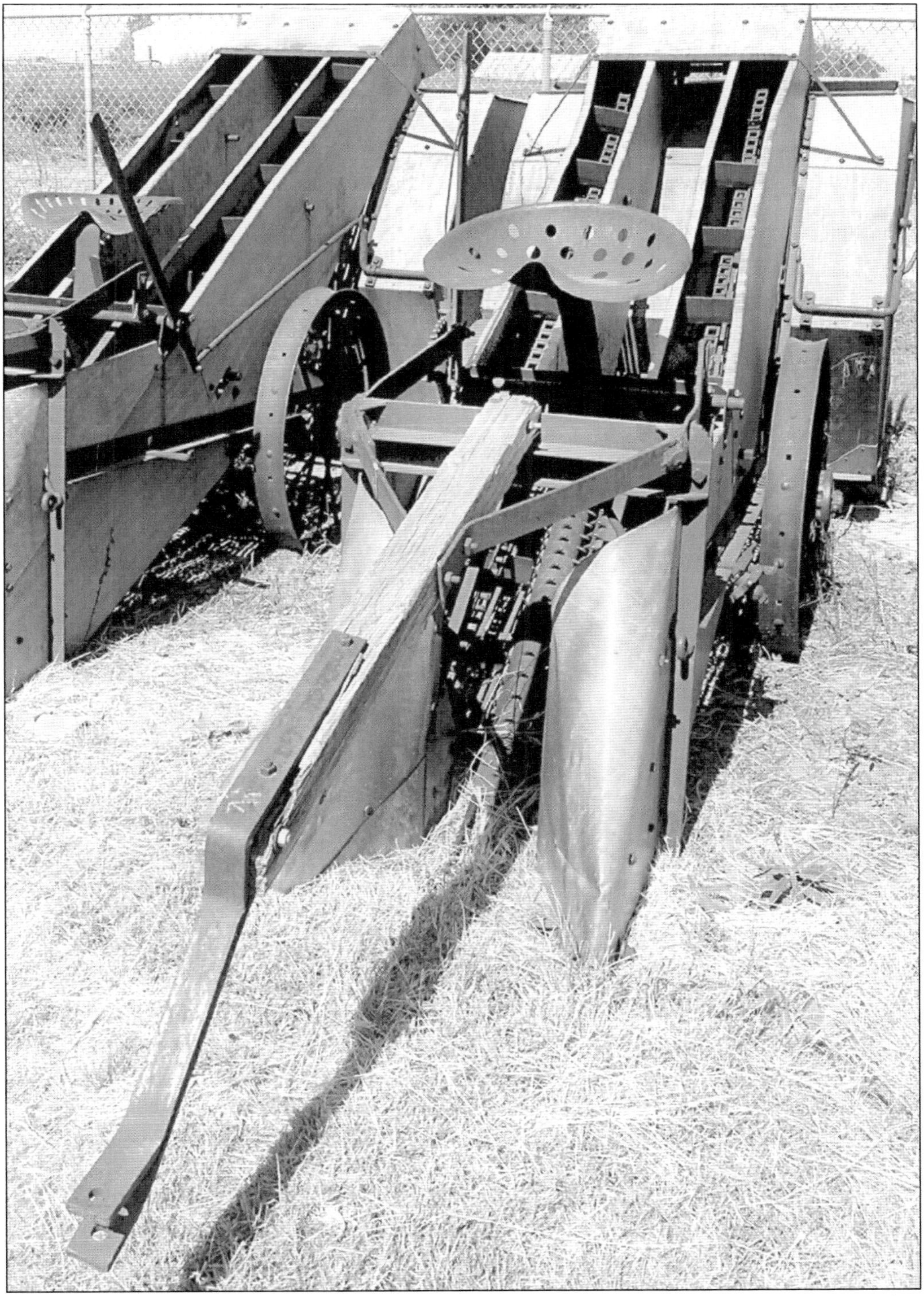

One man sat in the front of this John Deere one-row stripper driving the team, usually mules, as another man stood in the back pushing the cotton to the back of the stripper as it fell from the conveyor system behind the seat. The actual stripping took place under the driver's seat. (Photograph by Richard Porter, courtesy *Plainview Daily Herald*.)

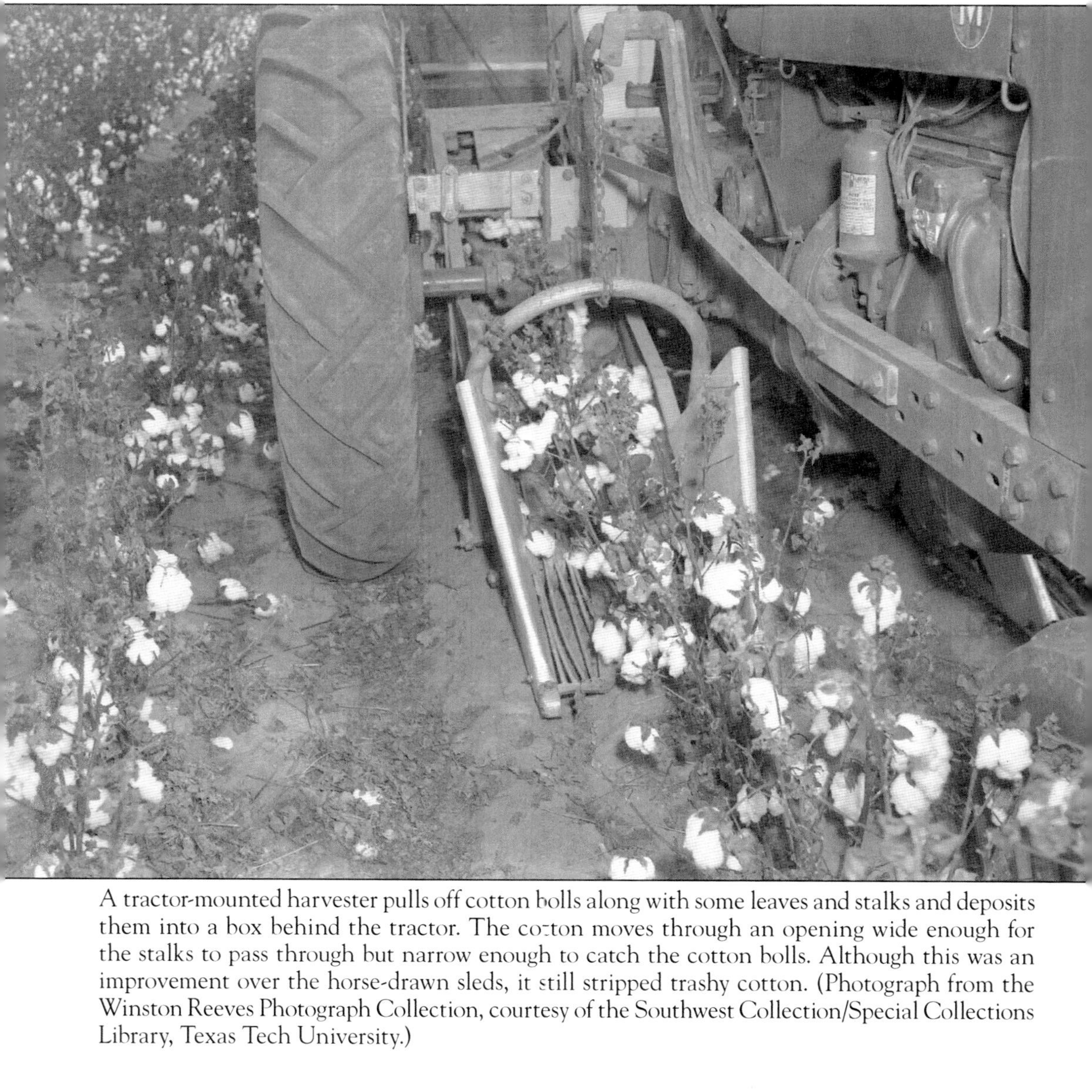

A tractor-mounted harvester pulls off cotton bolls along with some leaves and stalks and deposits them into a box behind the tractor. The cotton moves through an opening wide enough for the stalks to pass through but narrow enough to catch the cotton bolls. Although this was an improvement over the horse-drawn sleds, it still stripped trashy cotton. (Photograph from the Winston Reeves Photograph Collection, courtesy of the Southwest Collection/Special Collections Library, Texas Tech University.)

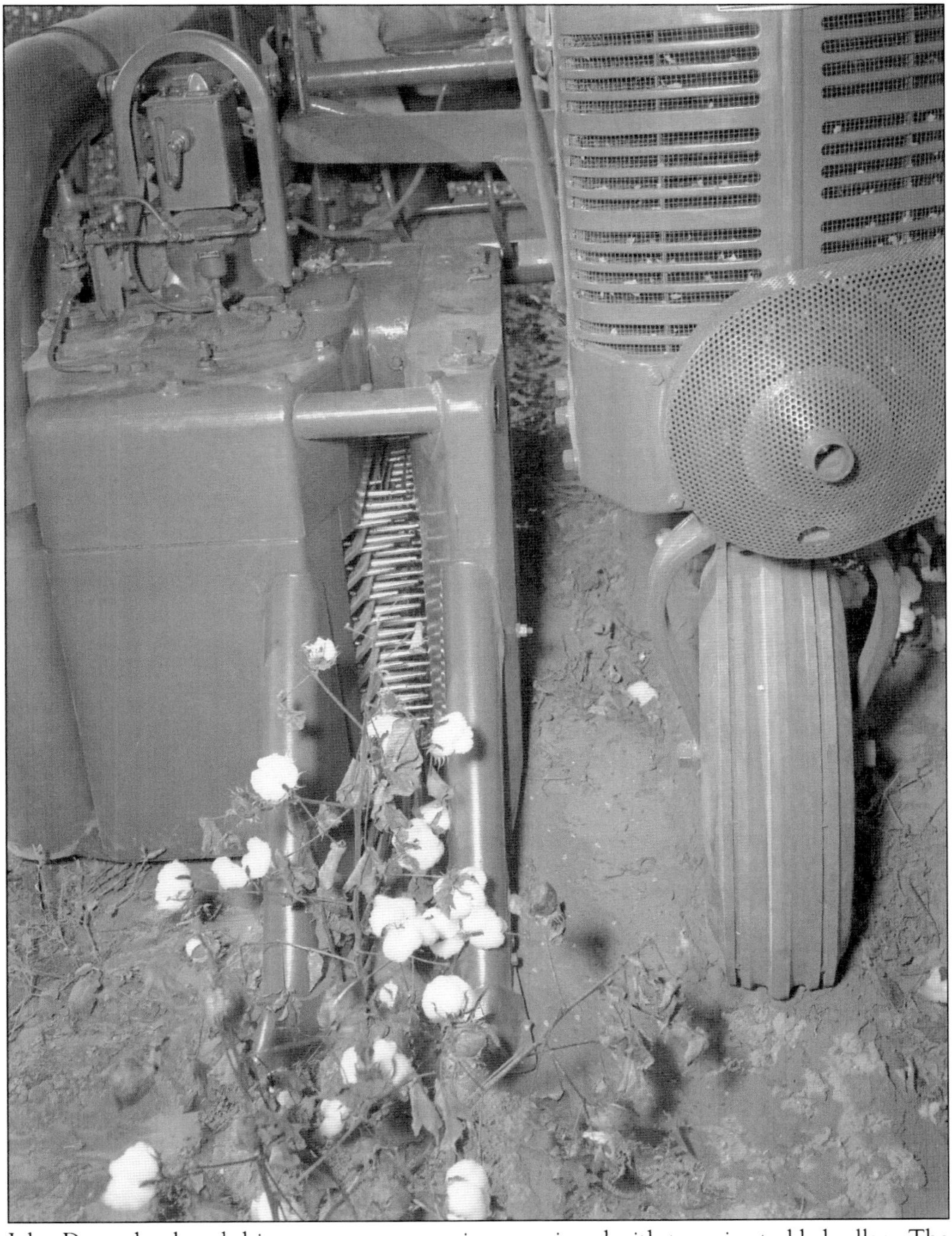

John Deere developed this one-row cotton stripper equipped with two pin-studded rollers. The rollers functioned by stripping the entire cotton boll off the stalk as well as some leaves and bits of stalk. One major drawback to this stripper and others like it was that it stripped unopened or green bolls off the plant. (Photograph from the Winston Reeves Photograph Collection, courtesy of the Southwest Collection/Special Collections Library, Texas Tech University.)

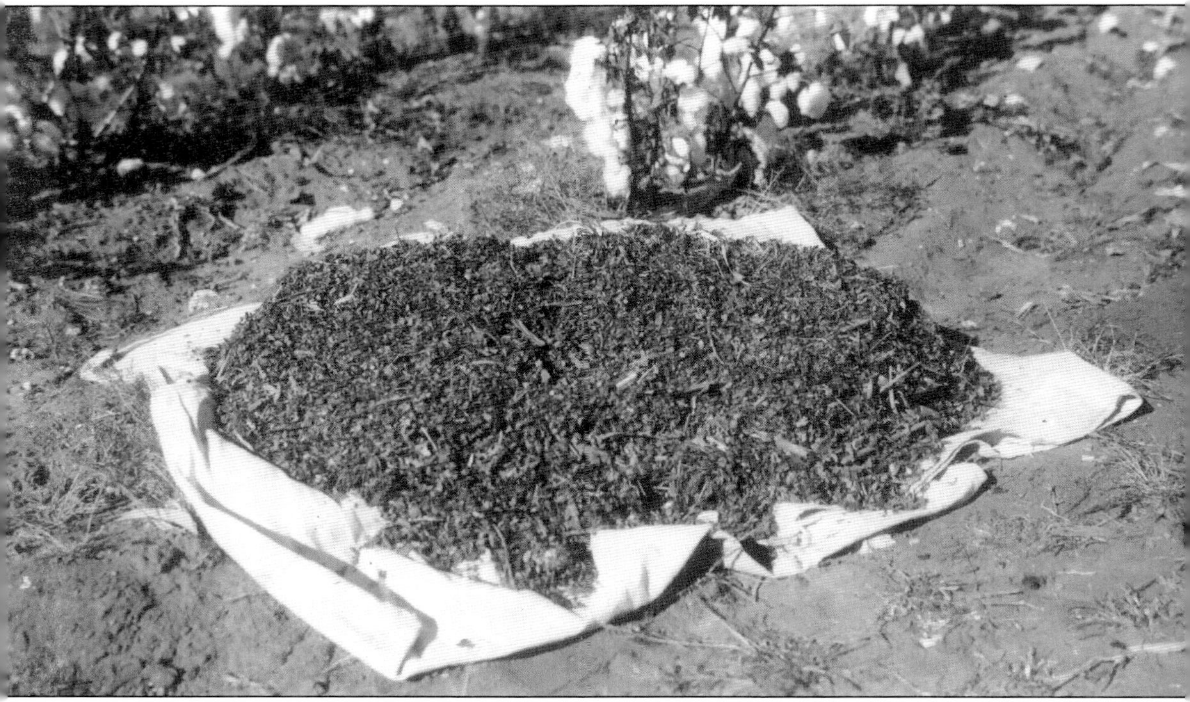

Research in collaboration with farmers led to improvements in harvesting equipment. This image shows the quality and quantity of leaf and stem trash taken out of the lint by an improved stripper unit and side conveyor screen on a John Deere stripper. About 7.4 pounds was rejected in the 425-foot test run of the single-row stripper on a Lubbock farm in 1946. (Courtesy of the Texas AgriLife Research and Extension Center – Lubbock, Texas.)

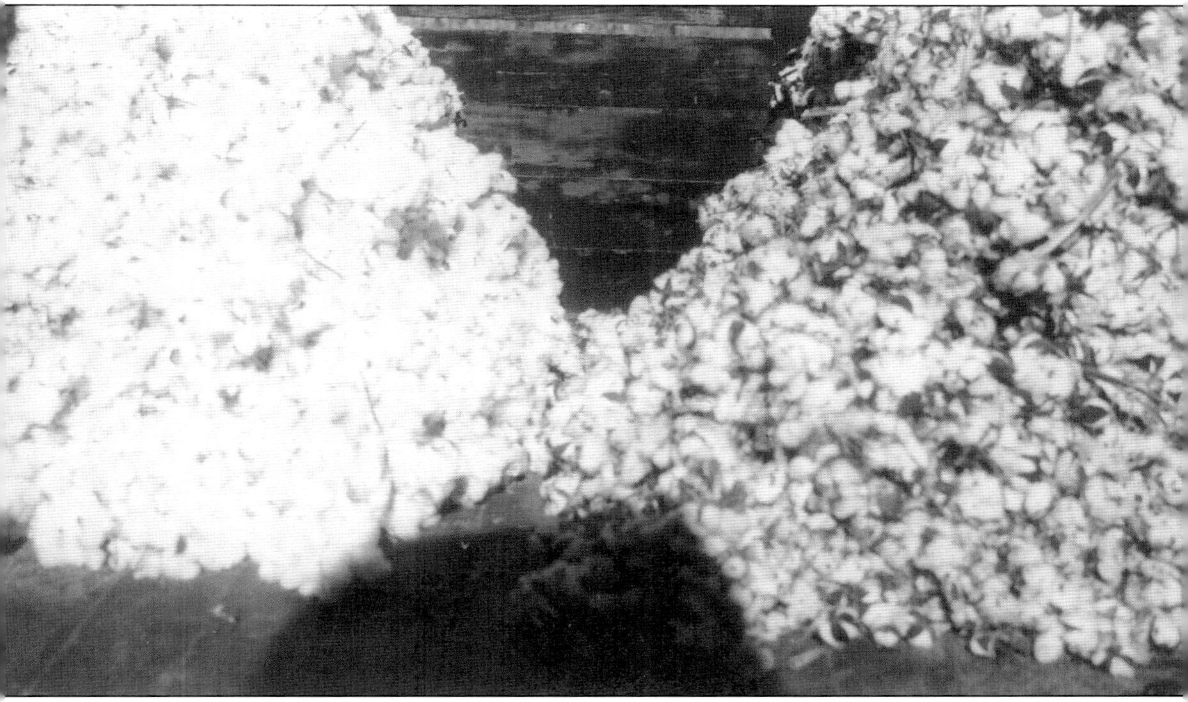

Improvements in agricultural mechanization improved the quality of cotton at harvest. This image shows the difference a stripper with a debris extractor can make. On the left is the cleaner cotton, which came from a stripper with an extractor, while the pile of the right came from a stripper without an extractor. (Courtesy of the Texas AgriLife Research and Extension Center – Lubbock, Texas.)

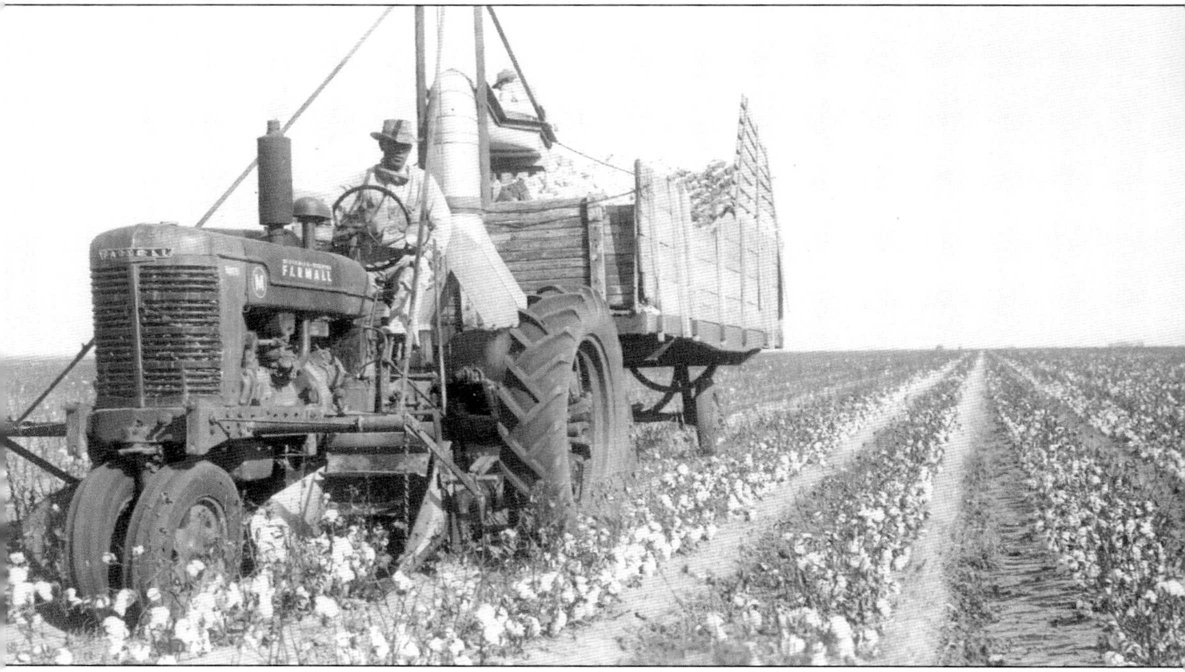

This farmworker by the name of Wallace works in an Anton cotton field in 1945, driving a two-row, tractor-mounted cotton stripper. The suction device behind Wallace blows the stripped cotton into a trailer pulled behind the tractor. The Farmall tractor was powerful enough to run the stripper and pull a large cotton trailer. (Courtesy of the Texas AgriLife Research and Extension Center – Lubbock, Texas.)

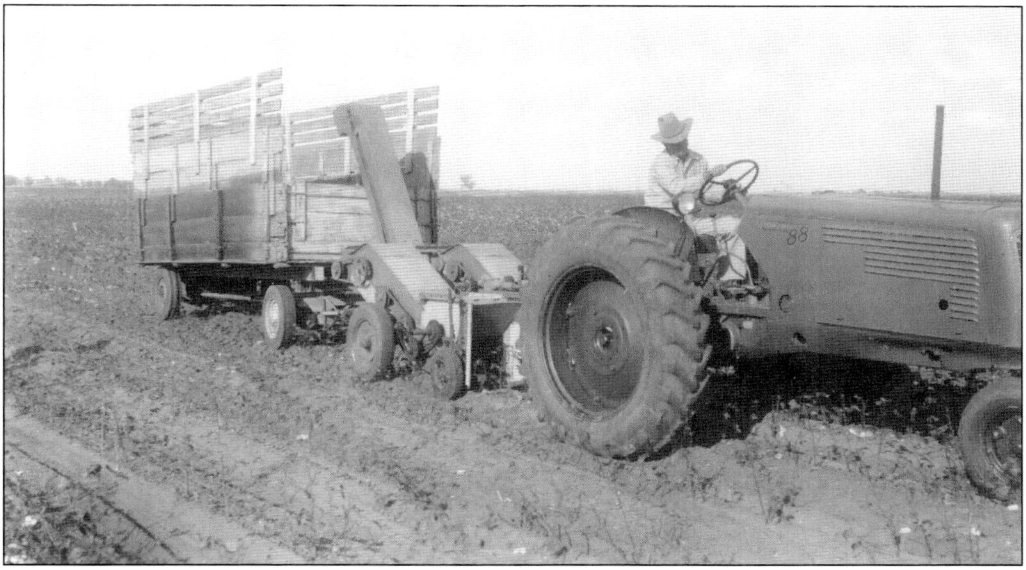

An Oliver two-row stripper runs through a field of previously stripped cotton. Notice the overall length of this pull-type stripper. One drawback of equipment being pulled behind a tractor is that the driver of the tractor has to constantly look back to see if the equipment is operating properly, while driving the tractor straight ahead. (Courtesy of the Texas AgriLife Research and Extension Center – Lubbock, Texas.)

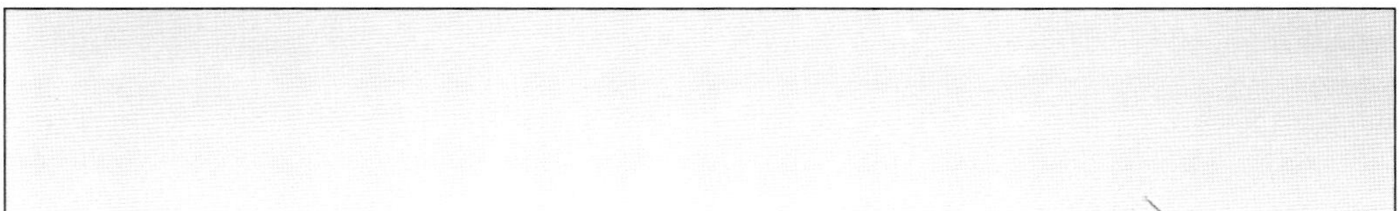

This two-row cotton stripper works on a Lubbock farm in 1948. An advancement over the one-row stripper, it still functioned the same. Advances include a motor that powers the stripper separate from the tractor, more powerful blowers and fans that produce cleaner cotton, and a basket attached to the stripper, which holds the stripped cotton until it can be emptied. (Courtesy of the Texas AgriLife Research and Extension Center – Lubbock, Texas.)

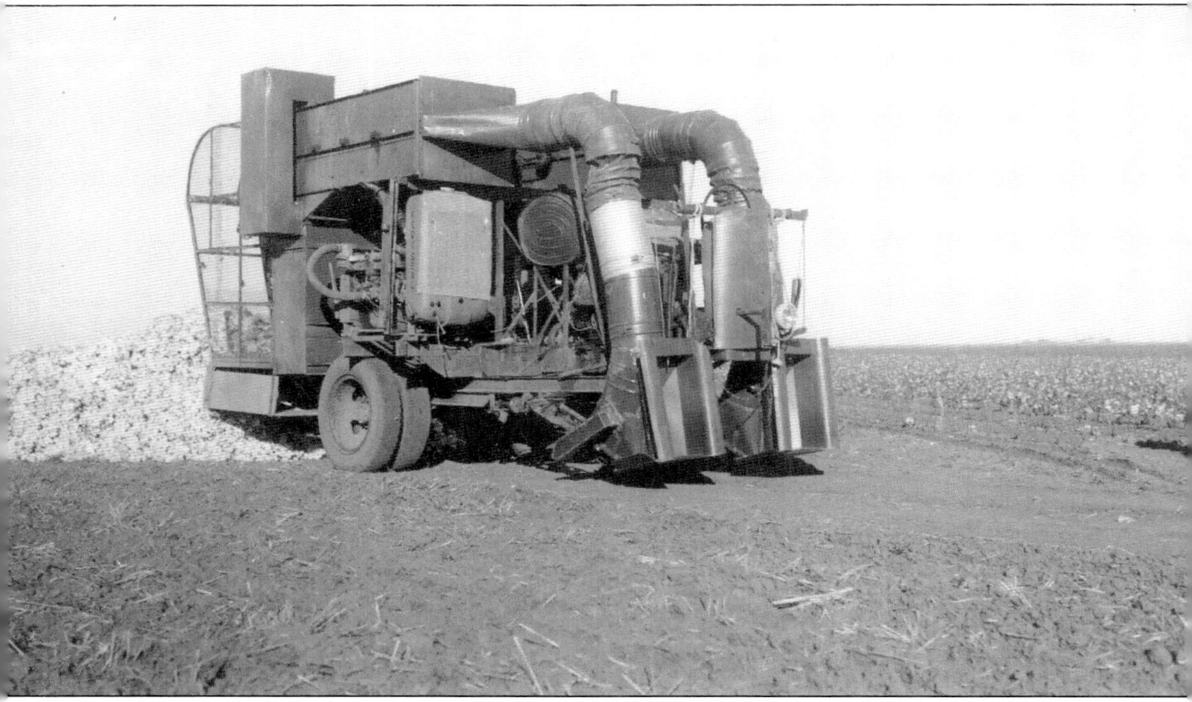

This is another view of a John Deere cotton stripper with an attached blower and boll rejecter, in 1949. More powerful tractors allowed farmers to pull heavier equipment through the cotton field. Although the blower sent the cotton into the trailer that followed the stripper, it still took another worker to push the cotton to the back of the trailer, while ejected bolls fell on the ground. (Courtesy of the Texas AgriLife Research and Extension Center – Lubbock, Texas.)

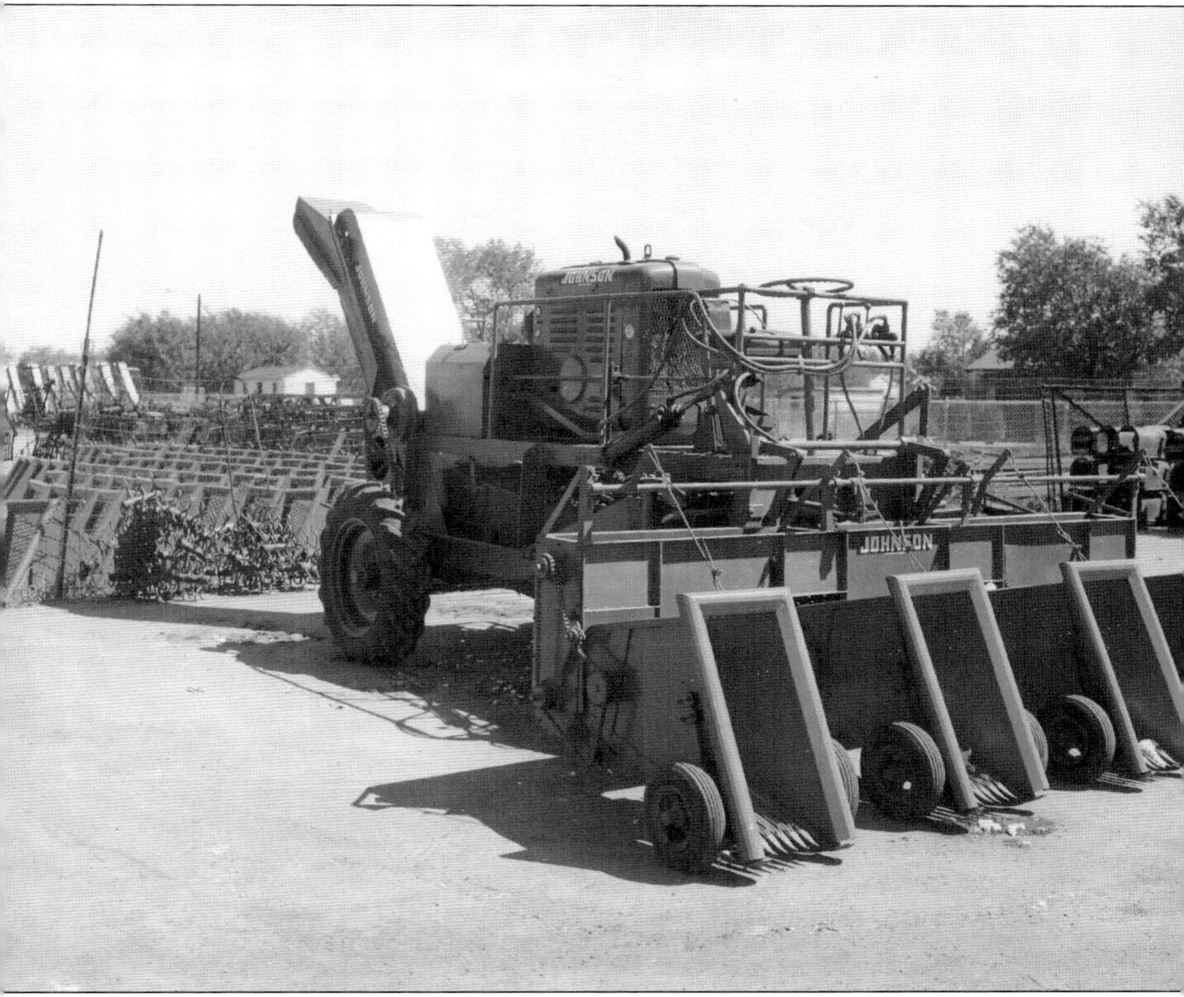

Farmers continued their quest for improved harvesting equipment. Here, a four-row Johnson cotton stripper stands idle on a Lubbock farm before the 1953 harvest begins. For the first time, the driver of the stripper had an excellent view of the cotton going into the stripper. However, the cotton was blown into a trailer pulled behind the stripper and not into a basket. (Courtesy of the Texas AgriLife Research and Extension Center – Lubbock, Texas.)

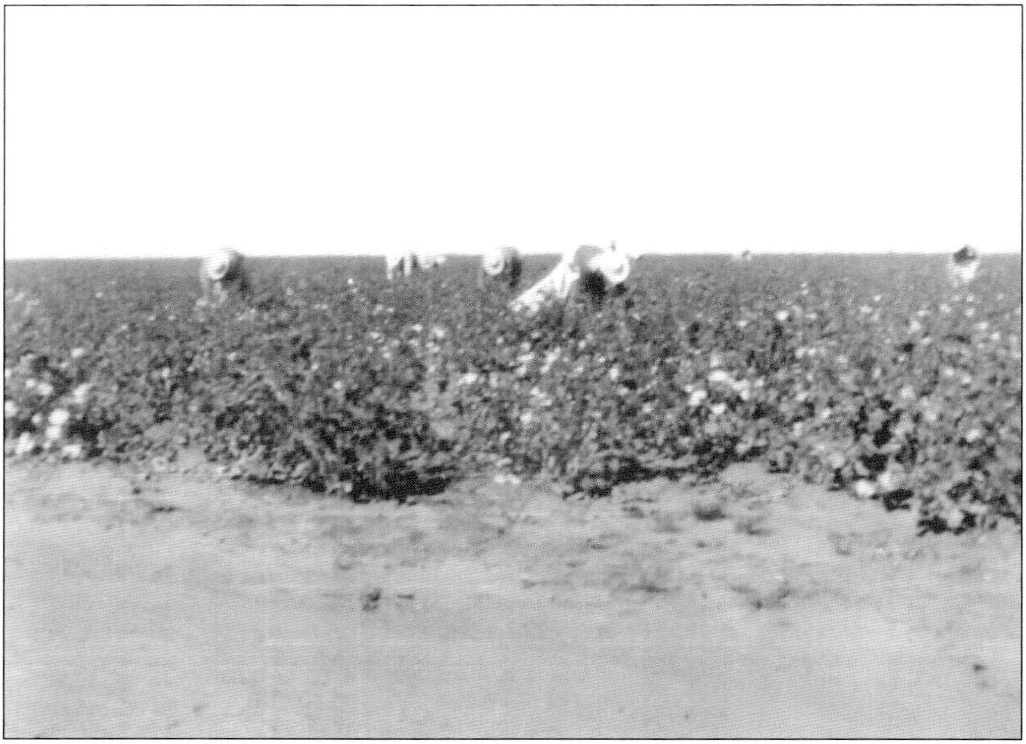

These workers are part of the Bracero Program—from the Spanish for "strong-armed"—which began in August 1942 to help in the war effort. In the 1950s, when this image was taken in a cotton field near Floydada, over 400,000 agricultural workers came to America annually. The program ended in 1964. (Courtesy of the Floyd County Historical Museum.)

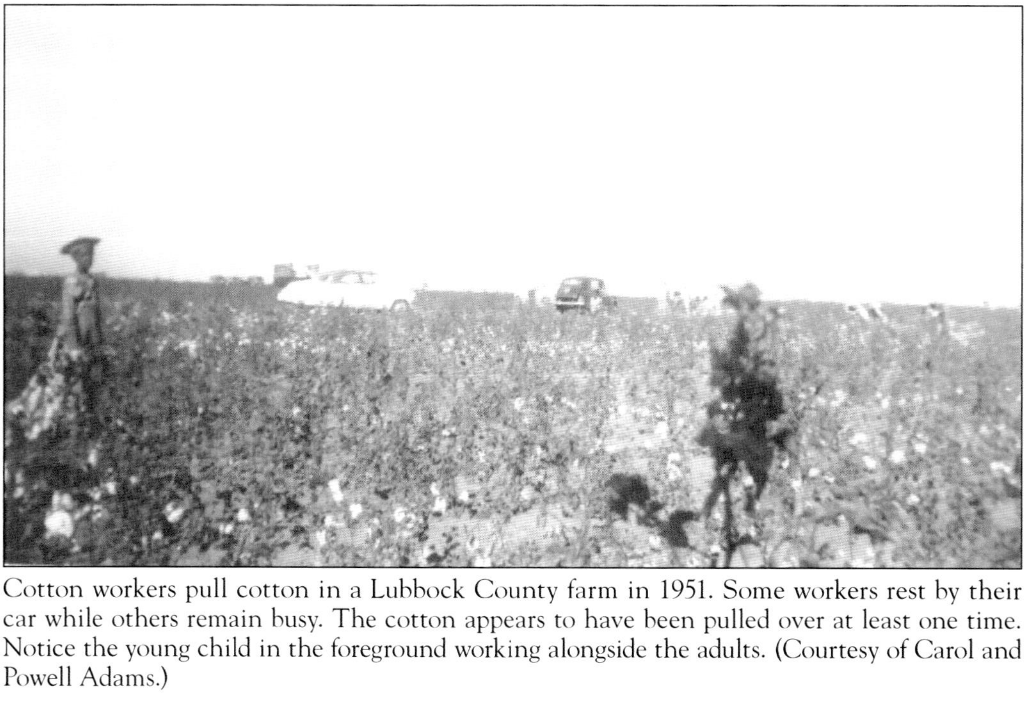

Cotton workers pull cotton in a Lubbock County farm in 1951. Some workers rest by their car while others remain busy. The cotton appears to have been pulled over at least one time. Notice the young child in the foreground working alongside the adults. (Courtesy of Carol and Powell Adams.)

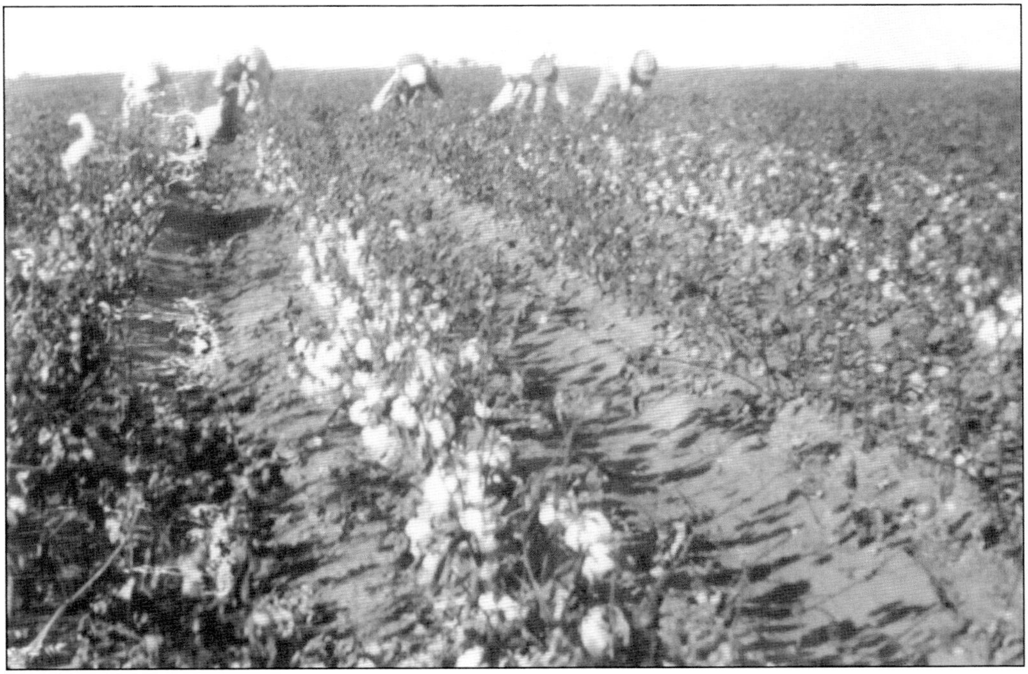

In the 1950s, cotton pulling was still a common site on the South Plains. Workers pull their way across a field, straddling the row they are pulling. Judging from the cotton, it is late in the season, but the cotton still seems to be of good quality. (Courtesy of Carol and Powell Adams.)

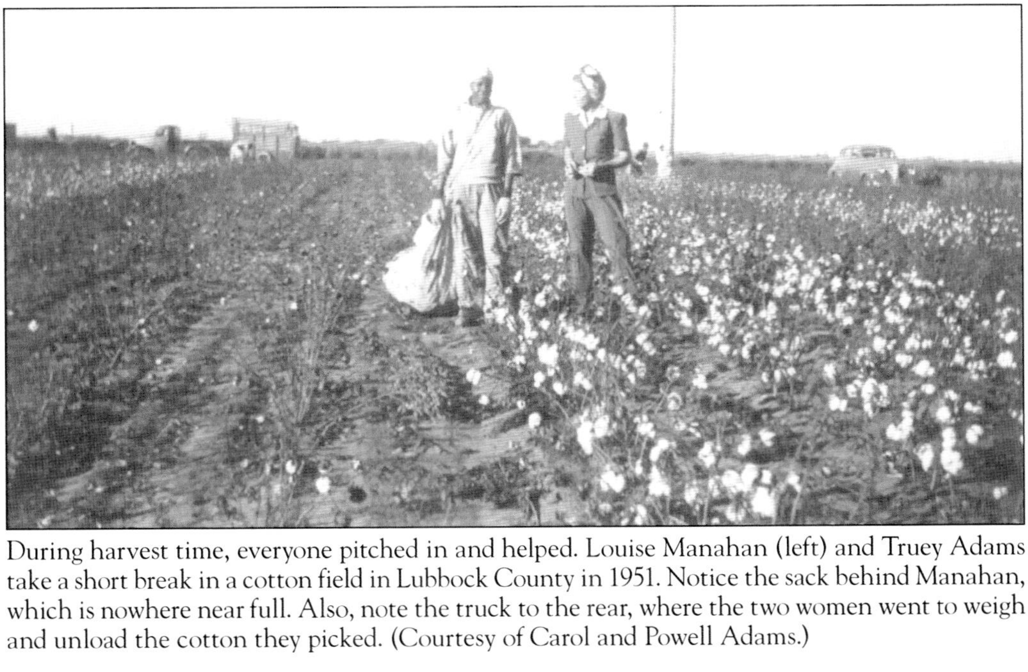

During harvest time, everyone pitched in and helped. Louise Manahan (left) and Truey Adams take a short break in a cotton field in Lubbock County in 1951. Notice the sack behind Manahan, which is nowhere near full. Also, note the truck to the rear, where the two women went to weigh and unload the cotton they picked. (Courtesy of Carol and Powell Adams.)

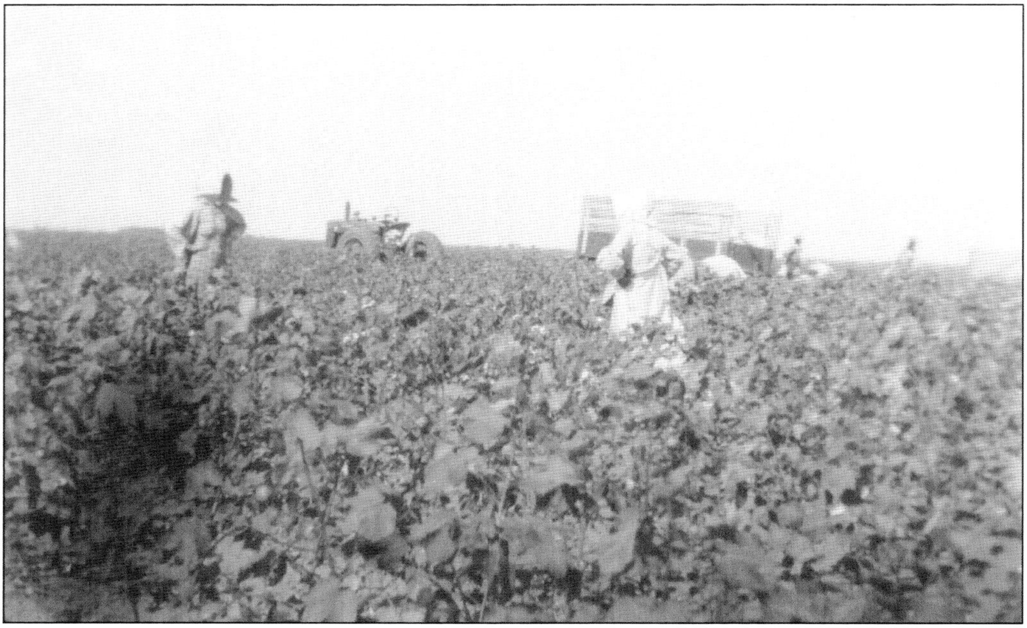

Two women take a break from pulling cotton in 1952 in a Lubbock County cotton field. Pulling cotton by hand meant two or three trips through the field, pulling the bolls as they ripened. Modern strippers only make one pass through a field. In the foreground are unopened bolls on cotton plants that have already been pulled once. (Courtesy of Carol and Powell Adams.)

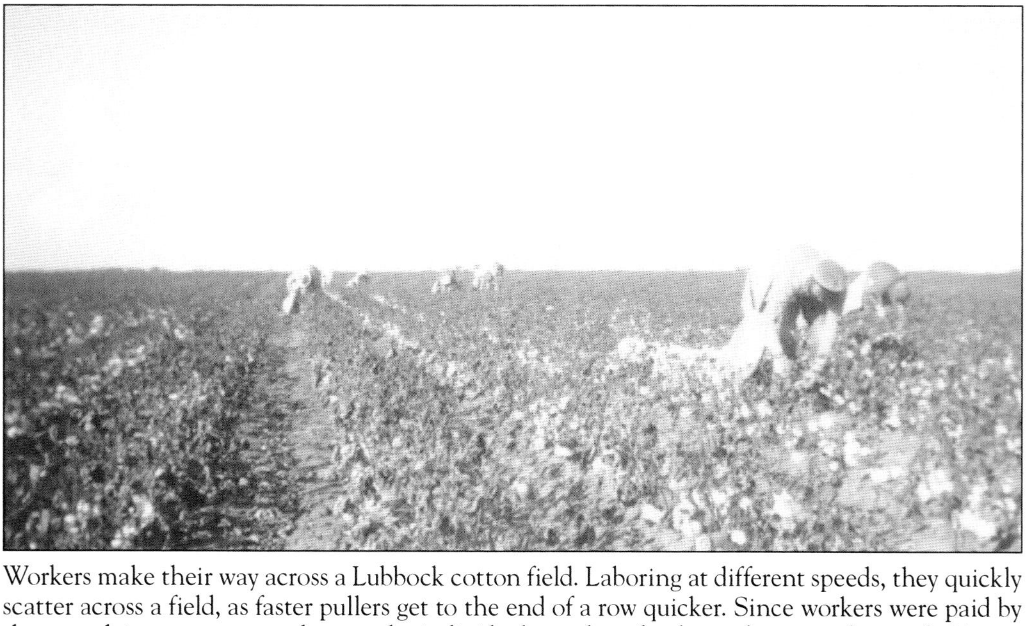

Workers make their way across a Lubbock cotton field. Laboring at different speeds, they quickly scatter across a field, as faster pullers get to the end of a row quicker. Since workers were paid by the pound, it was pretty much up to the individual as to how fast he or she wanted to work. Notice how low the cotton is to the ground. (Courtesy of Carol and Powell Adams.)

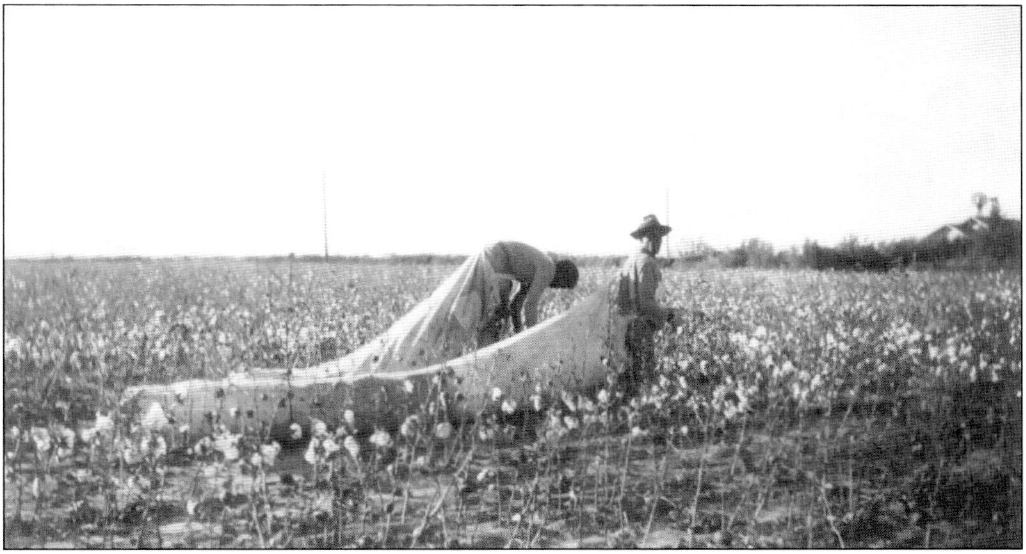

Frank and H.J. Monahan pick their way across a South Plains cotton field in 1953. On a good day, these two men could pull 1,000 pounds of cotton. Cotton bags were up to 20 feet long and were attached to the workers by a leather strap. When the bag was filled, it was taken to the scales and then dumped into a wagon. (Courtesy of Carol and Powell Adams.)

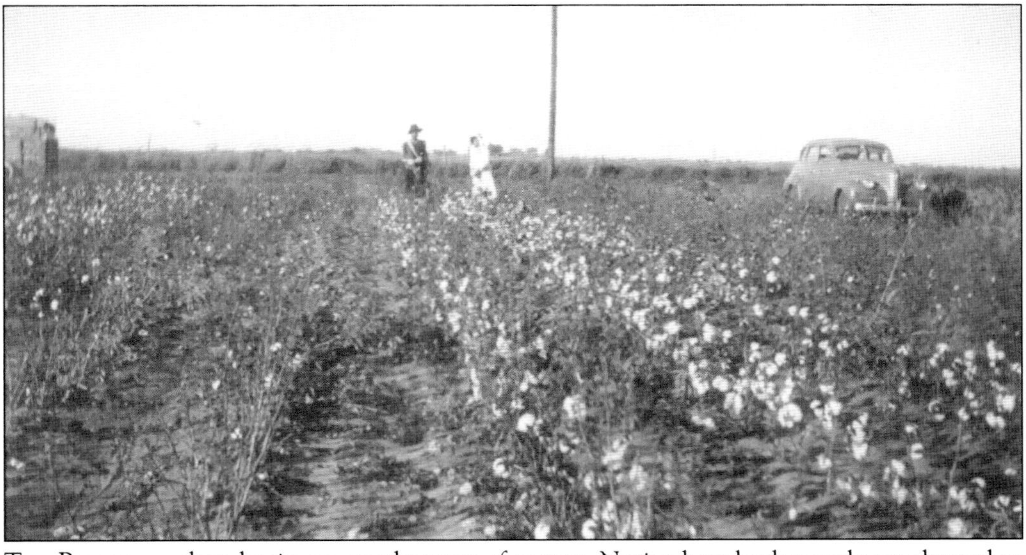

Two Bracero workers begin on another row of cotton. Notice how both people are dressed to protect themselves against the burning rays of the South Plains sun. Gloves were also worn to protect the hands from cotton burs. Since rows of cotton were often up to a mile long, a cotton sack could become pretty full before the end of a row. (Courtesy of Carol and Powell Adams.)

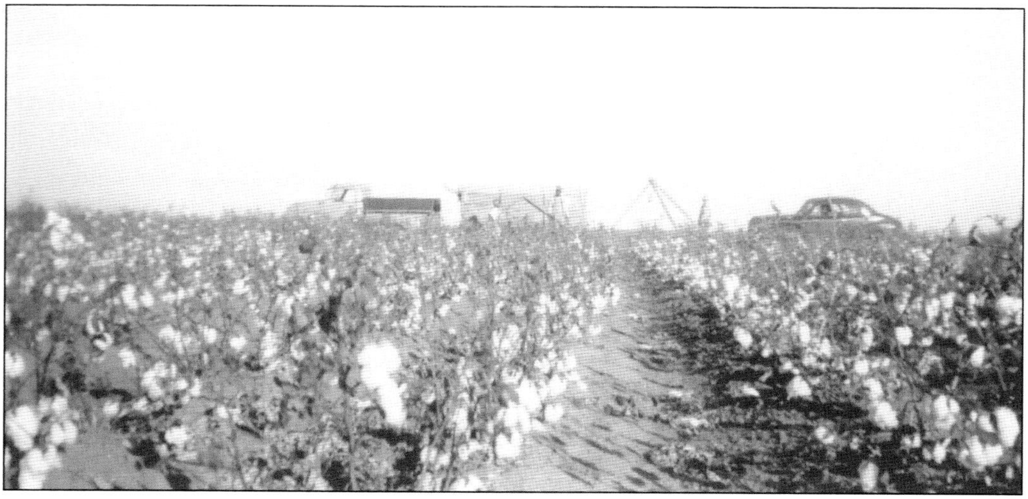

A cotton wagon sits empty and the scales stand ready to weigh cotton. It appears to be a cool morning in the fall of 1951, with plenty of cotton pulling yet to be done. Even today, cotton harvesting has to wait until the dew dries off the cotton, forcing farmers and workers to bide their time until mid-morning to begin work. (Courtesy of Carol and Powell Adams.)

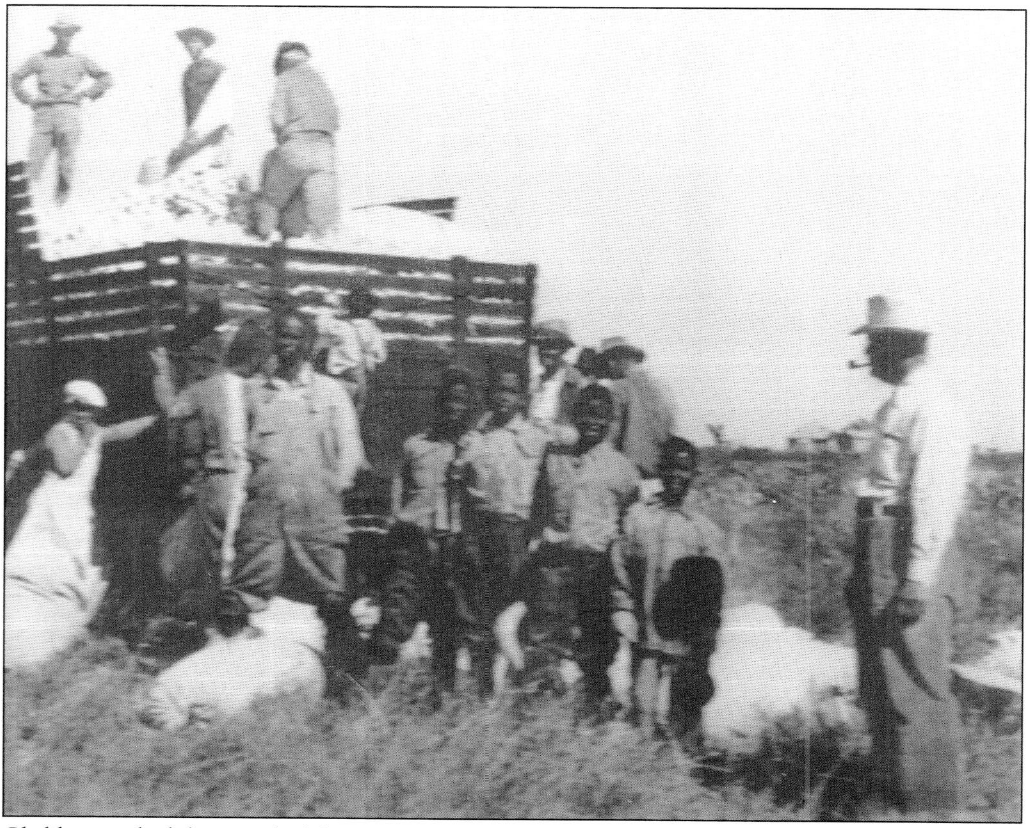

Children and adults, mostly African Americans, wait to empty their half-full bags into the waiting truck. The owner stands by and watches carefully. After loading the cotton onto the truck, it was driven to the gin. Hopefully, the truck could be emptied quickly so harvesting could continue without too much delay. (Courtesy of the Ralls Historical Museum.)

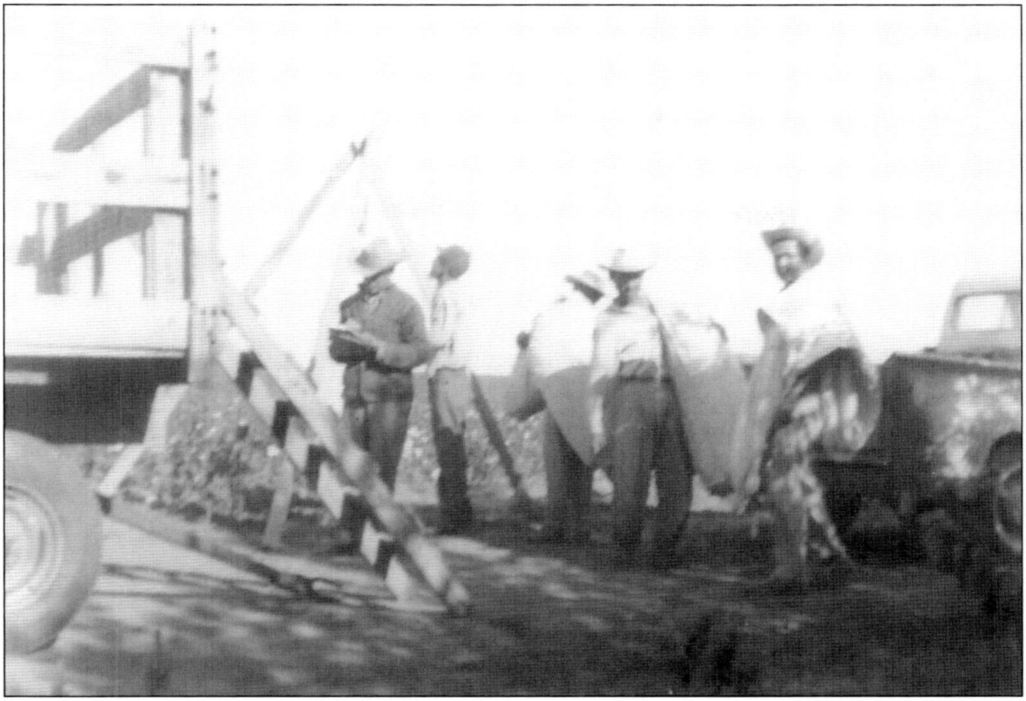

A Floydada cotton farmer writes down in his ledger the weight of the cotton picked by one of the Bracero workers he has hired. Others stand around waiting their turns. The weighted cotton is loaded into the wagon on the left. Notice that it takes two men to lift a full bag of cotton. (Courtesy of the Floyd County Historical Museum.)

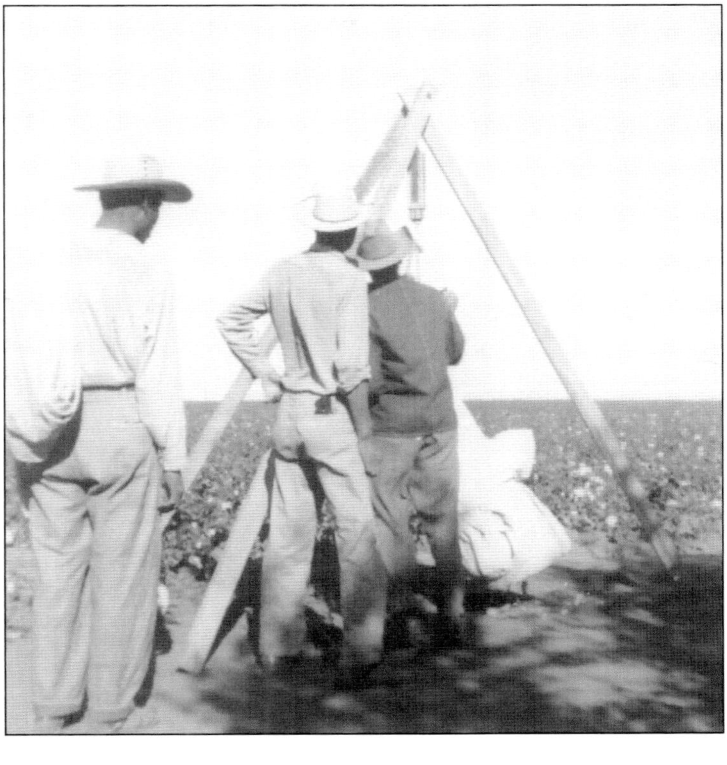

In this 1950s image of a cotton harvest, the tripod in the center holds the scale used to weigh the bags of cotton. The farmer would weigh the cotton and keep track of the pounds each worker pulled. At the end of the day or week, each cotton puller was paid. (Courtesy of the Floyd County Historical Museum.)

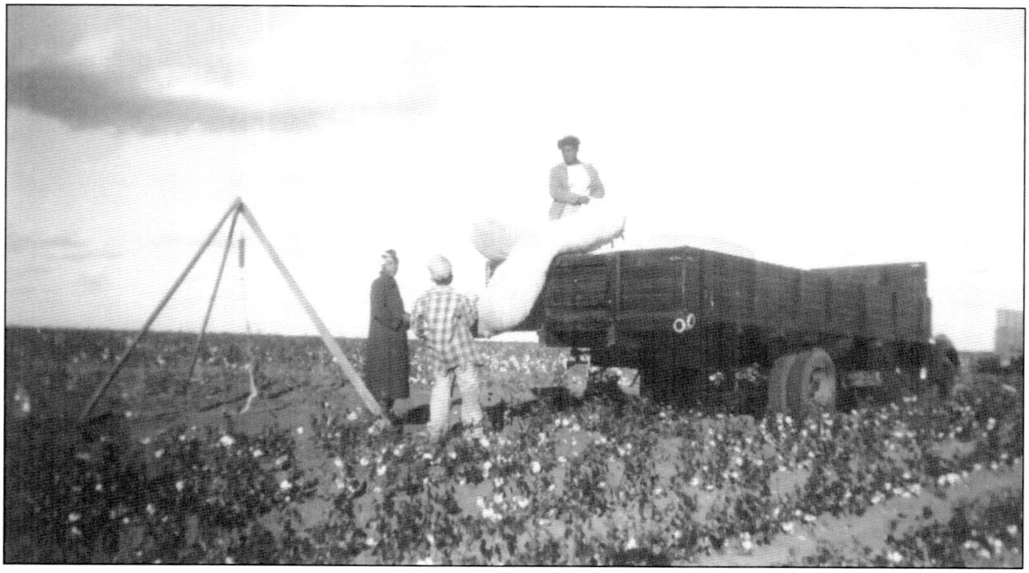

Women were not an uncommon site in the cotton field at any time of year, especially during cotton pulling time. Here, three African American women unload a bag of cotton into a cotton wagon. These women worked for the Adams family in eastern Lubbock County around 1950. (Courtesy of Carol and Powell Adams.)

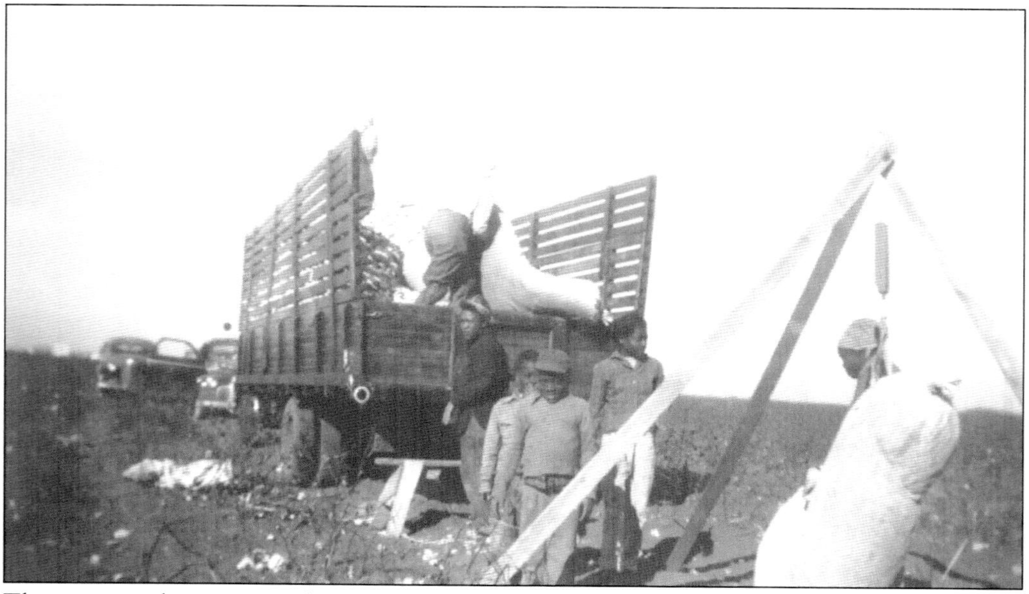

This crew, with one man, three women, and three children, was led by Ervetta Trimble, the woman by the scale. Many women worked long hours in the fields alongside the men, especially during the busiest times of the year. (Courtesy of Carol and Powell Adams.)

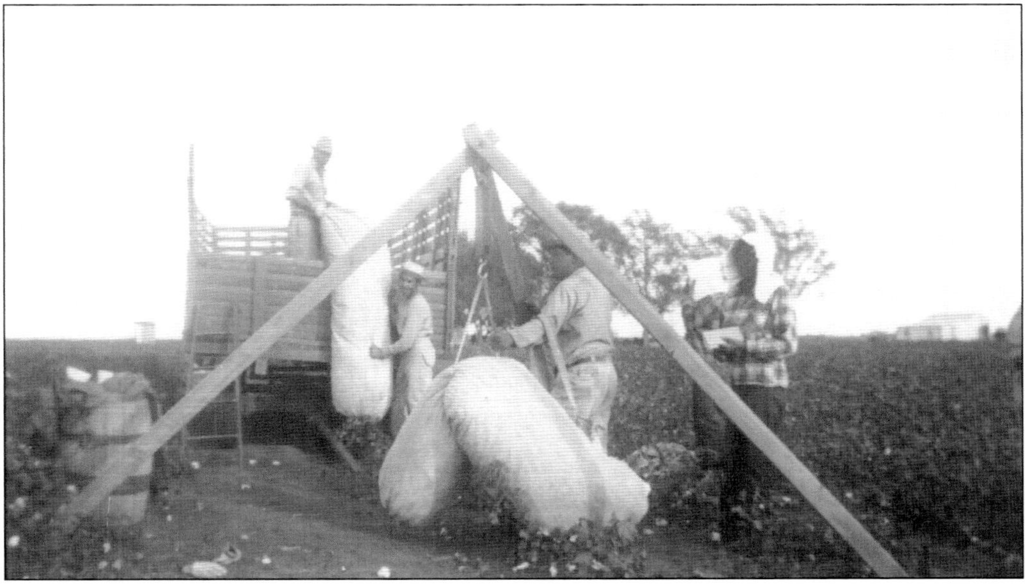

Ervetta Trimble, at the extreme right, supervises the weighing and loading of cotton on the farm in the 1950s. She wears a bonnet to protect herself against the sun, and everyone has on long sleeves to protect his or her arms while pulling cotton. Notice the gloves on the ground at the left used to protect hands. (Courtesy of Carol and Powell Adams.)

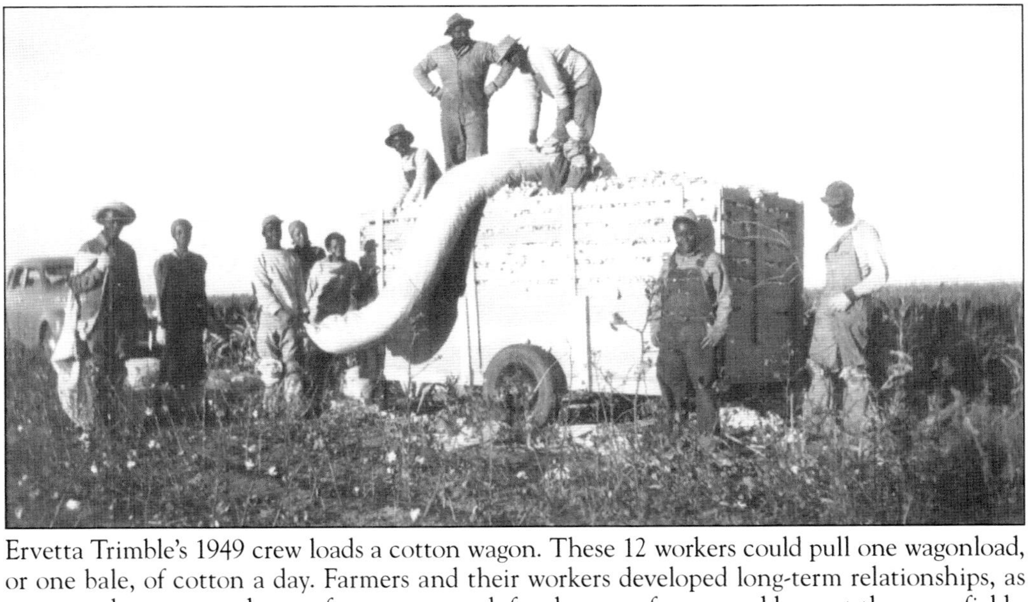

Ervetta Trimble's 1949 crew loads a cotton wagon. These 12 workers could pull one wagonload, or one bale, of cotton a day. Farmers and their workers developed long-term relationships, as many workers returned year after year to work for the same farmer and harvest the same fields. (Courtesy of Carol and Powell Adams.)

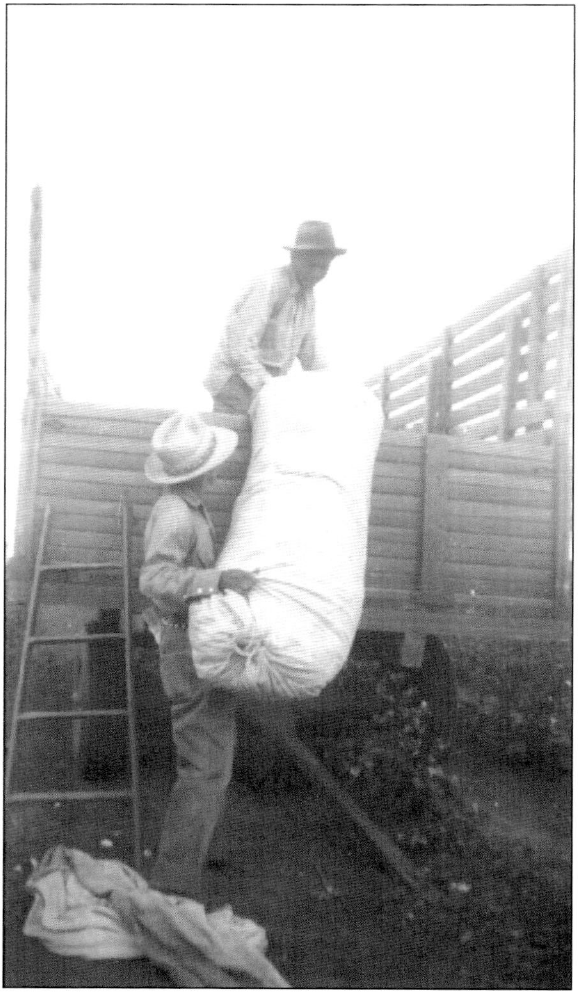

Two workers empty a bag of cotton into a wagon specially built by Powell Adams to carry three bales of cotton. Before the widespread use of module builders and mechanical strippers, cotton was pulled by hand and taken to the gin in trucks or wagons. (Courtesy of Carol and Powell Adams.)

This cotton is ready to be taken to the gin. In 1951, little had changed in how cotton was harvested and transported to the gin. Farmers were at the mercy of gin operators to unload their cotton wagons or trucks. In many instances, farmers had to stop harvesting their cotton and wait on a wagon or truck to be unloaded before pulling could begin again. (Courtesy of Carol and Powell Adams.)

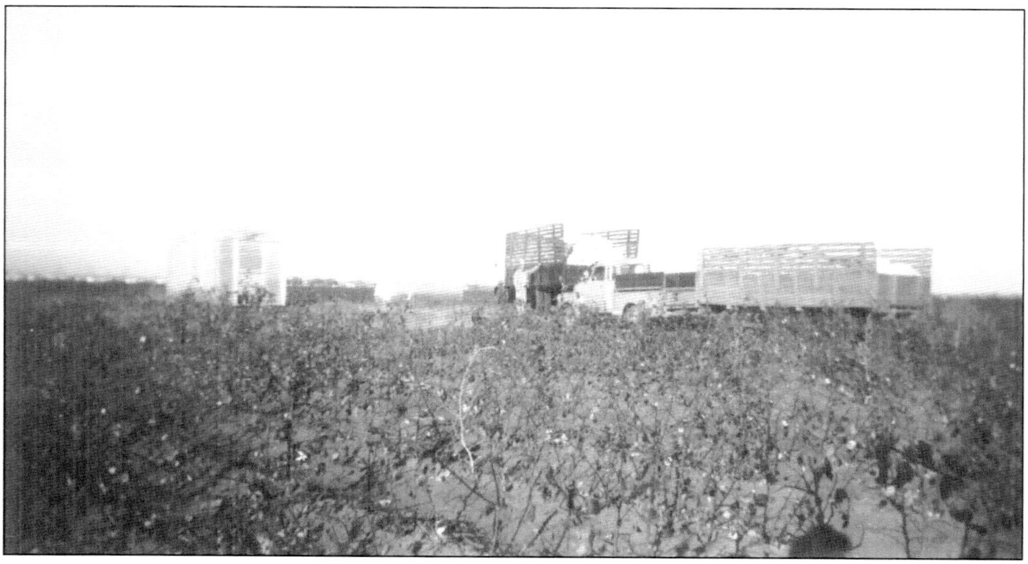

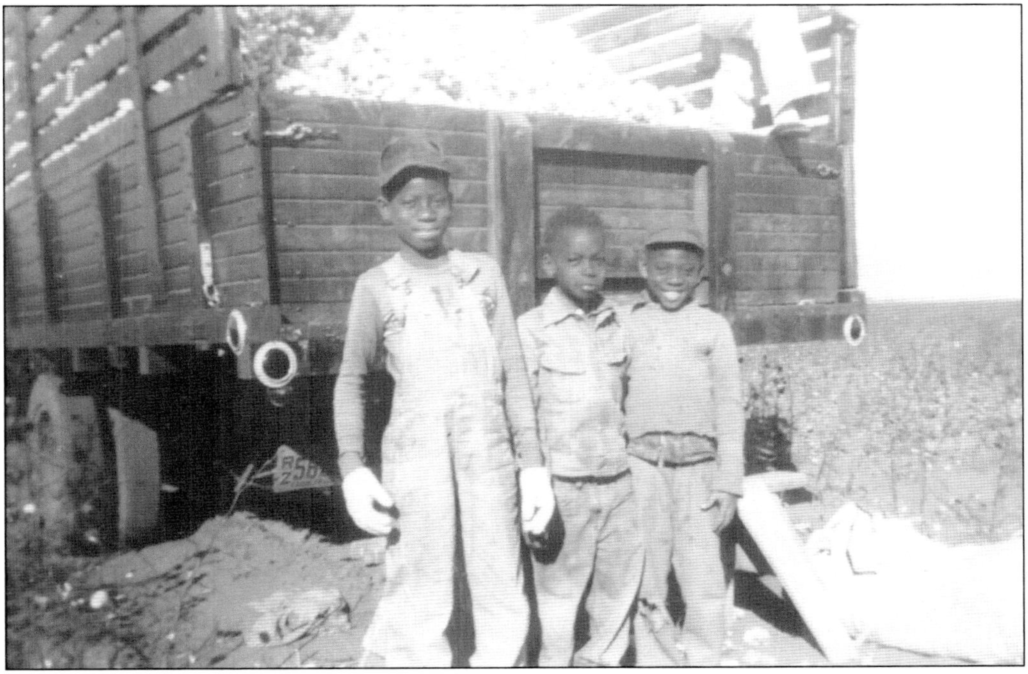

All ages helped when there was work. From left to right, Arthur Lee, J.L., and Doc Manahand appear to display a range of emotions—proud to be working alongside the grown-ups, not sure, and just plain happy. Notice Arthur Lee's brand new gloves. In 1949, many women and children worked alongside the men doing seasonal agricultural work. A lot of school was likely missed during harvest time. (Courtesy of Carol and Powell Adams.)

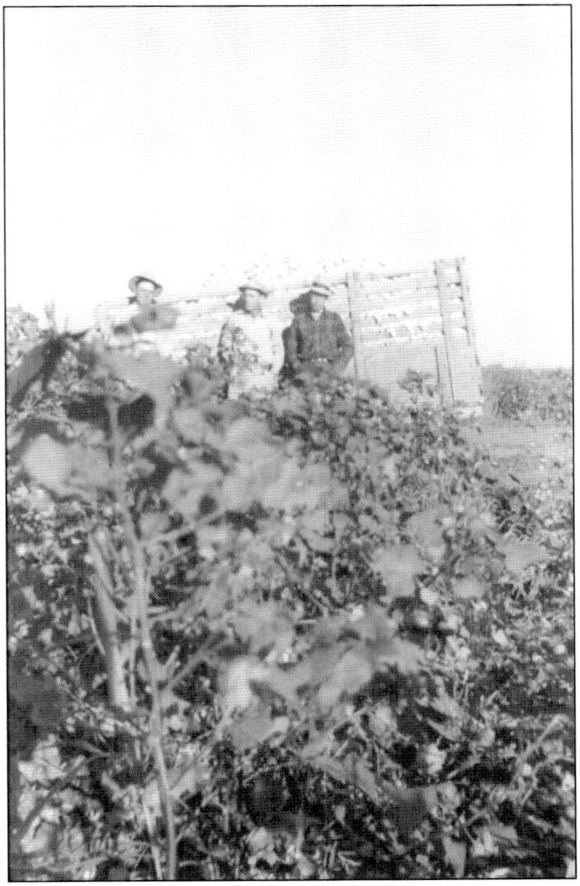

Farmers M.N. Thompson Sr. (left), W.T. Adams (center), and Wade Thompson stand in front of a wagon full of recently pulled cotton in Lubbock County in 1951. Judging from the cotton in the foreground, it has been pulled through once and will have to be harvested at least one more time. (Courtesy of Carol and Powell Adams.)

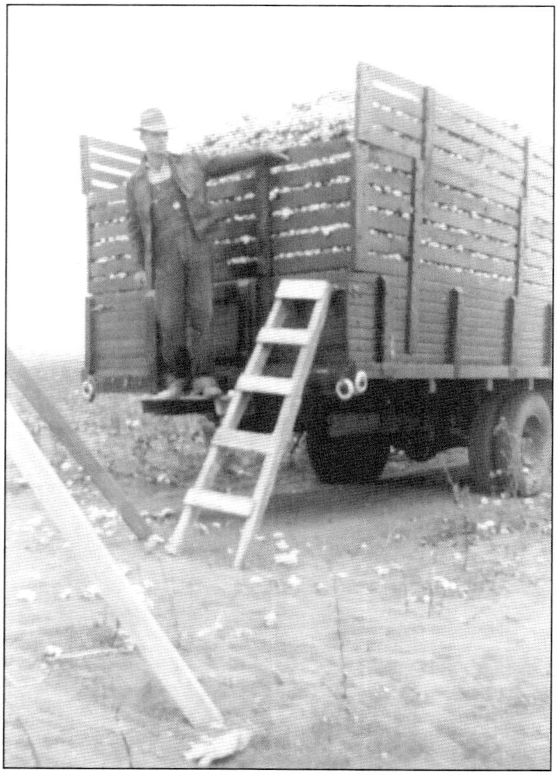

Powell Adams inspects a load of cotton ready to be delivered to the gin. Farmers could have as many as 90 wagons tied up at the gin waiting to be emptied, creating serious bottlenecks in the harvesting. When there were no wagons or trucks available, cotton harvesting stopped—regardless of conditions in the field, the price of cotton, or weather conditions. (Courtesy of Carol and Powell Adams.)

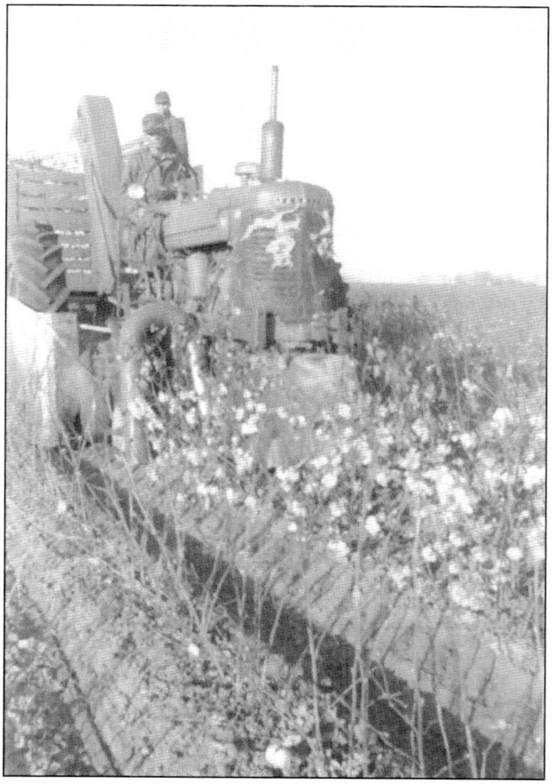

Here, Adams strips cotton with his new two-row cotton stripper. Mounting the two-row stripper on the front made it easier to operate. At least one other worker was needed to push cotton into the back of the wagon. Two or three men could strip as much cotton in one day using this two-row stripper as it took 12 men three days to pull. (Courtesy of Carol and Powell Adams.)

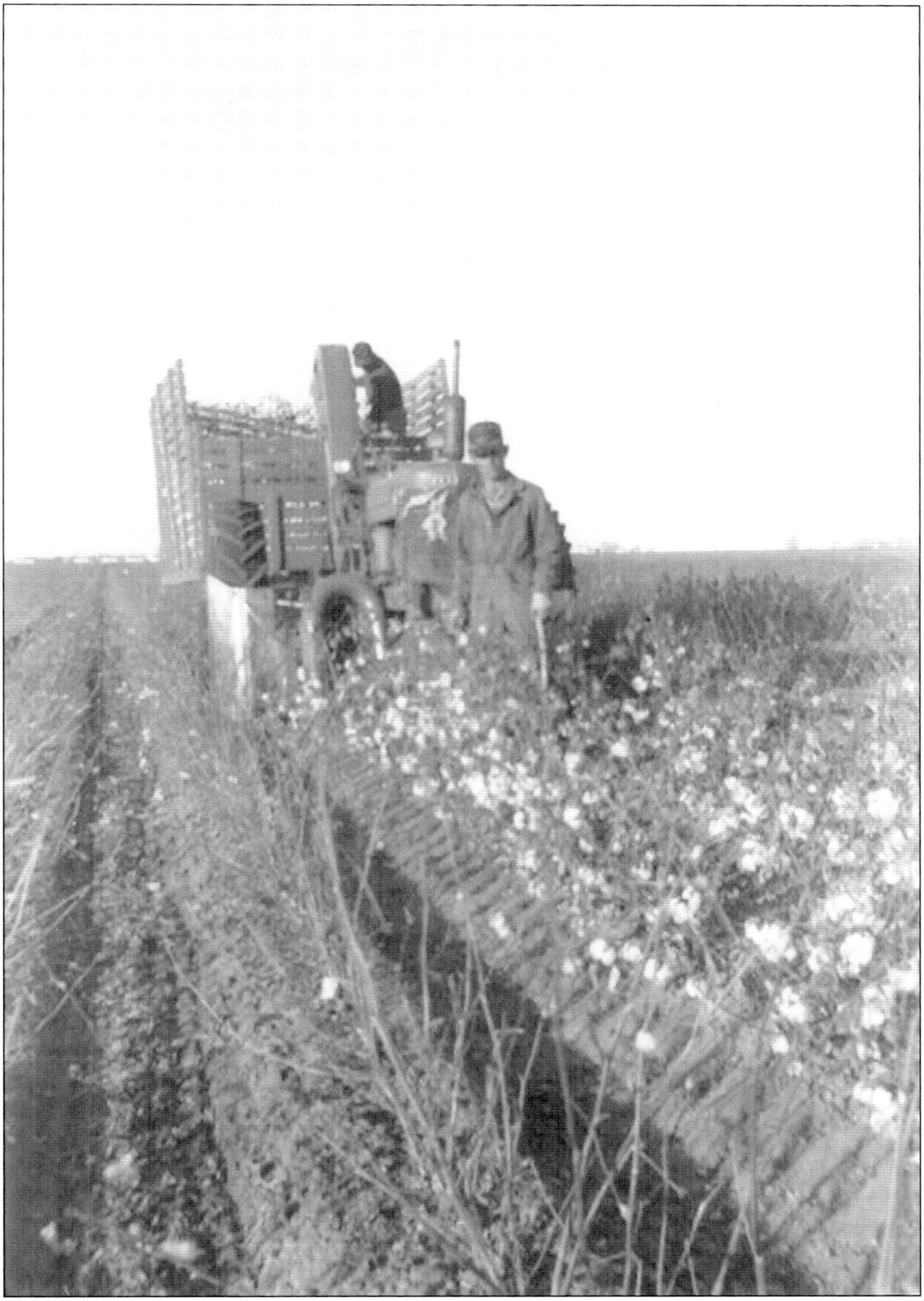

Powell Adams takes a break from stripping cotton while a worker pushes the cotton farther back into the wagon. Notice the stripped rows of cotton on the left. The stripper has removed not only the cotton lint, but also the leaves, unripened bolls, and other parts of the cotton plant. (Courtesy of Carol and Powell Adams.)

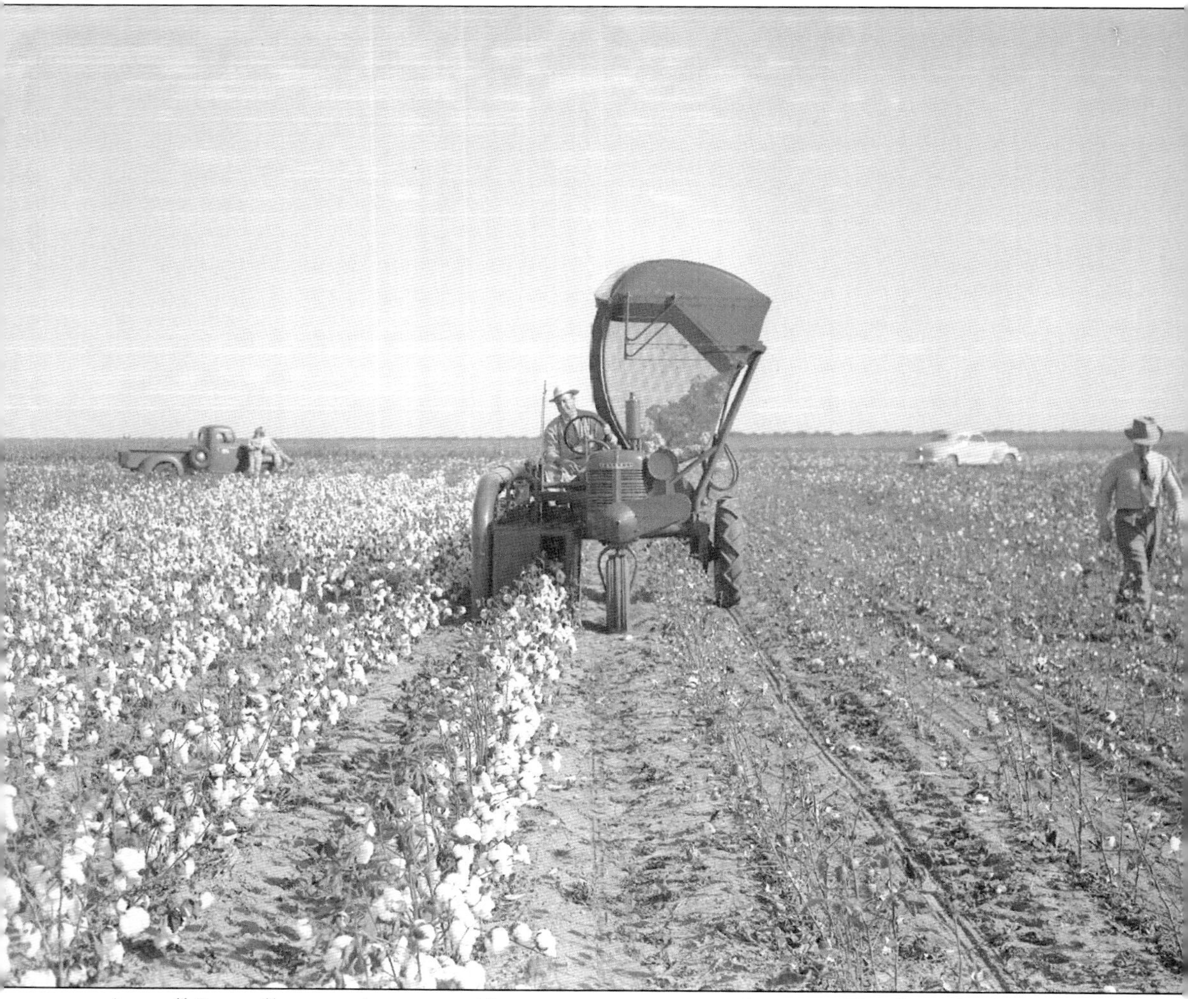

A small Farmall tractor has no problem stripping one row of cotton. The dump basket attached was a great improvement, for it allowed the farmer to dump the cotton into a wagon or trailer and not on the ground. Now, one man could strip a field and dump the bolls in a container for transport. (Photograph from the Winston Reeves Photograph Collection, courtesy of the Southwest Collection/Special Collections Library, Texas Tech University.)

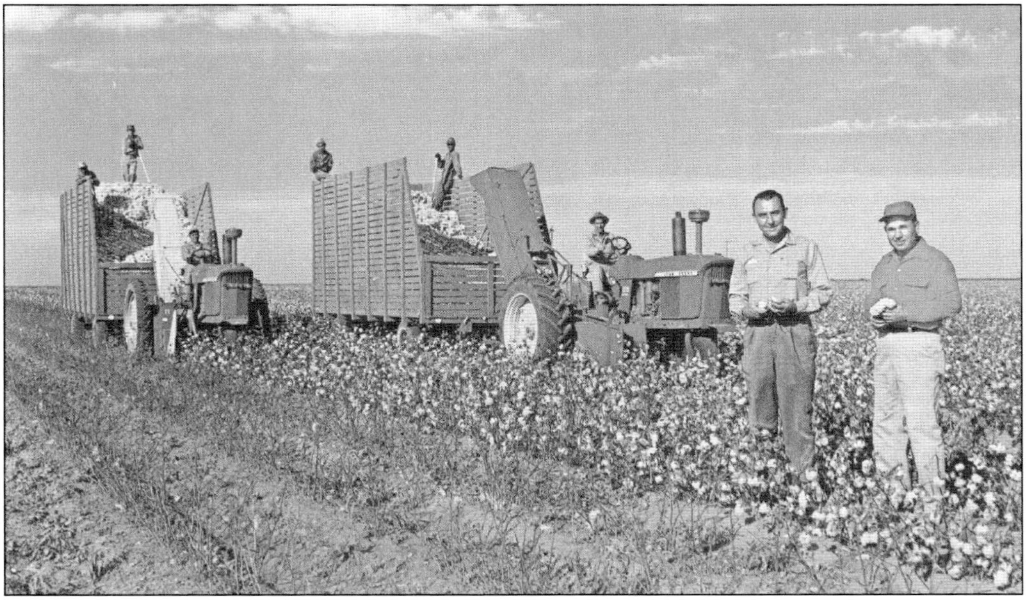

The 1961 fall cotton harvest is seen here on the Vardeman Farms near Lubbock. The powerful John Deere tractors had little problem pulling the mounted two-row strippers and the large trailers full of cotton. Notice the workers in the trailers holding equipment needed to compact the harvested cotton blown from the stripper. At one time, the Vardemans owned over 90 cotton trailers. (Photograph by and courtesy of Vardeman Farms.)

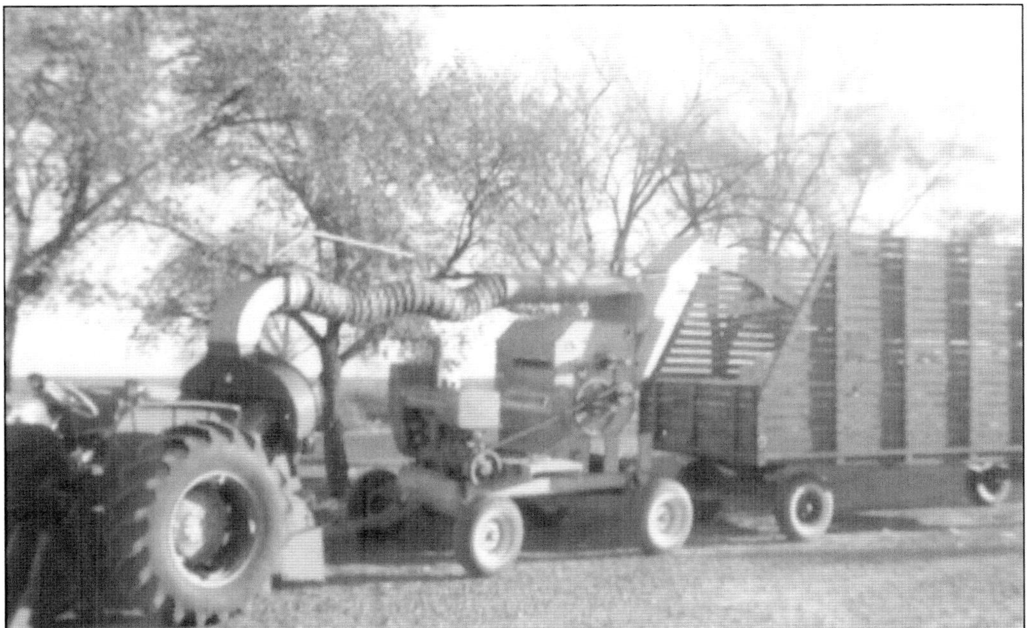

In 1963, another improvement to the cotton stripping process was developed. Behind the tractor and in front of the wagon is a burr extractor. As the name implies, the burr extractor separated cotton burrs and other cotton trash from the lint. Cotton farmers welcomed the burr extractor for it increased the quality of the cotton they produced and increased their profits. (Courtesy of Carol and Powell Adams.)

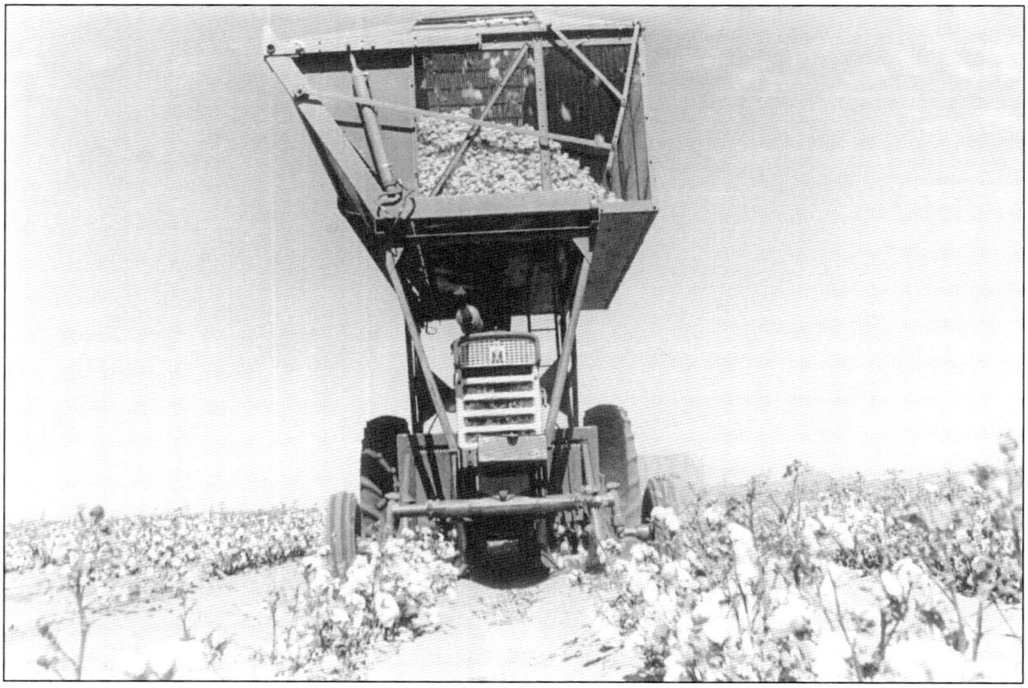

An International Harvester (IH) two-row cotton stripper is mounted on an IH tractor, with the cotton basket mounted overhead, thus making it unnecessary to pull a heavy wagon behind the stripper. Once the cotton basket was full, a boll buggy pulled alongside and the basket was emptied into it. This innovation allowed for faster and more economical harvesting of cotton. (Photograph by Lynette Thompson Wilson, courtesy of Plains Cotton Cooperative Association.)

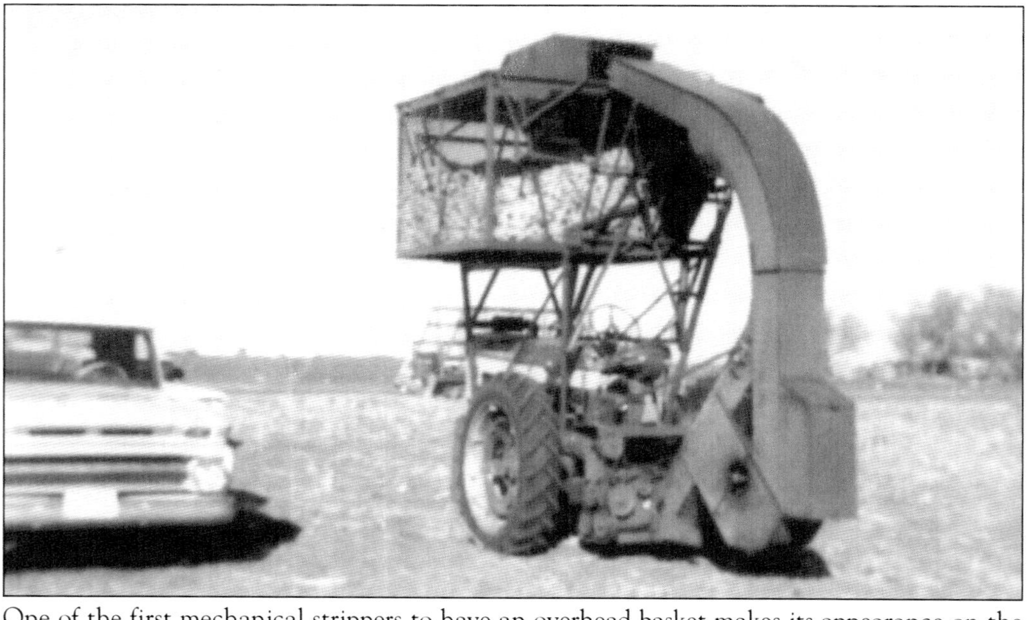

One of the first mechanical strippers to have an overhead basket makes its appearance on the South Plains in the fall of 1963. The overhead basket was an improvement over pulling a wagon behind the stripper, although one had to stop often to unload the buggy. (Courtesy of Carol and Powell Adams.)

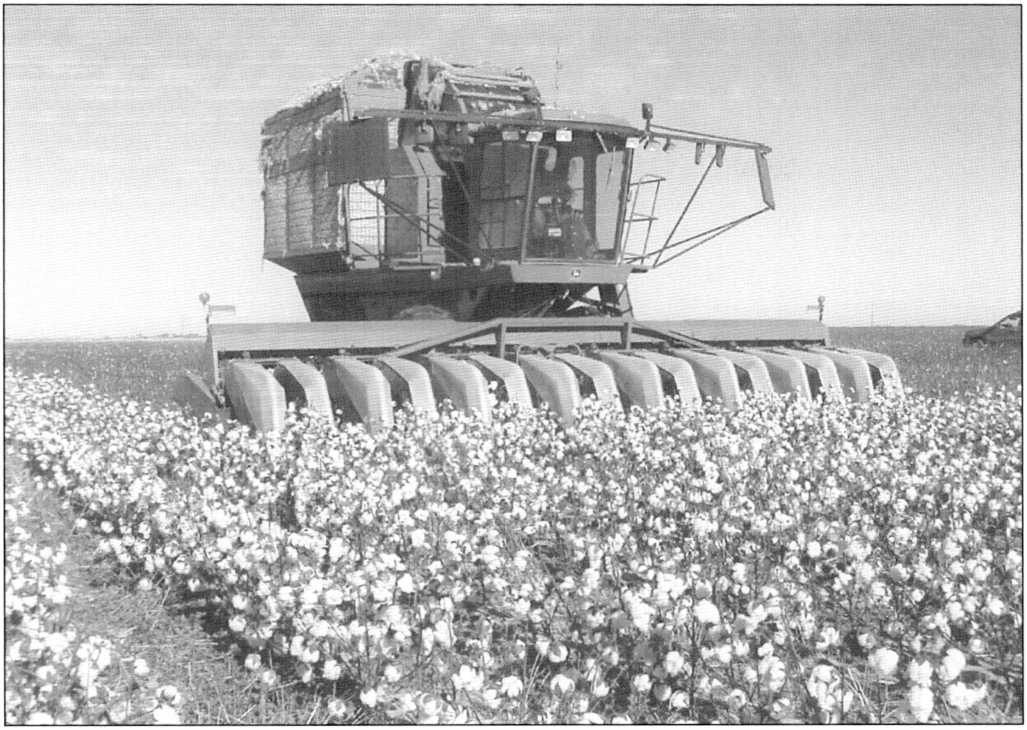

This John Deere 7455 eight-row cotton stripper strips a nice crop of cotton on the South Plains. The cotton enters the stripper through the grooves in front of the tractor and then it is blown up into the hopper behind the cab. Before stripping, the cotton was defoliated, causing the plant to drop its leaves and allowing the cotton to be stripped cleaner. (Courtesy of Dan Taylor.)

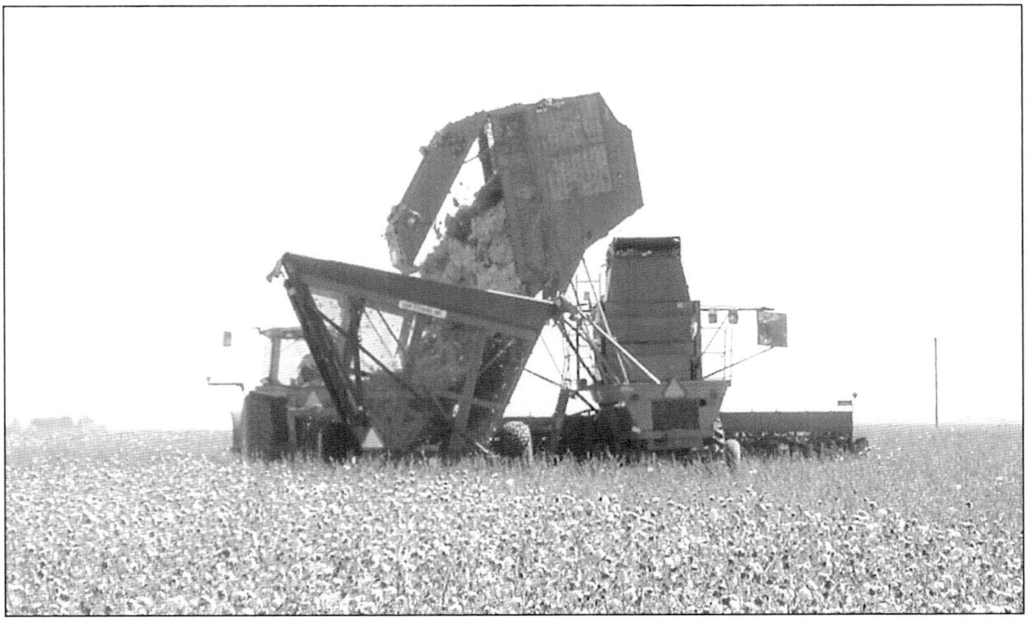

A South Plains cotton farmer unloads a hopper of recently stripped cotton from his stripper (right) to the boll buggy (left). It takes two hoppers of cotton to fill the boll buggy, which takes the cotton to the module builder. (Courtesy of Dan Taylor.)

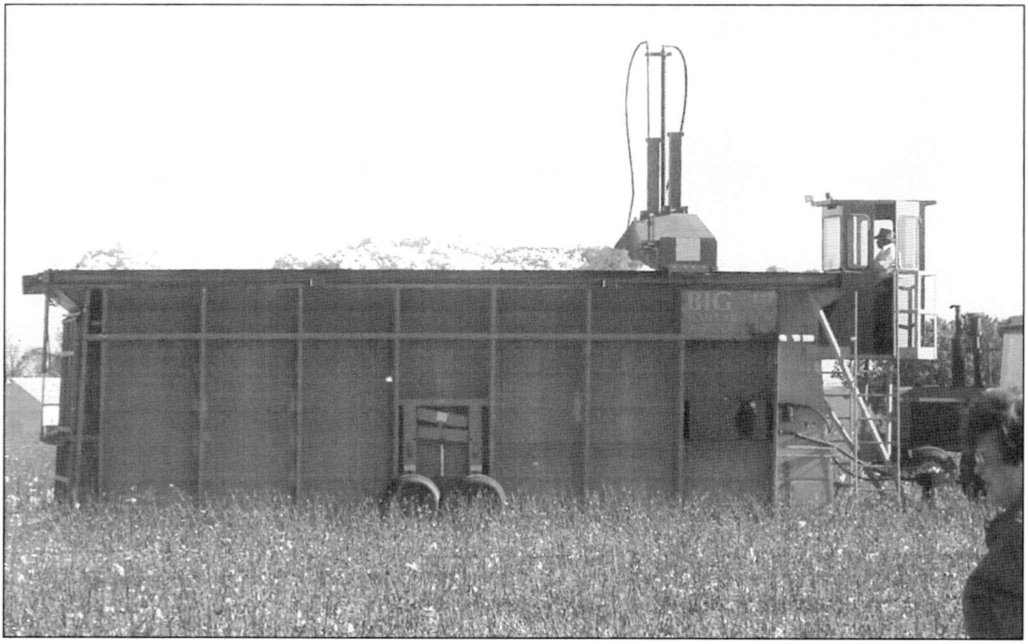

As harvesting proceeds, a nearly full cotton module builder sits beside a stripped field of cotton. The compressor moves along the top of the module builder, compacting the cotton in the module. The cotton inside the module can weigh up to 10 tons. During the harvest, module builders sit on the edges of the fields so that boll buggies have easy access to them. (Courtesy of Dan Taylor.)

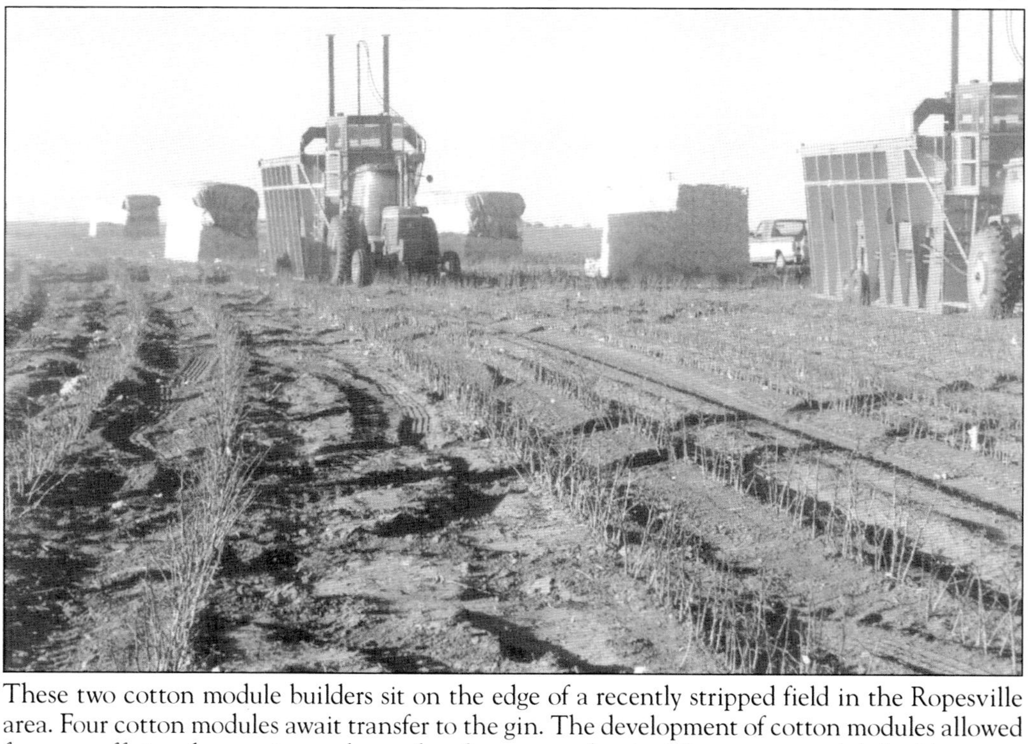

These two cotton module builders sit on the edge of a recently stripped field in the Ropesville area. Four cotton modules await transfer to the gin. The development of cotton modules allowed for more efficient harvesting and transfer of cotton to the gin. The cotton module builders were first used on the South Plains in early 1970s. (Courtesy of Dan Taylor.)

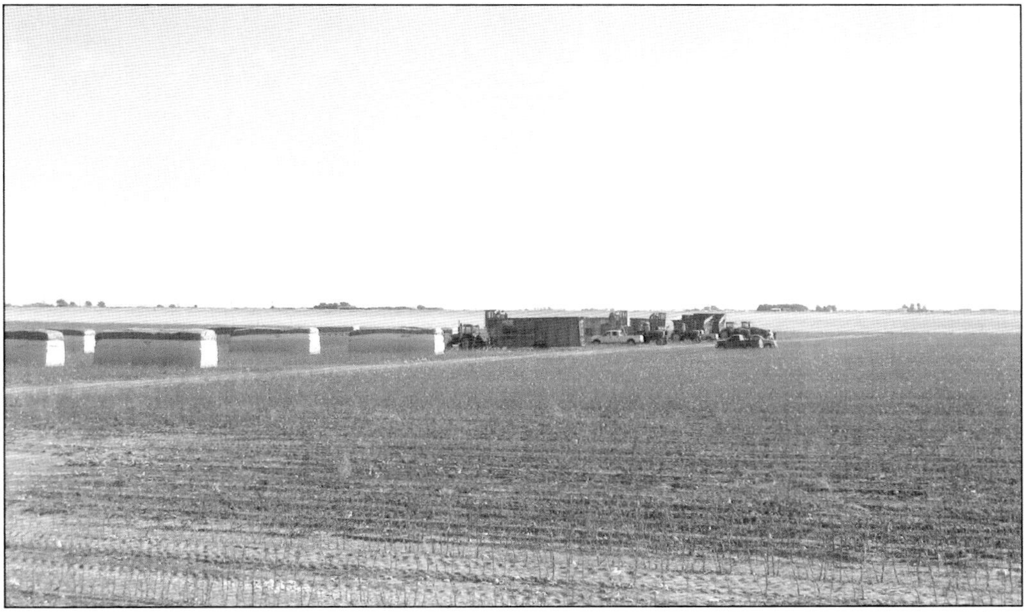

Cotton strippers and a tractor pulling a boll buggy keep the module builder busy on this modern cotton harvesting operation. It takes no more than six workers to keep this operation going. The development of cotton modules revolutionized cotton harvesting, allowing farmers to continuously harvest cotton and not wait on the gin to empty their cotton wagons. (Courtesy of Carol and Powell Adams.)

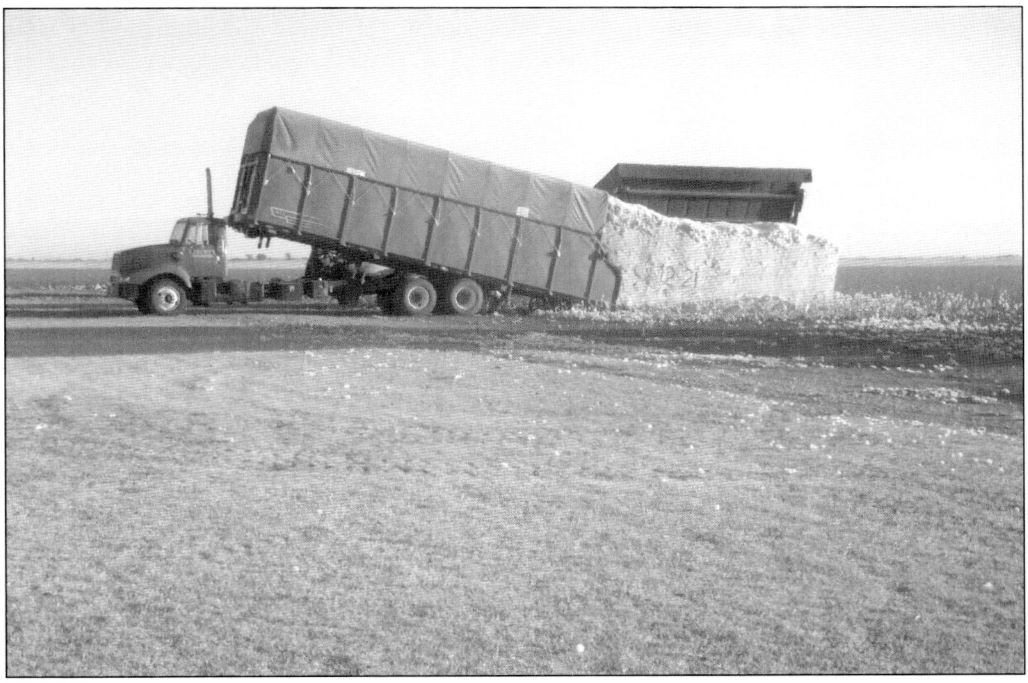

Cotton module trucks pick up cotton modules left beside a field. Traditionally, cotton gins owned and operated the trucks, picked up the cotton modules, and took them to the gin as a service to the farmer. Today, using a GPS mounted in the truck's cab, the truck drivers know exactly where each module is located and can drive directly to it. (Courtesy of Powell Adams.)

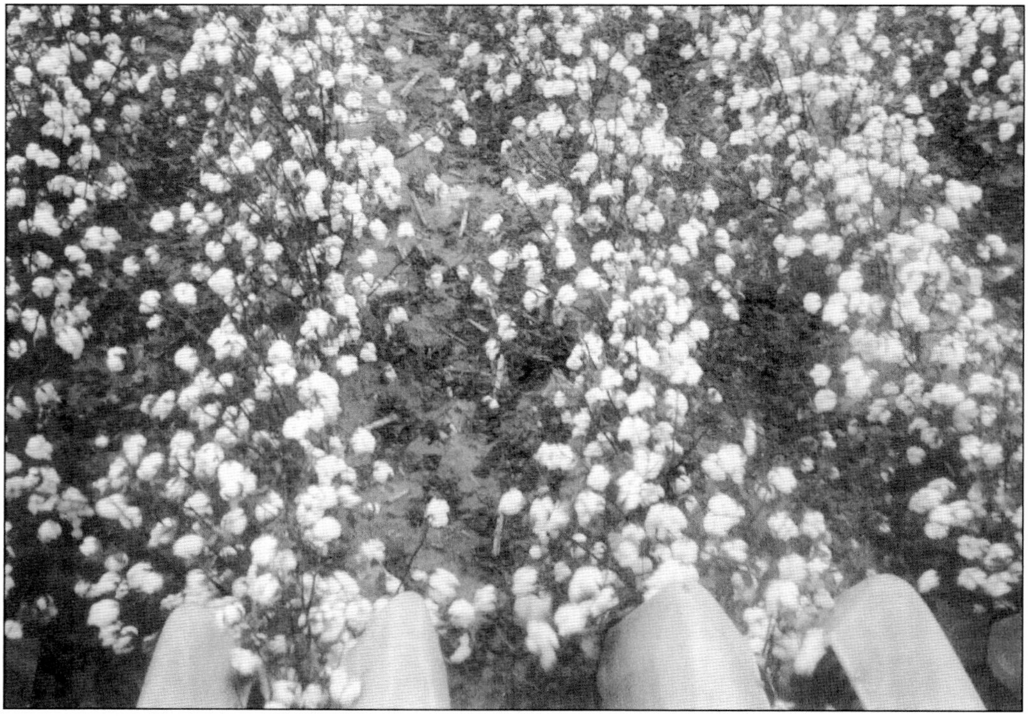

Cotton is harvested on the Vardeman cotton farm in 2009 using a John Deere 7460 eight-row cotton stripper. The above view is what the driver of the cotton stripper sees. Mirrors mounted on the sides of the cab and above the outside rows help the farmer to see how the stripping is progressing. Another improvement over past strippers was the mounting of two boll baskets instead of one (below). Placed behind the driver, they allowed the farmer to strip twice as much cotton before he had to stop and unload. (Above, photograph by and courtesy of Vardeman Farms; below, photograph by and courtesy of Kimberly Vardeman.)

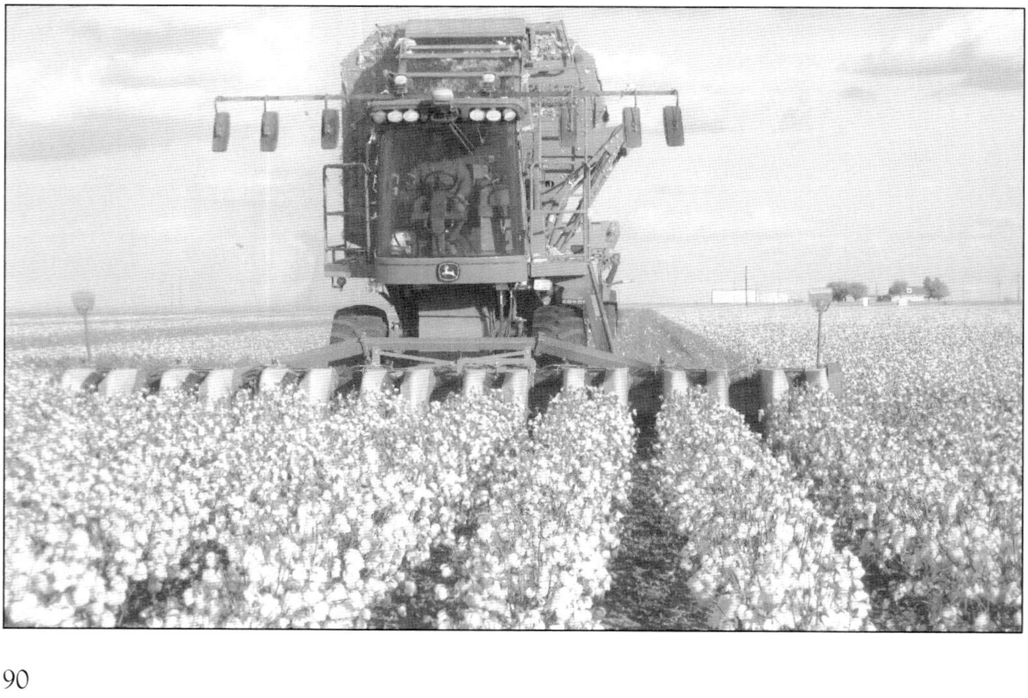

Five
Ginning, Marketing, and Milling

In the mid-1900s, cotton gins and mills dotted the South Plains, but today, only a few gins and one mill remain. As roads and ginning technology improved, fewer gins were needed to handle the area's cotton, although cotton production steadily increased, as did the number of acres planted. South Plains cotton mills eventually succumbed to foreign competition, as the area mills could not compete with foreign labor costs.

Despite the foreign competition, marketing of cotton has improved with the organization of the Plains Cotton Cooperative Association (PCCA). The cooperative was organized by area farmers as a way to increase prices, secure demand, and improve the image of area cotton. The PCCA pooled farmer's cotton and sold it to buyers for a better price than each individual farmer could get working strictly in his own interest. The PCCA also found markets for low-quality cotton and cotton by-products. If prices dropped, the PCCA had the ability to hold back cotton until prices rose.

Cotton gins perform an important service for area cotton farmers, removing the seed from the lint and cleaning it, thus preparing it for milling. Most of the trash—parts of dried stems, leaves, and hulls—is removed by a series of fans and blowers, while the seeds are removed from the lint mechanically by a series of sawlike teeth that pull, or comb, the seeds from the lint. All by-products of the ginning process—seeds, trash, and motes—are sold separately. The trash and seed make up about 30 percent (by weight) of the cotton brought to the gin. After the cotton is ginned, it is pressed into bales and is ready for milling. Each bale ginned is tagged and numbered so the owner, grade, and location of the cotton can be traced through the entire manufacturing process.

Cotton grown and ginned on the South Plains is sent all over the world for manufacturing, or milling, into useful products. The grade of the cotton determines what products it will be made into. A great deal of South Plains cotton finds its way into denim jeans.

At present, only one mill is in operation on the South Plains—the Littlefield Denim Mill in Littlefield. It employs over 600 people who work three shifts in an effort to keep up with the demand for denim. The mill weaves 100,000 yards of cotton a day and produces between 30 and 36 million yards of denim every year—25 million pairs of jeans.

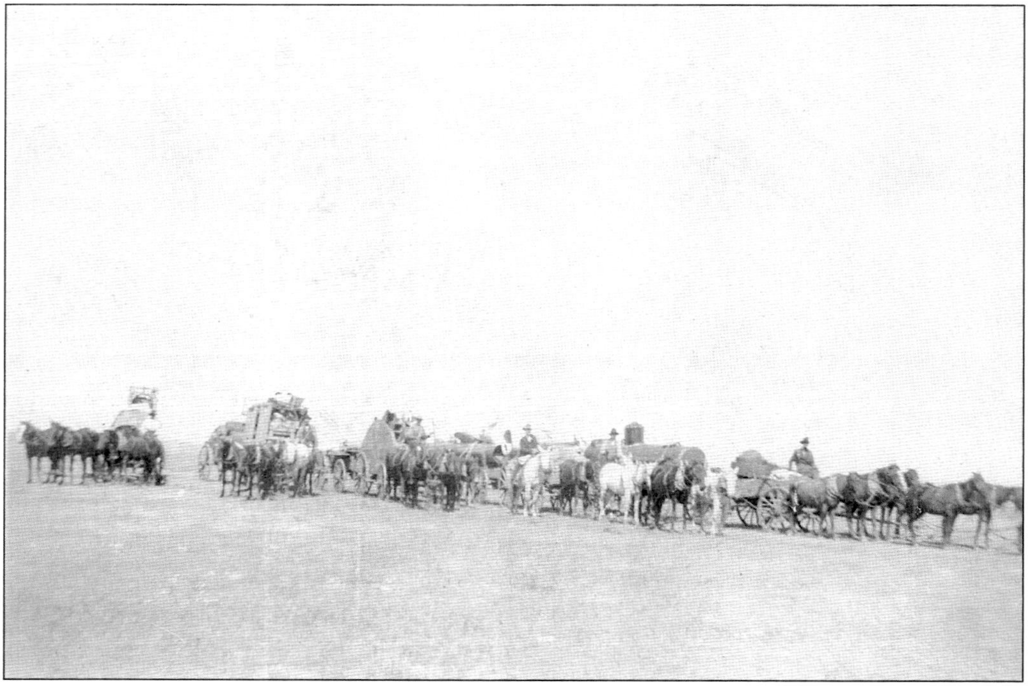

A small wagon train takes a break while transporting a cotton gin to Ralls, the area's first gin. The wagon train picked up the gin in Plainview, probably at the train station, before heading out cross-country to Ralls. The large tank on one wagon is the boiler, which will generate the steam to power the gin. (Courtesy of the Ralls Historical Museum.)

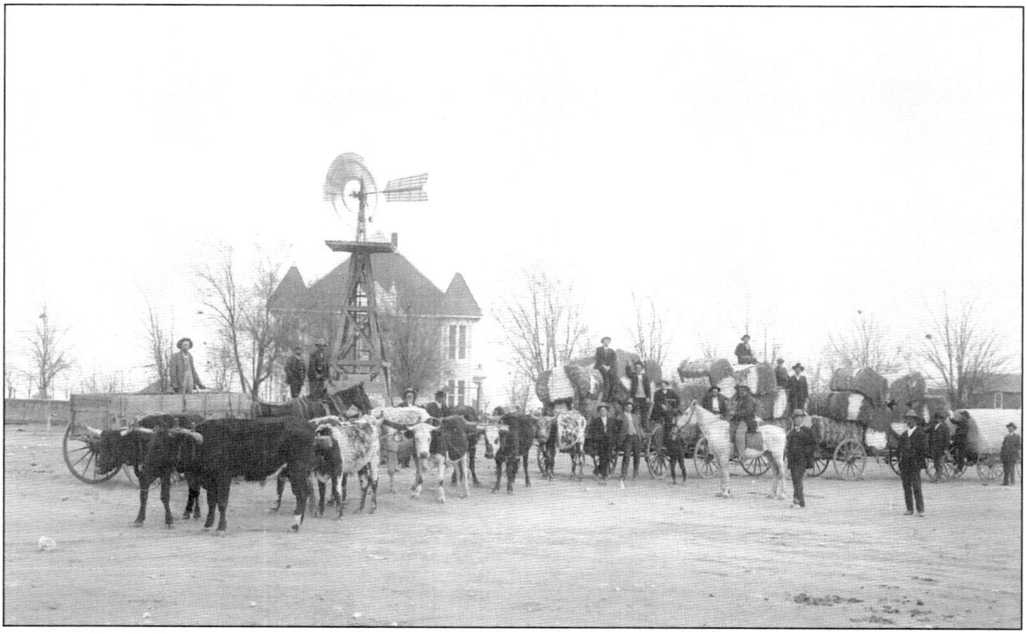

Wagons loaded with cotton grown in Lubbock and Crosby Counties stop in front of the Lubbock County Courthouse in 1904. The three wagons piled high with cotton bales are attached together and are pulled by five double yokes of oxen. The cotton has already been ginned and is being transported to the rail yard. (Courtesy of the Ralls Historical Museum.)

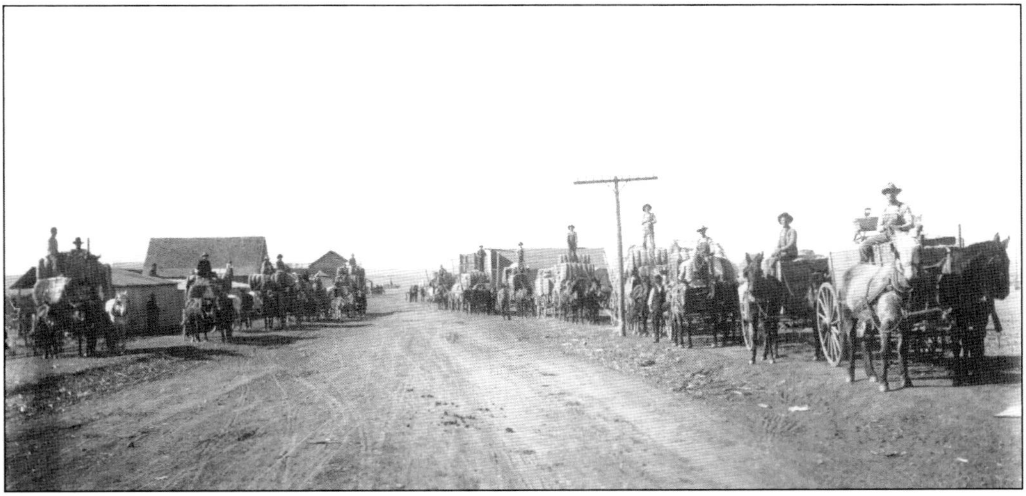

On November 29, 1910, men and teams of horses and mules take a break from hauling cotton to the railroad station in Floydada, where it will be shipped to cotton mills across the country. A division of the Santa Fe Railway—the Pecos & Northern Texas Railway—had just reached Floydada earlier that year, making the transportation of Floyd County cotton easier. As these images indicate, it took a lot of people to plant, harvest, gin, and transport cotton on the South Plains in the early 1900s. (Both photographs courtesy of the Floyd County Historical Museum.)

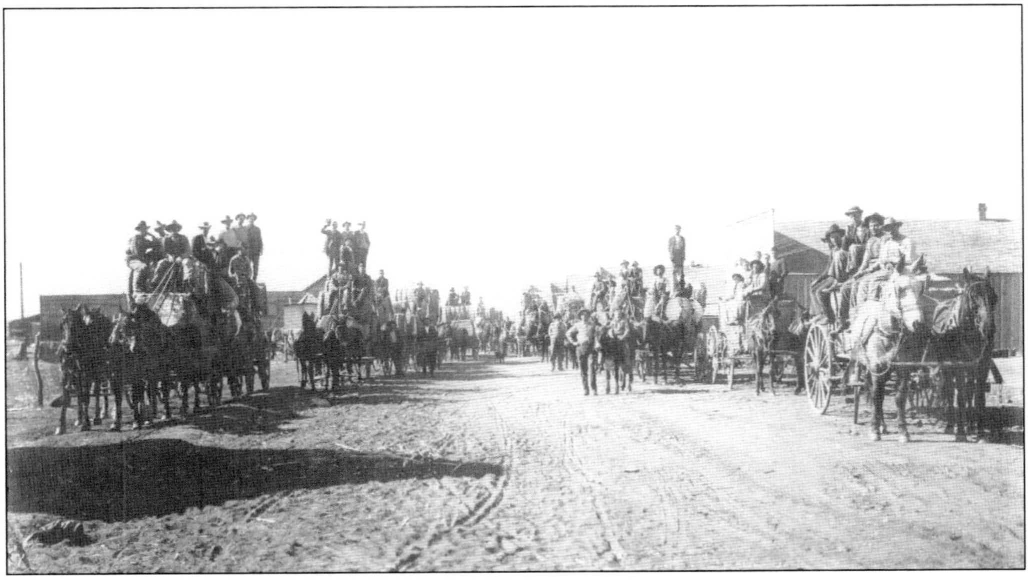

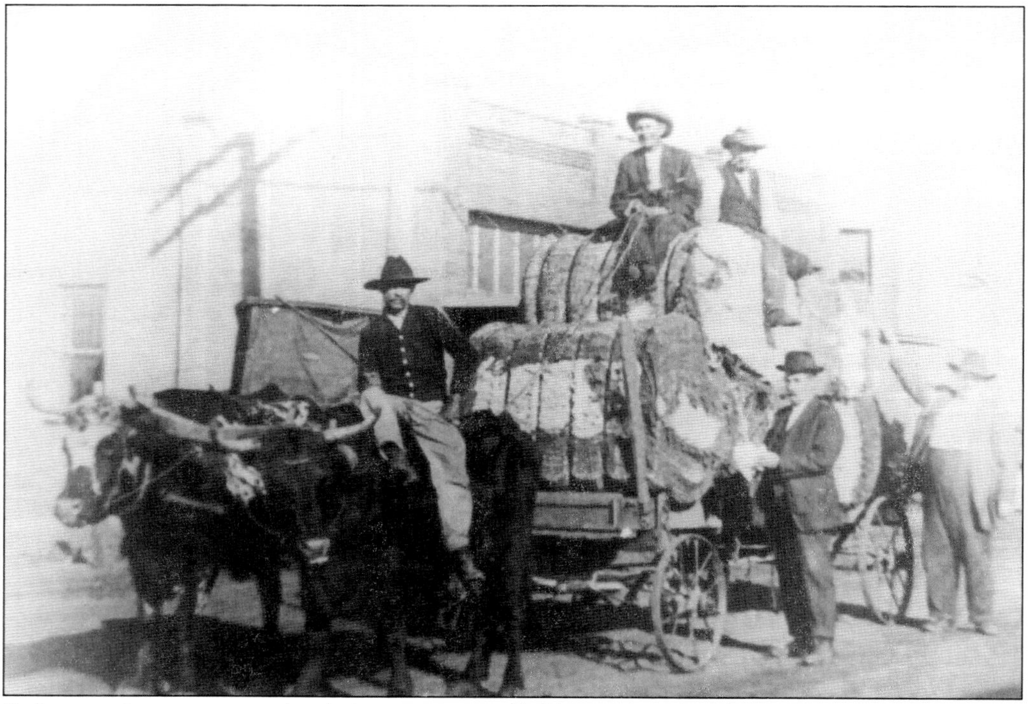

Before trucks, cotton was hauled in wagons pulled by teams of mules, horses, or even oxen. In this image from around 1920, the cotton has already been ginned and bagged. The five cotton bales bagged in a hemp covering are being hauled to a warehouse to await transport to a cotton mill. (Courtesy of Dan Taylor.)

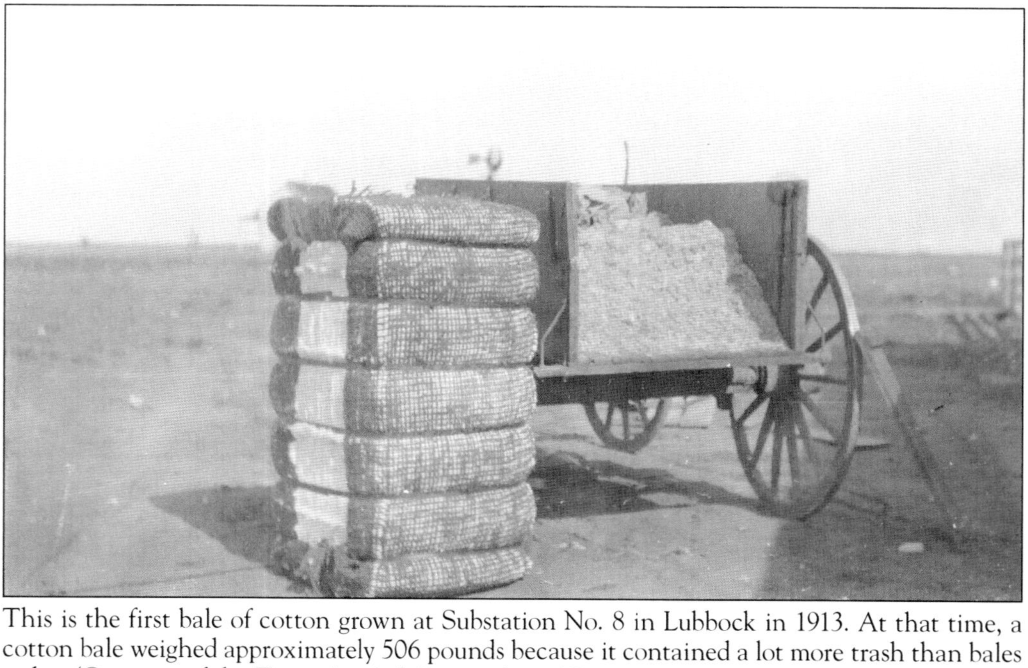

This is the first bale of cotton grown at Substation No. 8 in Lubbock in 1913. At that time, a cotton bale weighed approximately 506 pounds because it contained a lot more trash than bales today. (Courtesy of the Texas AgriLife Research and Extension Center – Lubbock, Texas.)

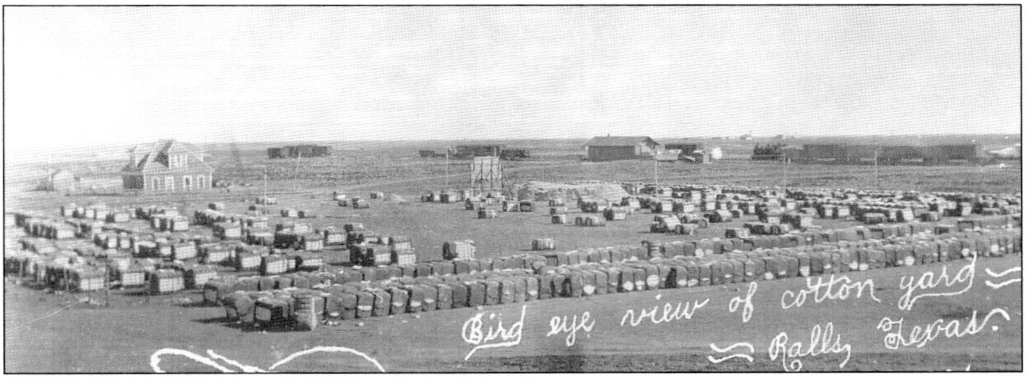

This bird's-eye view shows the cotton yard at Ralls in 1916. Benefiting from its location on the Santa Fe Railway, Ralls thrived as a shipping point for cotton. The cotton bales were deposited in the cotton yard close to the railroad to facilitate eventual loading onto trains carrying the bales to distant mills. (Courtesy of the Ralls Historical Museum.)

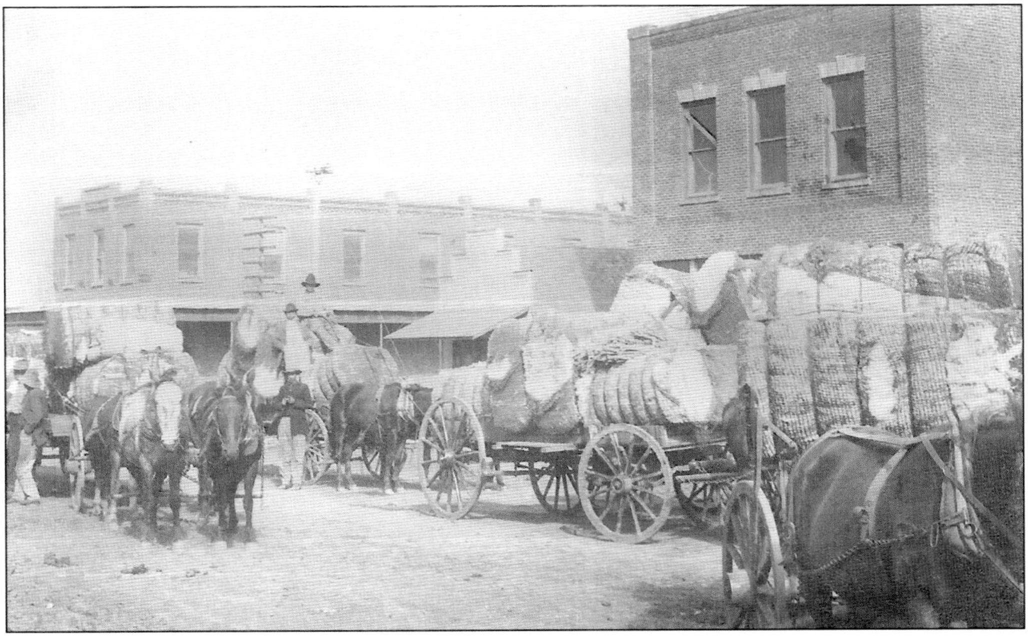

Horse-drawn wagons are loaded with cotton bales in Ralls in 1916. Ralls was an important commercial center at the time, with a cotton gin and a Santa Fe Railway station. This cotton, grown on Crosby and eastern Lubbock County farms, was brought to Ralls for ginning before it was sent off to be milled. (Courtesy of the Ralls Historical Museum.)

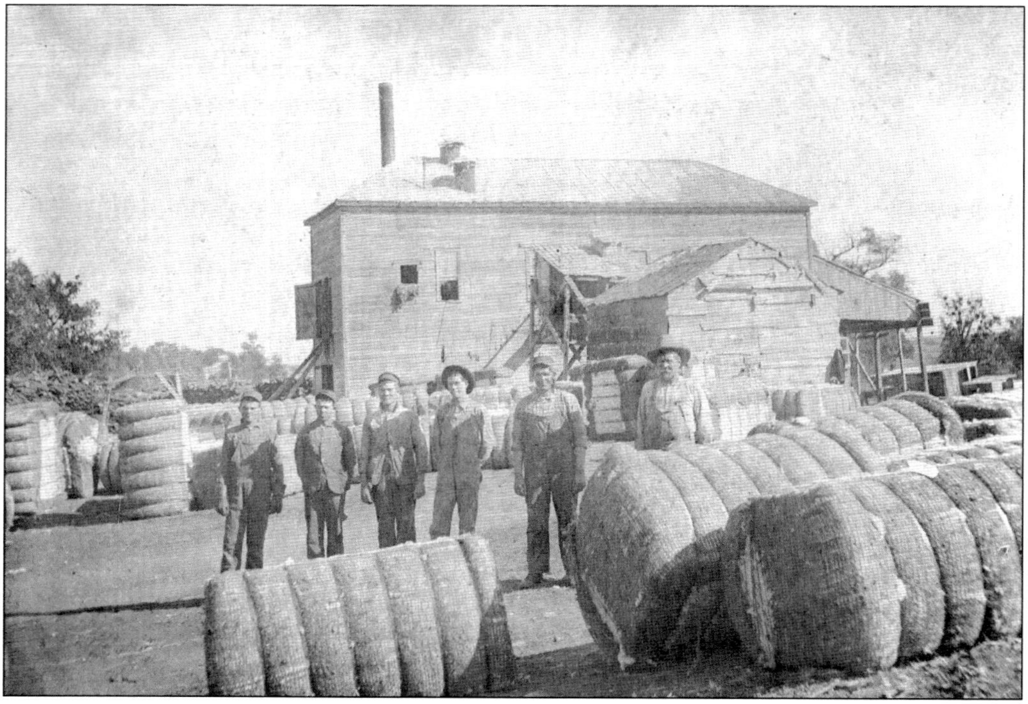

Gin workers stand behind cotton bales in front of a Floydada gin. Back then, cotton bales in various sizes were wrapped in jute bags and stored outside, exposing them to the weather, especially the bright sunlight, which harmed the lint. Today, plastic material is used to wrap cotton bales, and federal law prohibits storage out of doors. (Courtesy of the Floyd County Historical Museum.)

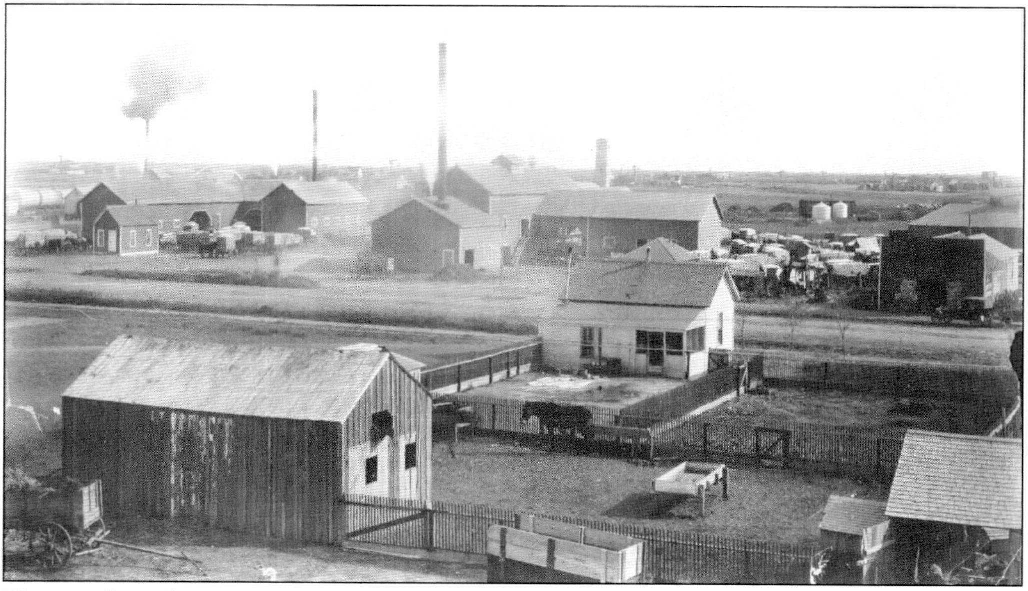

The number of acres in cotton grew rapidly in Floyd County, making up 20 percent of the land in cultivation by 1910. Production rose from 430 bales in 1910 to 42,801 in the mid-1920s, creating the need for more gins. Three cotton gins are seen here in Floydada in 1917. Take note of horse-drawn carts, which hauled the cotton into the gins. (Courtesy of the Floyd County Historical Museum.)

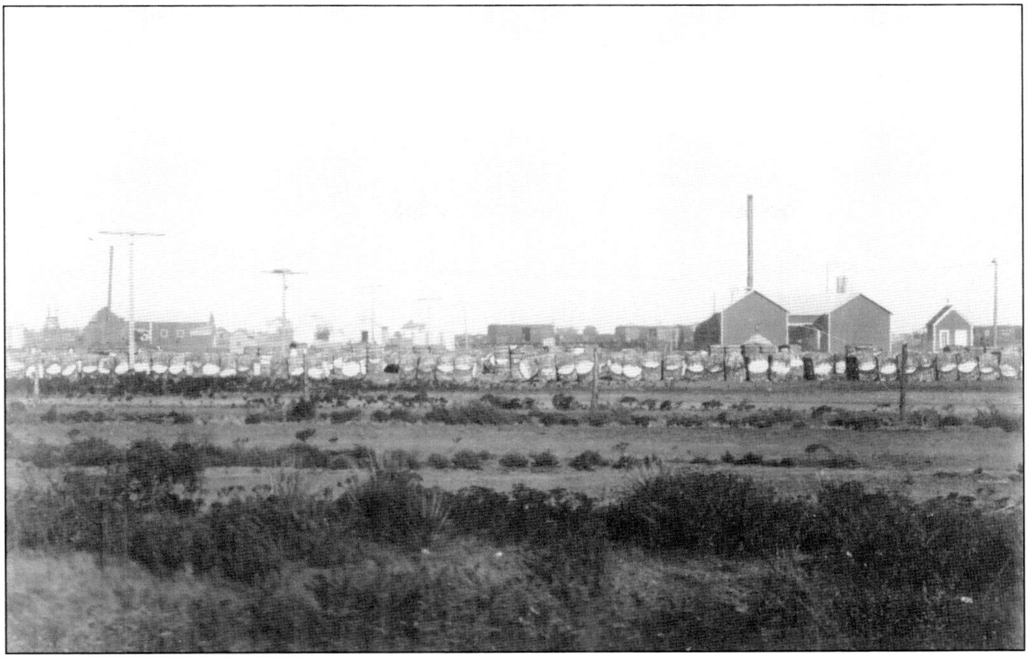

Even with the addition of several new gins, the gins could not keep up with the rush of cotton needing ginning and transportation to storage facilities at harvest time. Here, cotton bales await shipment at a Floydada cotton gin. During the busy cotton-ginning season, a shortage of railroad cars caused ginned cotton to literally pile up waiting for transport. (Courtesy of the Floyd County Historical Museum.)

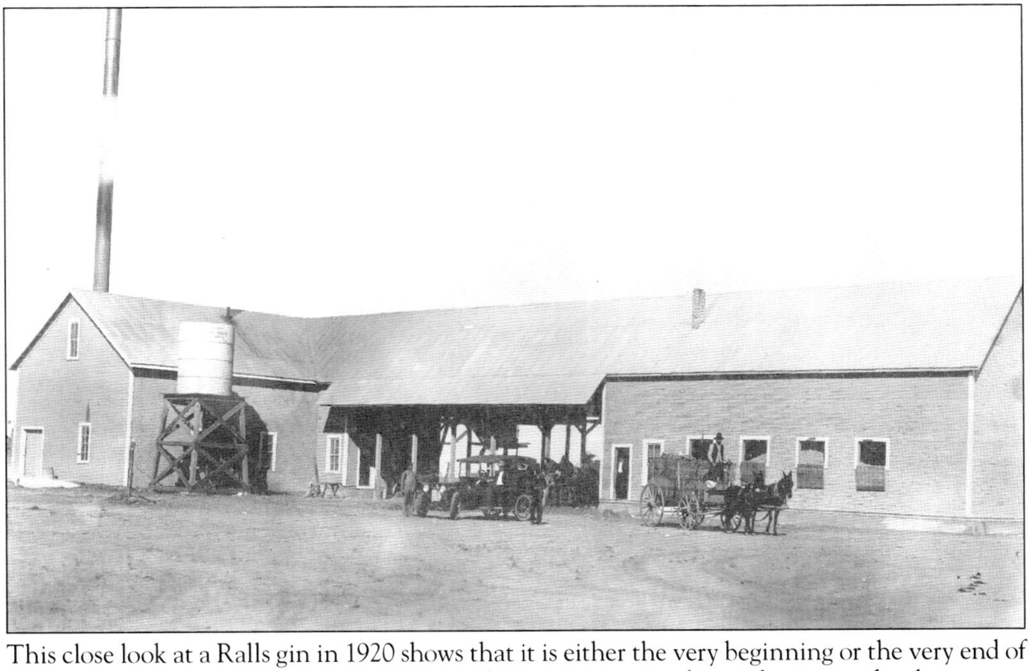

This close look at a Ralls gin in 1920 shows that it is either the very beginning or the very end of the harvest season, as the gin looks clean and neat. A man in a horse-drawn cart hauls a cotton bale away from the gin under the watchful eyes of businessmen visiting the gin and standing in front of it. (Courtesy of the Ralls Historical Museum.)

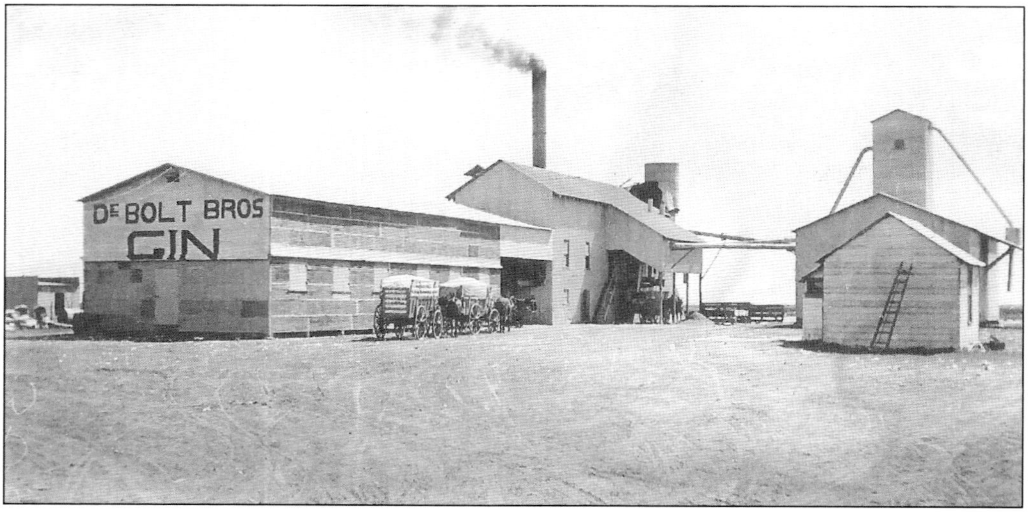

Two wagons full of cotton wait their turn to be emptied at the De Bolt Bros. gin in Ralls in 1919. In front of the two teams, under the shed, a wagon full of cotton is being emptied by a giant suction pipe that sucks the cotton up out of the wagon and into the gin for processing. (Courtesy of the Ralls Historical Museum.)

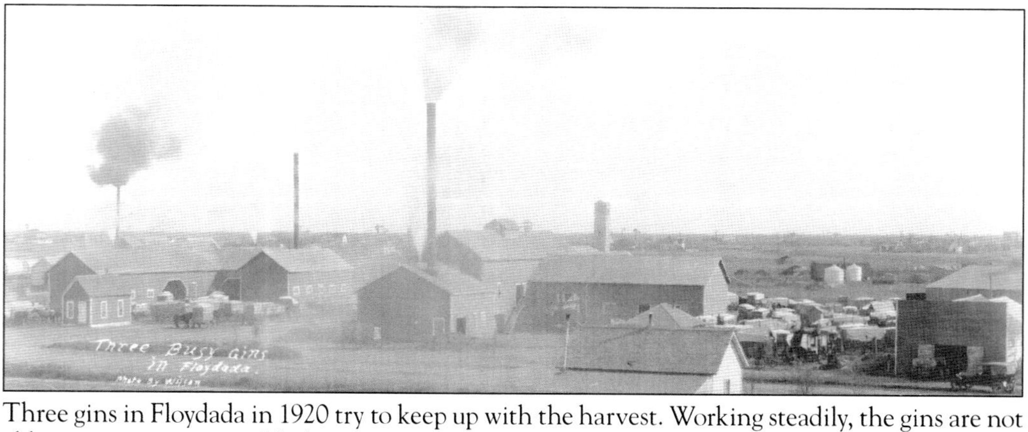

Three gins in Floydada in 1920 try to keep up with the harvest. Working steadily, the gins are not able to cope, as wagons filled with cotton stack up. Often, the harvest had to halt while farmers waited for their wagons to be emptied. Stopping the harvest was risky, as delays could damage the waiting crop. (Courtesy of the Floyd County Historical Museum.)

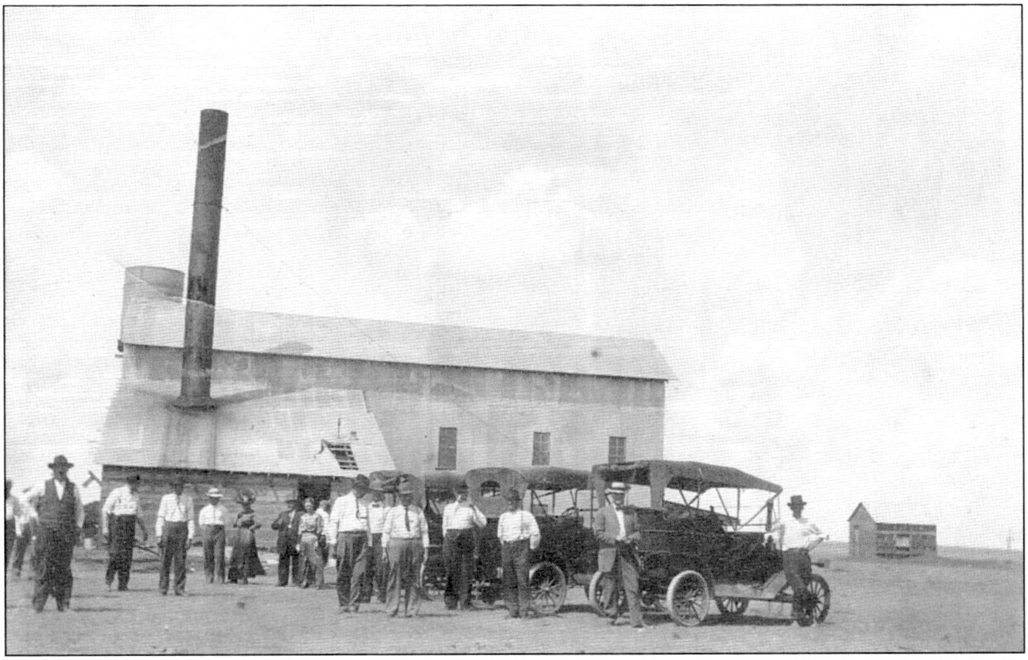

A group of farmers visits a cotton gin in the Ralls area at the invitation of either John R. Ralls or his brother, Percy. The brothers promoted Ralls and Crosby County by bringing farmers to the area in hopes they would stay. The visit allowed for a close inspection of the entire cotton production chain, from the field to the gin. (Courtesy of the Ralls Historical Museum.)

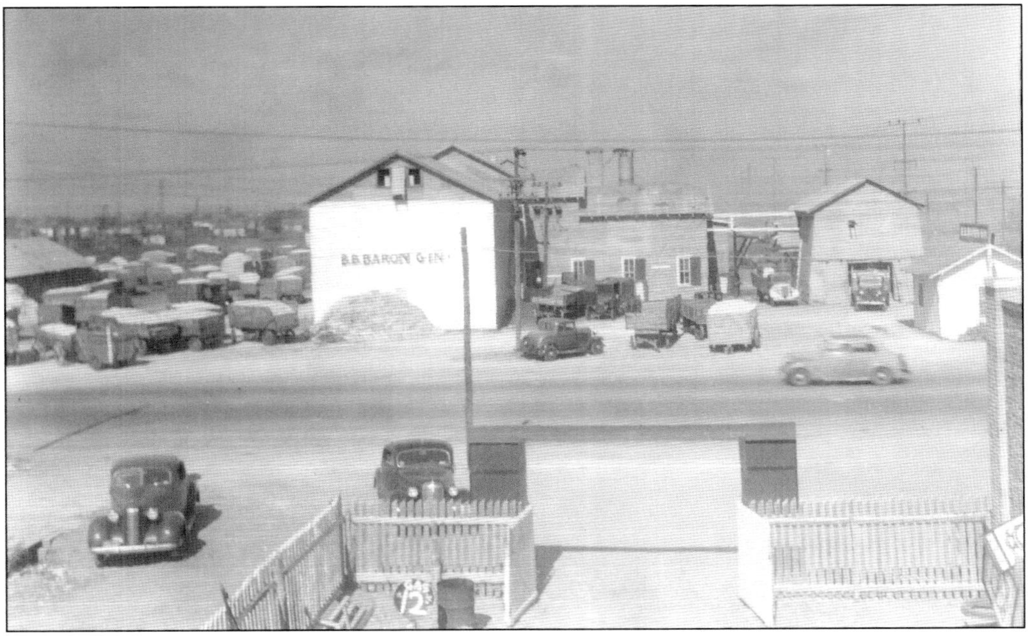

The B.B. Baron Gin in Lubbock is seen here in 1930. Farmers produced large crops of cotton during the 1930s in an effort to work their way out of the Depression. The large number of trailers needing emptying testifies to the size of the crop. Notice the advertisement for gas at 12¢ a gallon. (Photograph from the Agriculture Photo Collection, courtesy of the Southwest Collection/Special Collections Library, Texas Tech University.)

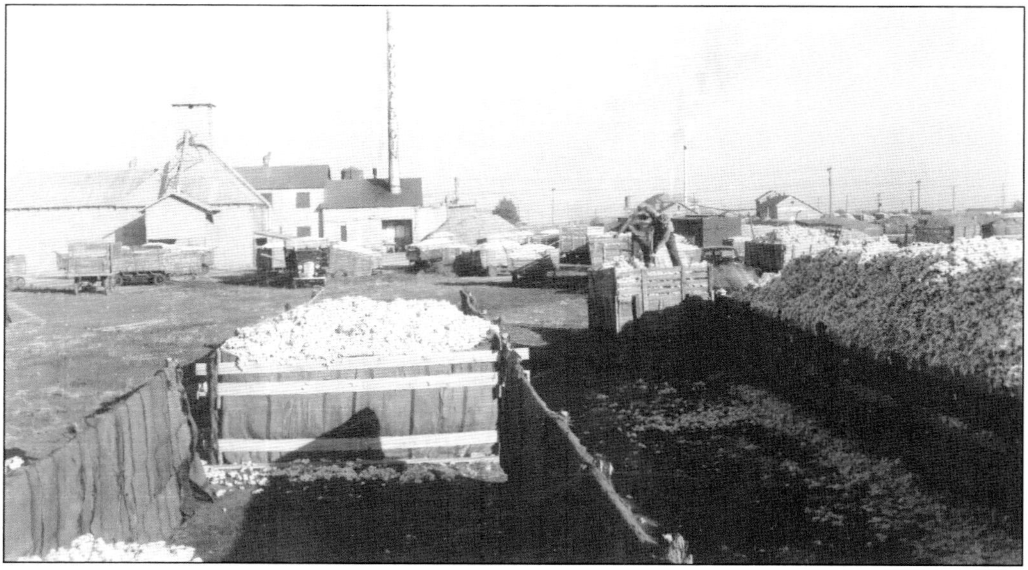

In 1937, a large harvest required farmers to unload their cotton directly onto the ground at this Lubbock gin. Research and development at Texas Technological College and agricultural research stations led to improved seed varieties, irrigation, and other technologies, which played a part in creating this congestion at the gin. (Photograph by John Rigg, courtesy of the *Hockley County News-Press.*)

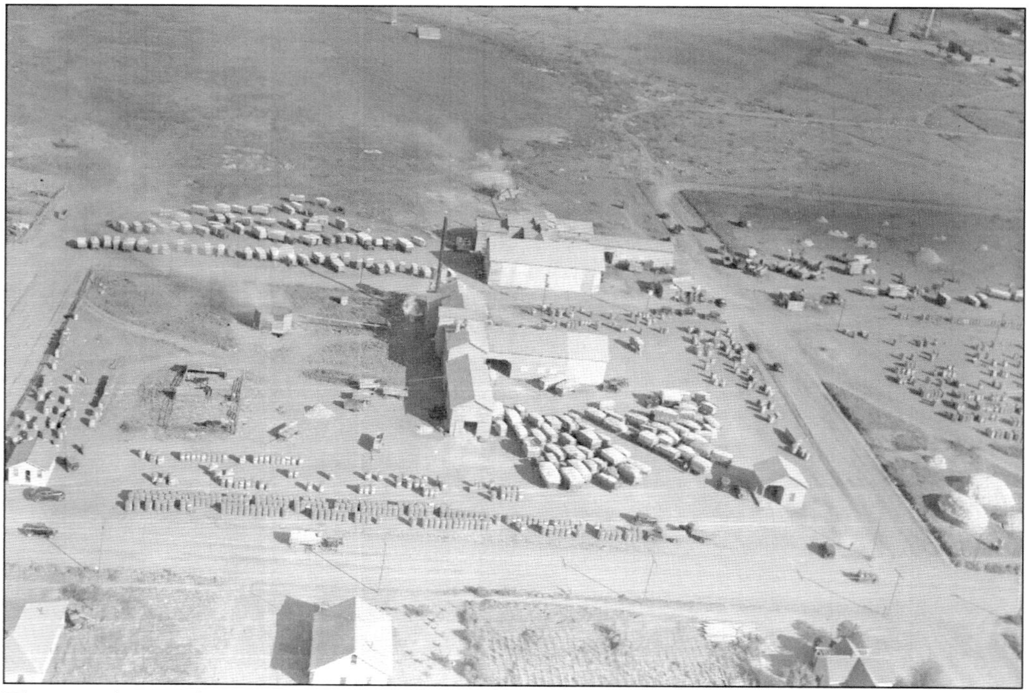

This aerial view shows two cotton gins somewhere on the South Plains. Wagons and trailers filled with cotton and at least four large piles of cotton wait to be ginned. Bales of cotton and piles of cottonseed also mound up. Sites like this were common at harvest time. (Photograph from the Winston Reeves Photograph Collection, courtesy of the Southwest Collection/Special Collections Library, Texas Tech University.)

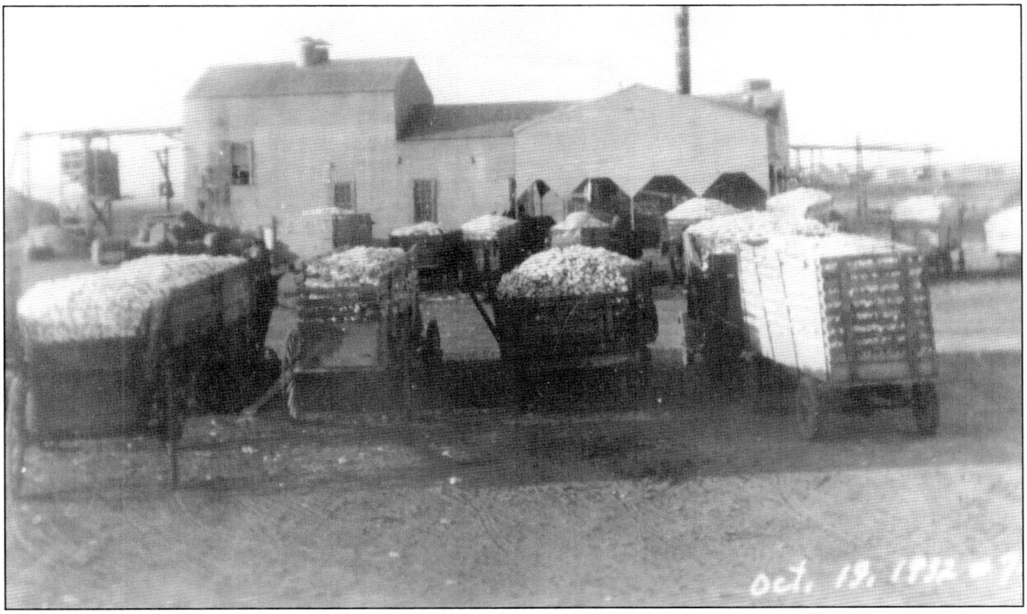

Cotton wagons wait their turn at a Lubbock gin on October 19, 1932. At the far left is the seed—a by-product of cotton ginning. At this time, farmers would gather some of the cottonseed after ginning and use it to plant the next year's crop. Before the development of cottonseed oil, there was not much demand for the seed. (Photograph from the Lubbock Agriculture Collection, courtesy of the Southwest Collection/Special Collections Library, Texas Tech University.)

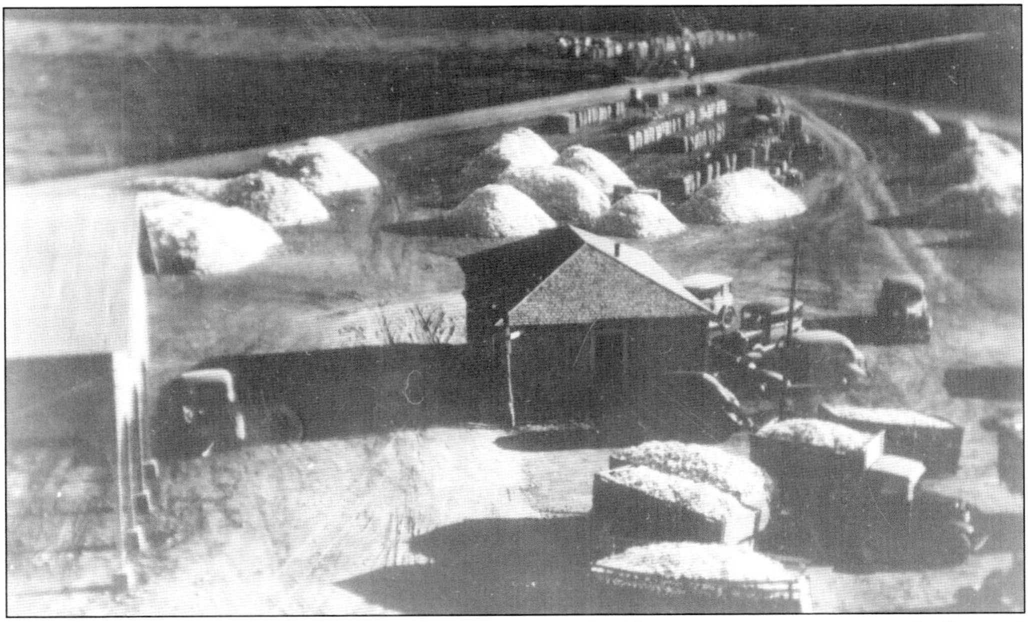

Cotton waits to be ginned at a Lubbock area gin in 1930. Notice some cotton is simply dumped on the ground near the gin, indicating how it was harvested. In all likelihood, this cotton was harvested by an early cotton stripper—possibly a sled pulled by a team of horses or mules. Stripping cotton accelerated the gathering but did not speed up ginning. (Photograph from the Lubbock Agriculture Collection, courtesy of the Southwest Collection/Special Collections Library, Texas Tech University.)

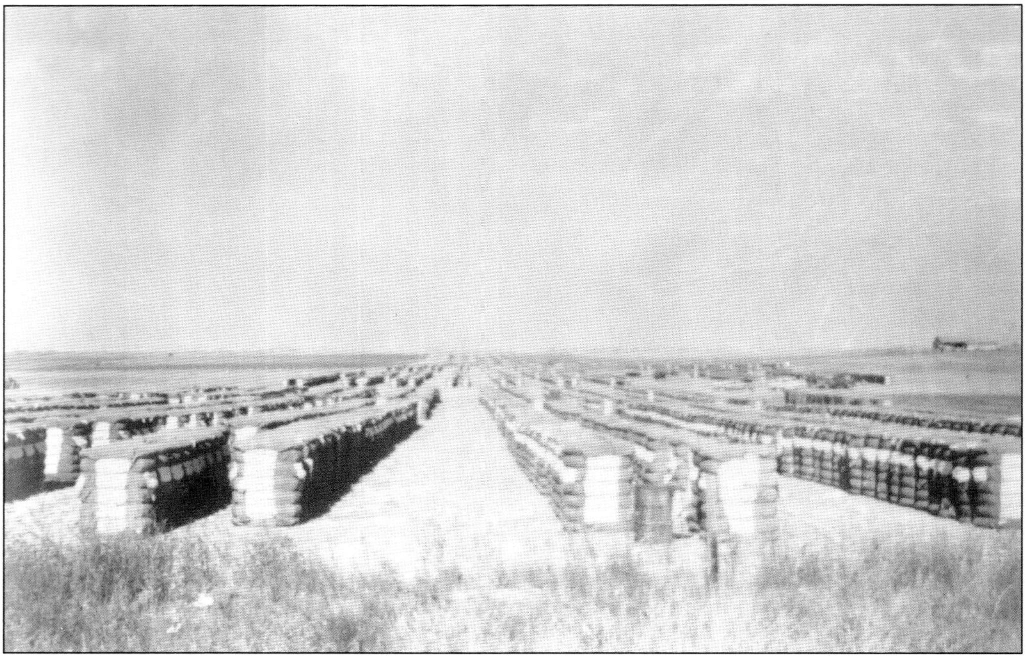

Cotton bales in the gin yard wait to be transferred to a storage facility. Cotton raised and ginned on the South Plains could go almost anywhere in the world. Most, if it did not stay in America, went to Europe or South America, and some went as far away as Asia. (Photograph from the Cotton Industry Photography Collection, courtesy of the Southwest Collection/Special Collections Library, Texas Tech University.)

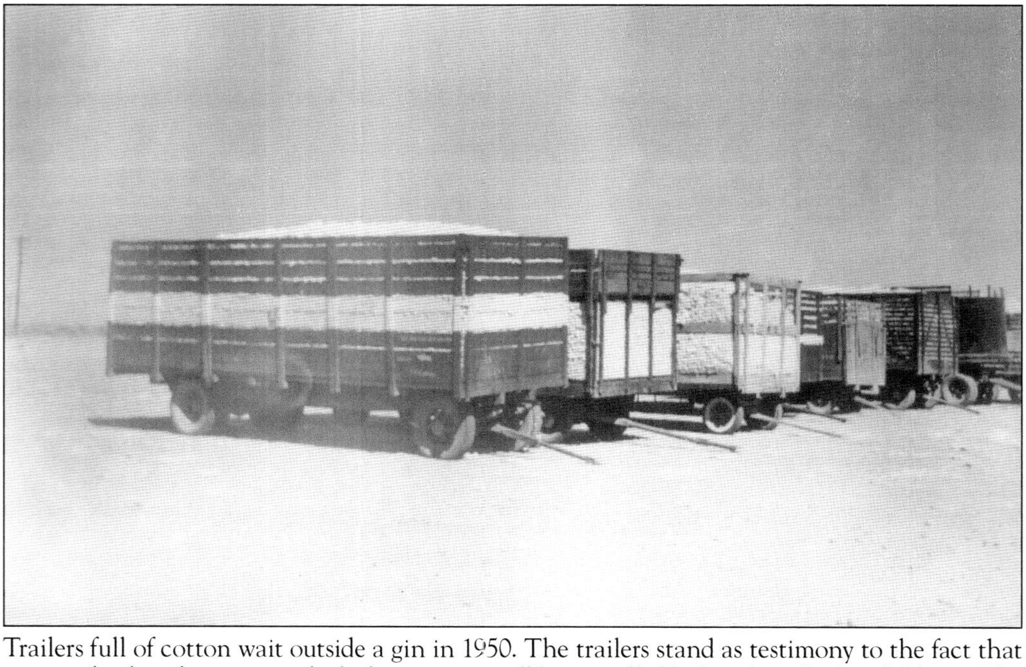

Trailers full of cotton wait outside a gin in 1950. The trailers stand as testimony to the fact that even at this late date, a great deal of cotton was still being pulled by hand on the South Plains. The cotton appears to be of high quality. (Photograph from the Cotton Industry Photography Collection, courtesy of the Southwest Collection/Special Collections Library, Texas Tech University.)

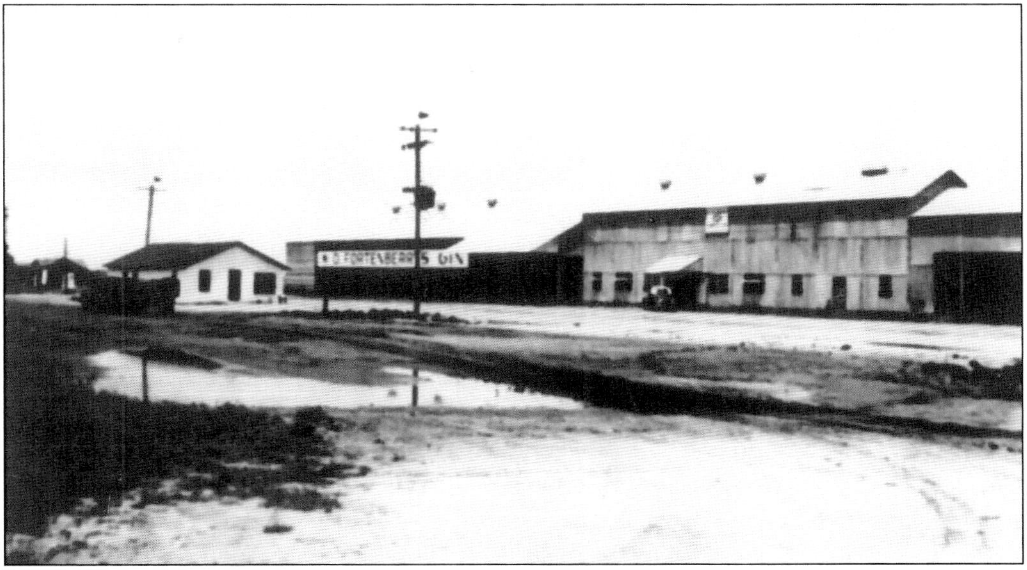

The Forte & Berry Gin near New Deal is seen here in 1939. The gin stands quiet after the harvest. Although cotton production was expanding and most gins found plenty of work during the harvest season, they struggled to remain open. Better roads meant farmers could choose where they ginned their cotton. (Photograph from the Cotton Industry Photography Collection, courtesy of the Southwest Collection/Special Collections Library, Texas Tech University.)

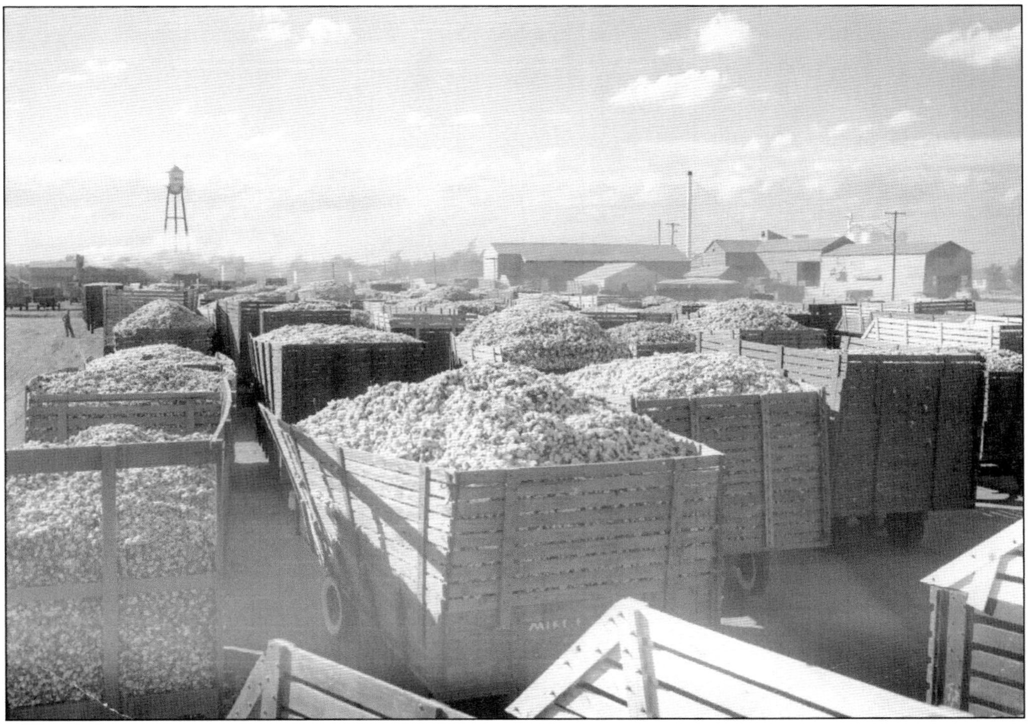

An Idalou gin is covered up with cotton trailers sometime in the 1930s. As this picture vividly emphasizes, the overproduction of cotton during the decade kept prices low all during the period. (Photograph from the Cotton Industry Photography Collection, courtesy of the Southwest Collection/Special Collections Library, Texas Tech University.)

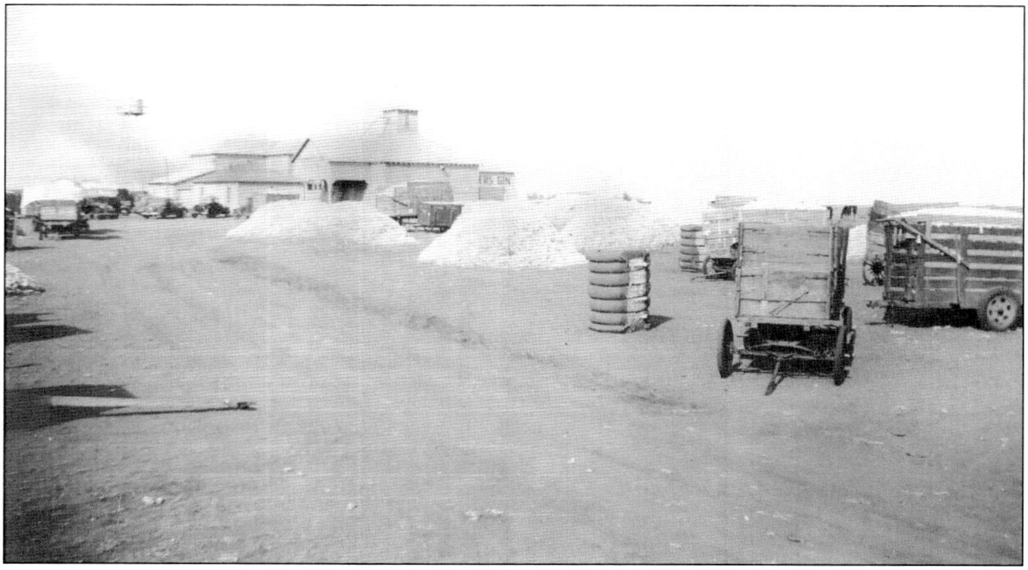

There is congestion at this Lubbock cotton gin in 1937 due to a large cotton crop, which forced farmers to unload cotton on the ground. Research and development at Texas Technological College as well as at the agricultural research stations in the 1930s led to improved seed varieties and the expansion of irrigation and mechanization, which in turn led to increased and improved harvests. (Courtesy of the Texas AgriLife Research and Extension Center – Lubbock, Texas.)

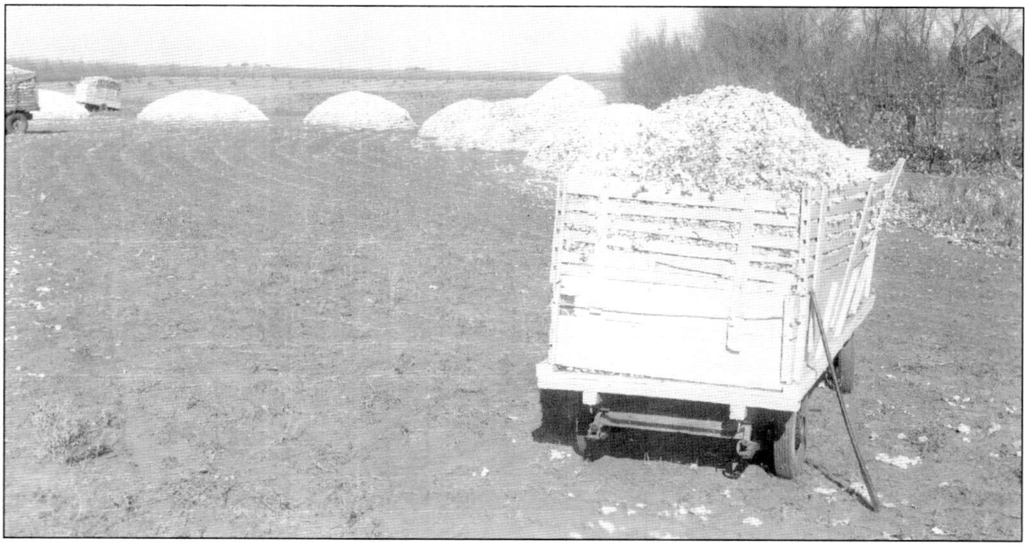

Cotton is dumped on the ground for ginning at a later date near Littlefield in 1944. During the war years, cotton production expanded, as cotton was an essential war material. This did not, however, speed up cotton ginning. Wartime shortages in laborers and spare parts continued to create bottlenecks in the production of cotton. (Courtesy of the Texas AgriLife Research and Extension Center – Lubbock, Texas.)

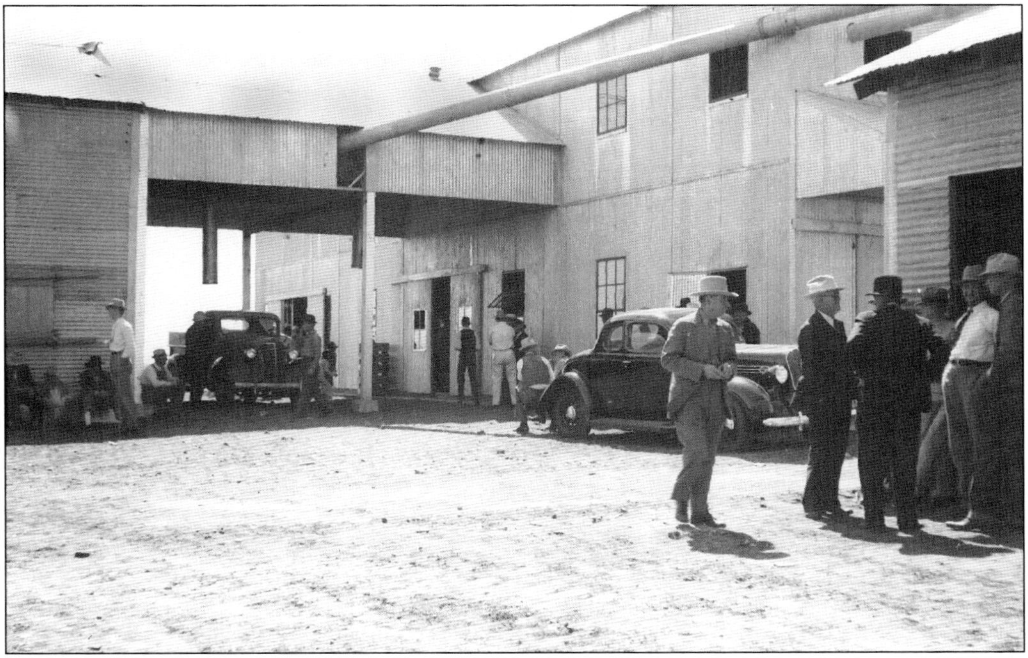

Above, a group of men congregates outside a Floydada cotton gin in 1938. They are part of an agricultural field day organized by the Crosby Country agriculture agent. The trip showed off the latest improvements in the cotton industry. Already having seen newly developed cotton varieties and the latest improvements in irrigation, they are getting ready to inspect this gin and its equipment, which would hopefully speed up the ginning process. Below, the appearance of new cars and clothes suggests that the Depression seems to be lifting in some places. (Both photographs courtesy of the Floyd County Historical Museum.)

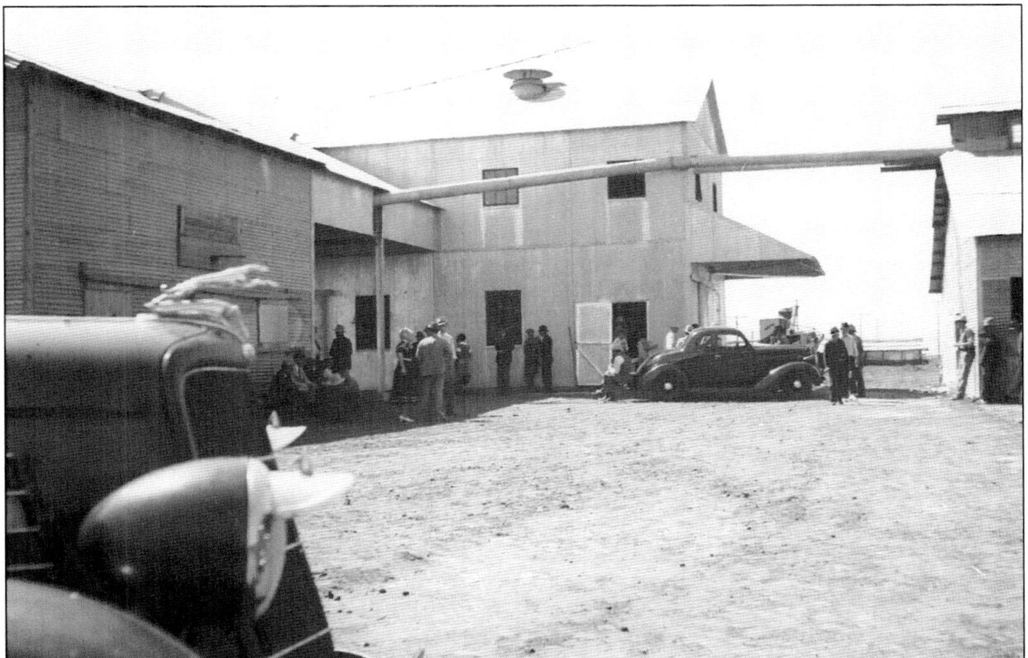

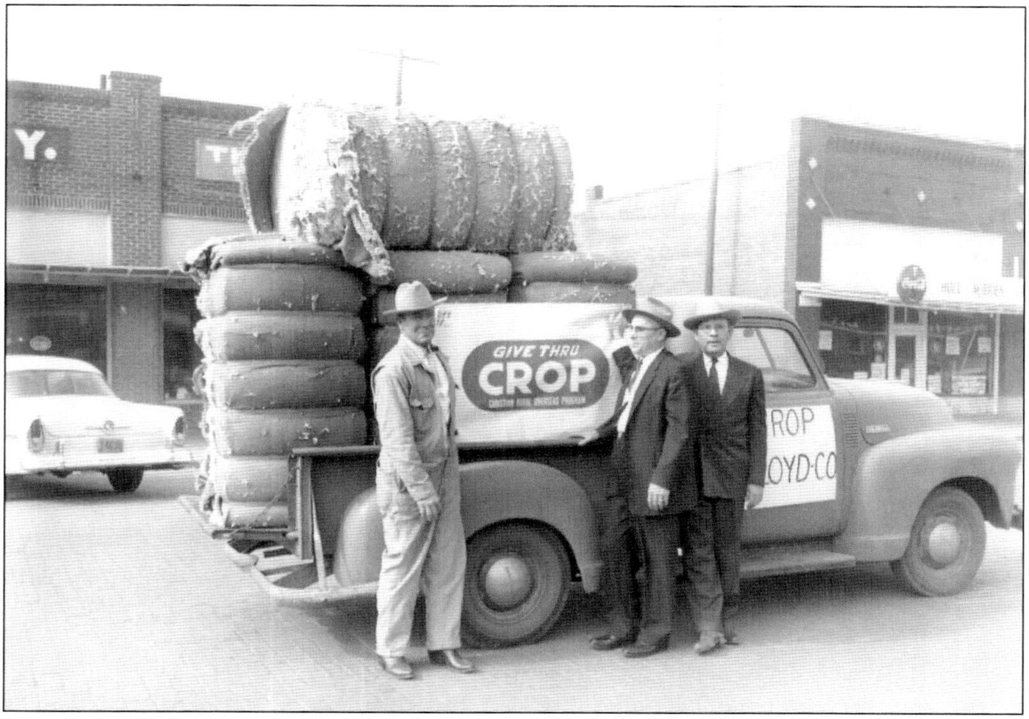

The Christian Rural Overseas Program (CROP) began operation in August 1947 under the sponsorship of Church World Service to solicit and receive bulk gifts-in-kind from American farmers during the harvest season for needy people overseas. Bill Colston (left) and T.B. Armstrong (center) of Floydada pose here with their gifts of baled cotton, along with an unidentified man. (Courtesy of the Floyd County Historical Museum.)

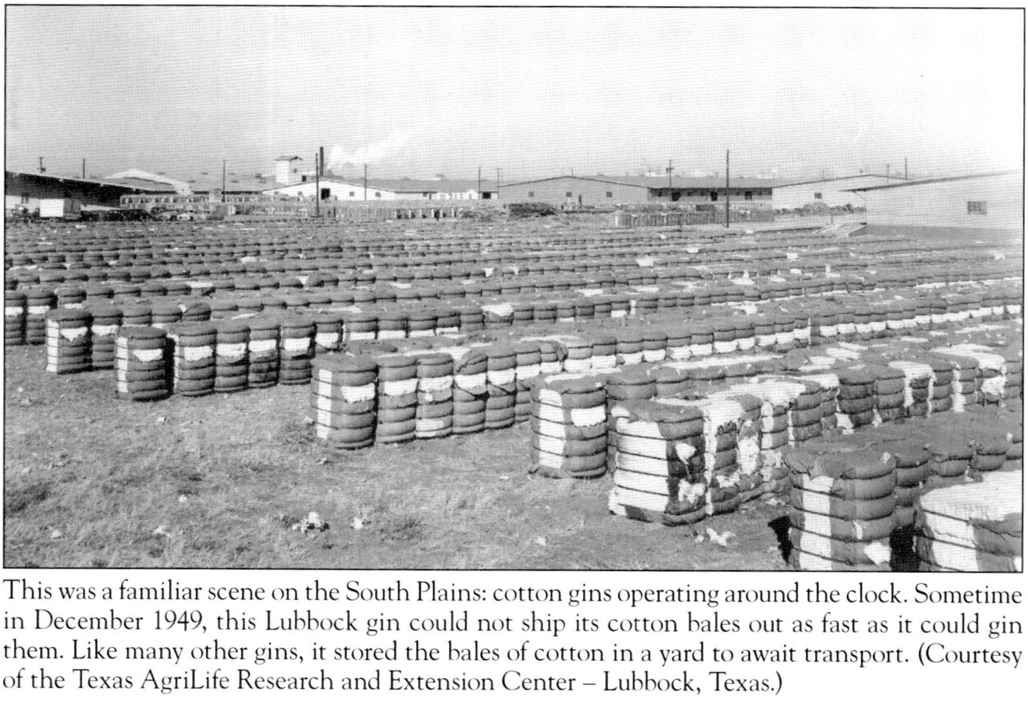

This was a familiar scene on the South Plains: cotton gins operating around the clock. Sometime in December 1949, this Lubbock gin could not ship its cotton bales out as fast as it could gin them. Like many other gins, it stored the bales of cotton in a yard to await transport. (Courtesy of the Texas AgriLife Research and Extension Center – Lubbock, Texas.)

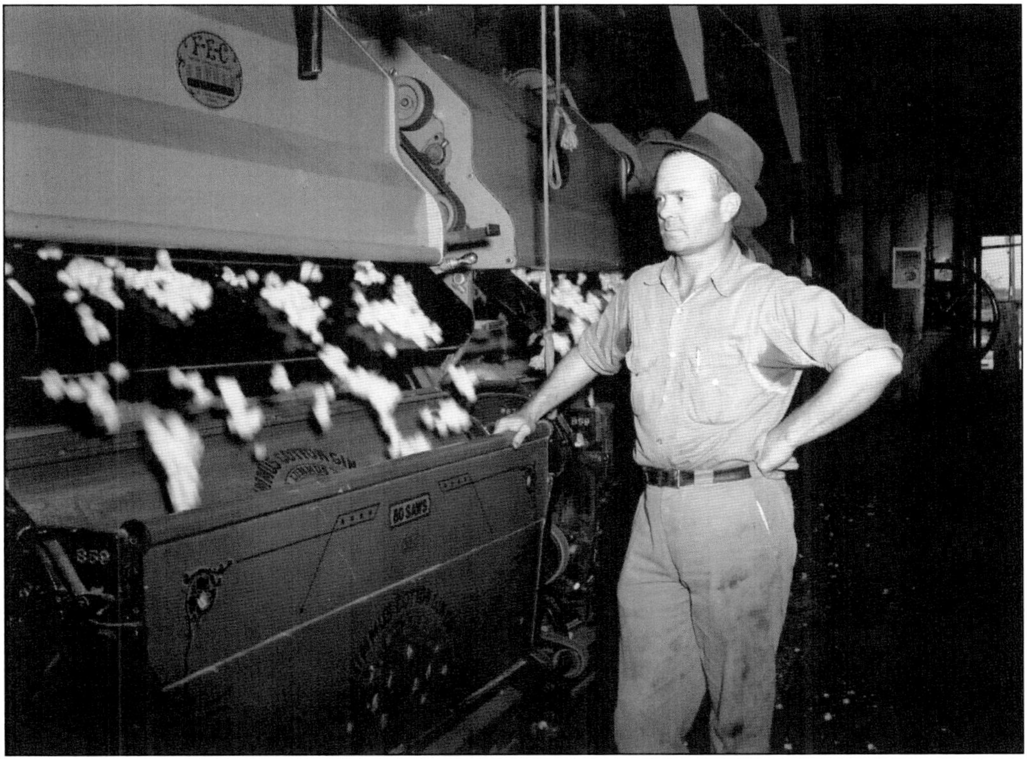

An unidentified worker stands in front of a ginning machine, monitoring its operation, making sure the machine does not clog up, and periodically taking samples of cotton to test for cleanliness. Most of the trash has already been blown out of the cotton, and this machine, an actual gin, removes the seed. (Photograph from the Winston Reeves Photograph Collection, courtesy of the Southwest Collection/Special Collections Library, Texas Tech University.)

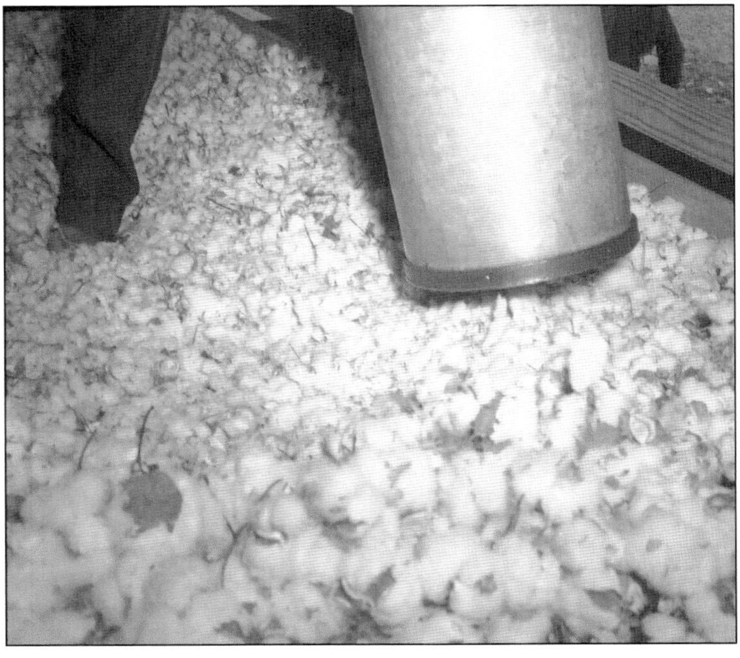

This close-up view shows how cotton was vacuumed out of a trailer over to the gin—the first step in the ginning process. The extension nozzle needed a skillful operator to work efficiently; keeping a steady hand at this position was hard, since it was hot, dirty, and very noisy work. (Photograph from the Winston Reeves Photograph Collection, courtesy of the Southwest Collection/Special Collections Library, Texas Tech University.)

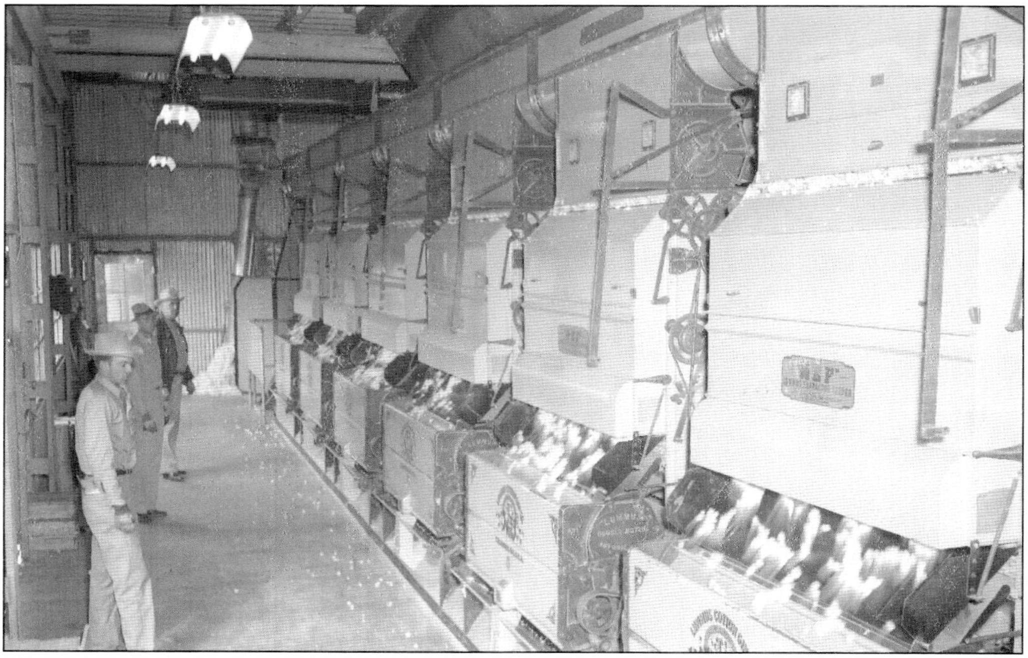

The ginning process essentially separates the seed from the lint. The cotton goes through dryers to reduce moisture and then through cleaning equipment to remove foreign matter. It is blown to the gin (seen here), where seed is removed from the lint by a series of saw teeth. Then, it is ready for baling. (Photograph from the Winston Reeves Photograph Collection, courtesy of the Southwest Collection/Special Collections Library, Texas Tech University.)

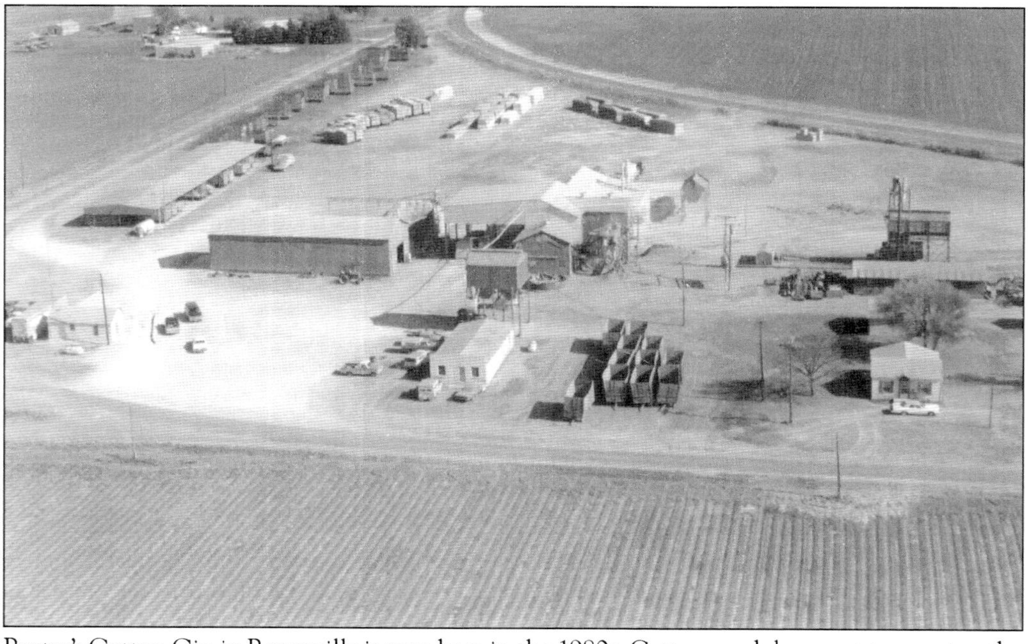

Buster's Cotton Gin in Ropesville is seen here in the 1980s. Cotton modules are at top center; the residence of the workers, mostly migrants and seasonal employees, is to the left; and the gin is at the center. Improved machinery such as pickers and strippers has reduced the need for migrant labor on farms and gins. (Courtesy of Dan Taylor.)

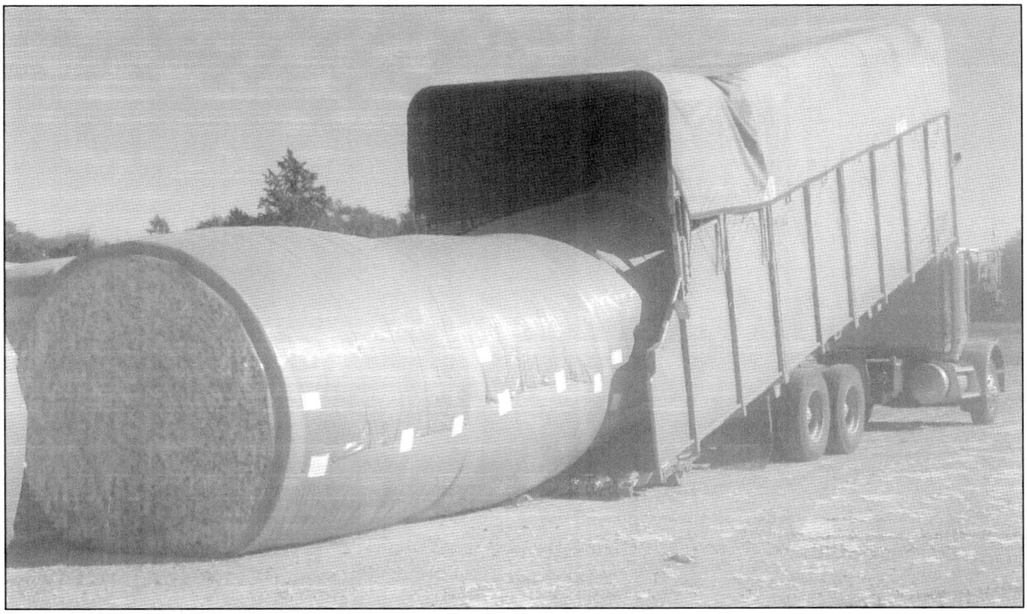

A module truck unloads a round bale of cotton at a gin in Lubbock County. In 2011, farmers were experimenting with round bales, the latest innovation in cotton production on the South Plains. This innovation eliminated the need for a module builder and made cotton easier to transport. (Courtesy of Dan Taylor.)

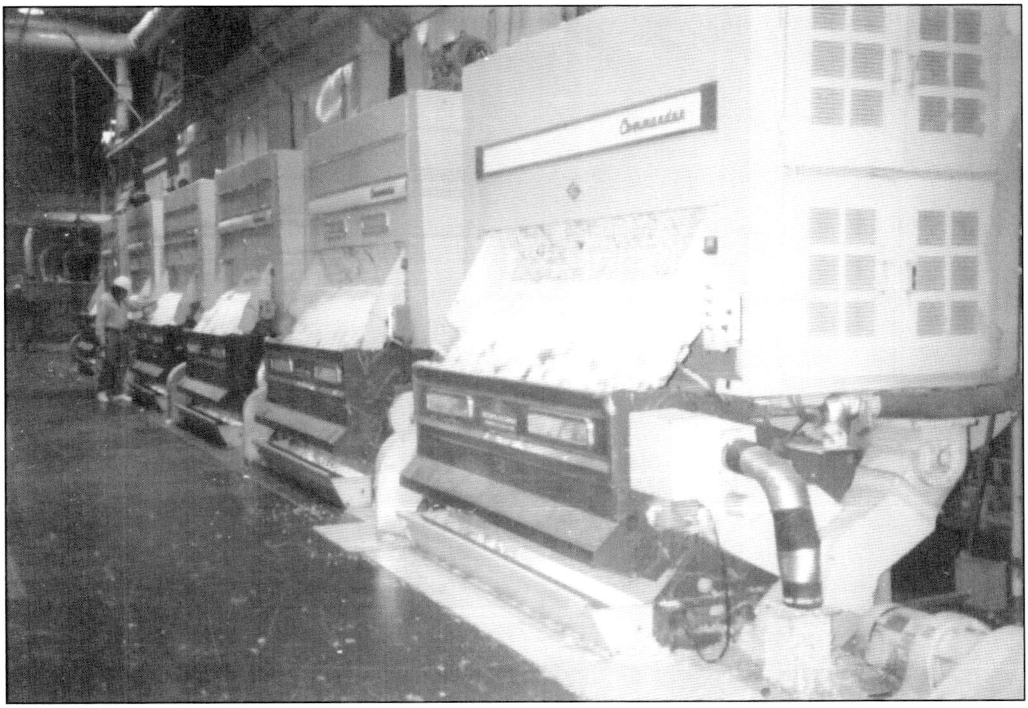

Before ginning, the cotton is cleaned, and trash and motes are removed from the lint. During the ginning process, the cottonseed is removed. In the gin, revolving circular saws pull the lint through closely spaced ribs, which prevent the seeds from passing through. Today, valuable products can be made from the trash and motes. (Courtesy of Dan Taylor.)

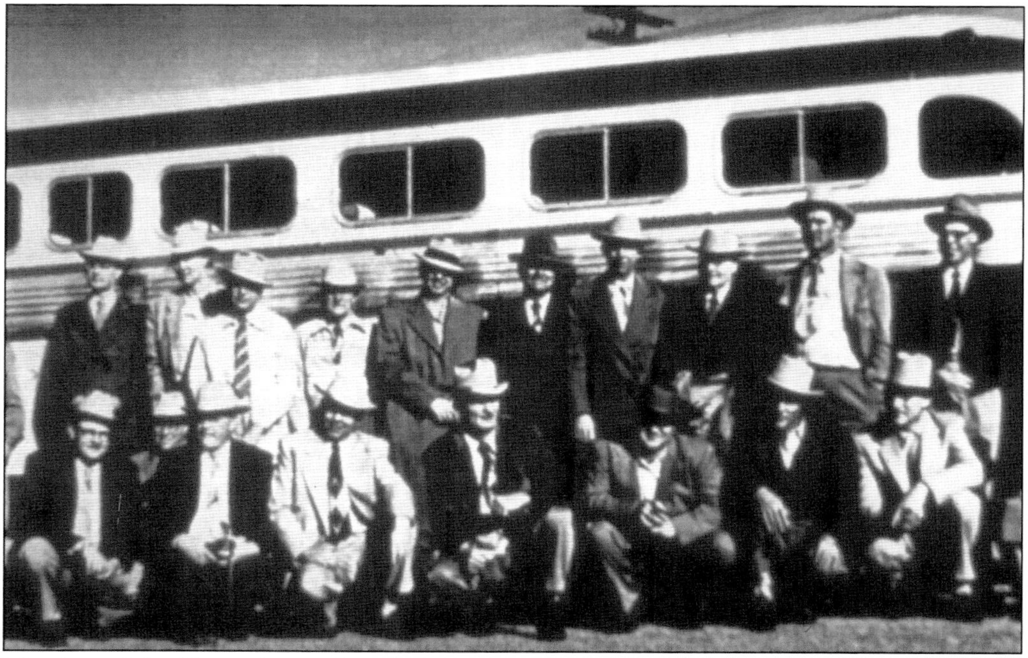

Members of the Plains Cotton Cooperative Association (PCCA) stand by their tour bus. These men helped form the PCCA on the South Plains in the 1950s. The PCCA developed to collectively sell farmers' cotton for the highest available price while working to improve its grade. (Photograph by Lynette Thompson Wilson, courtesy of Plains Cotton Cooperative Association.)

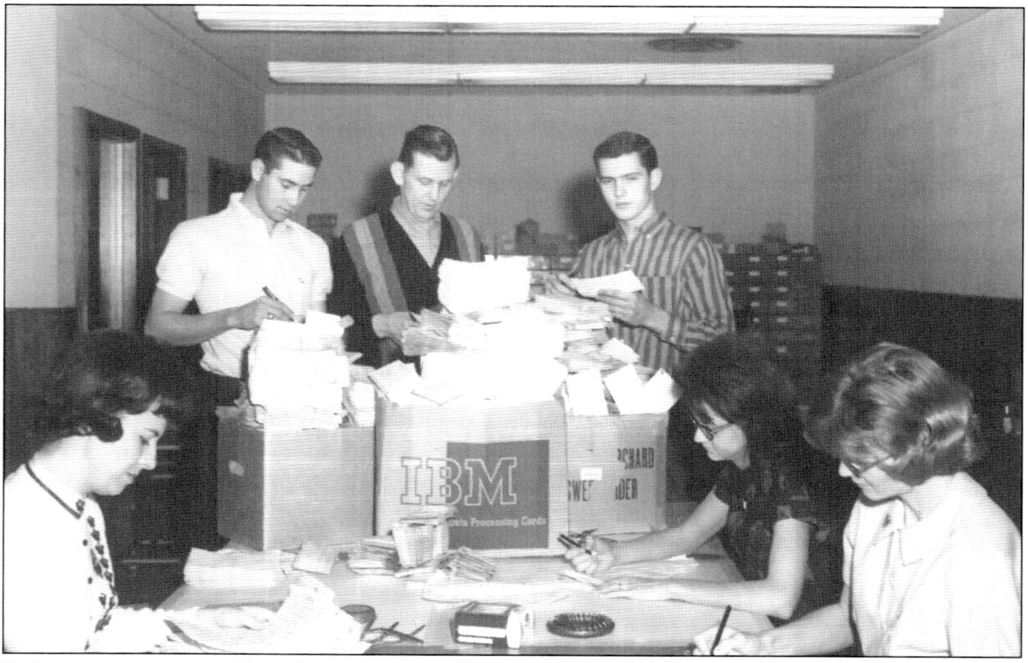

Before computers could track cotton from the field to the mill and beyond, the process had to be done with paper slips, creating a lot of paperwork. Here, PCCA employees plow through several box loads of slips containing information about the cotton bales processed that day. (Photograph by Lynette Thompson Wilson, courtesy of Plains Cotton Cooperative Association.)

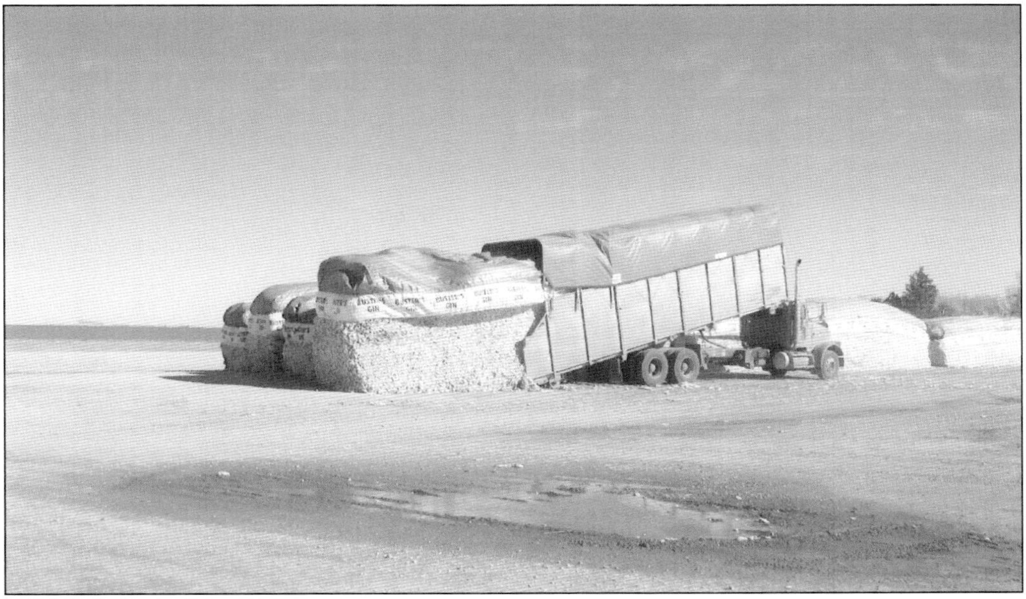

A module truck unloads a module in the yard of Buster's Gin in Ropesville. This cotton, stripped in 2011, was brought to the gin the previous day. In 2011, cotton modules did not have to sit in the field or in the yard waiting to be ginned. The very short crop year meant gins could keep up easily with demand. (Courtesy of Dan Taylor.)

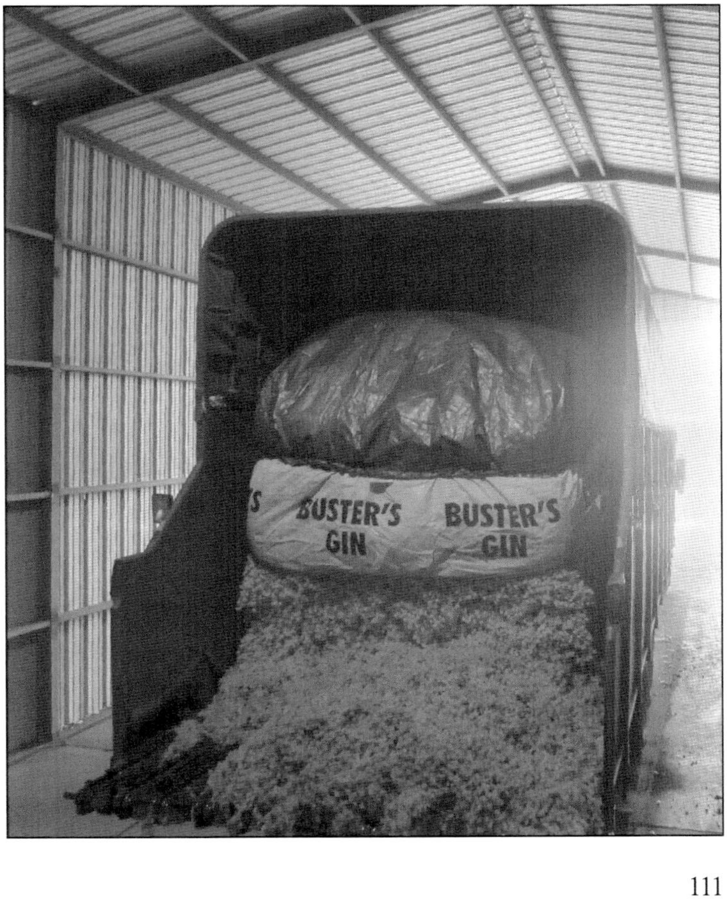

A cotton module hauling truck, developed on the South Plains in the early 1970s, unloads a cotton module. The module is placed onto a conveyer system, which moves the cotton into the gin. Modern trucks have cameras and monitors that allow drivers to view the loading and unloading of modules from a screen inside the cab. (Photograph by and courtesy of Jack Becker.)

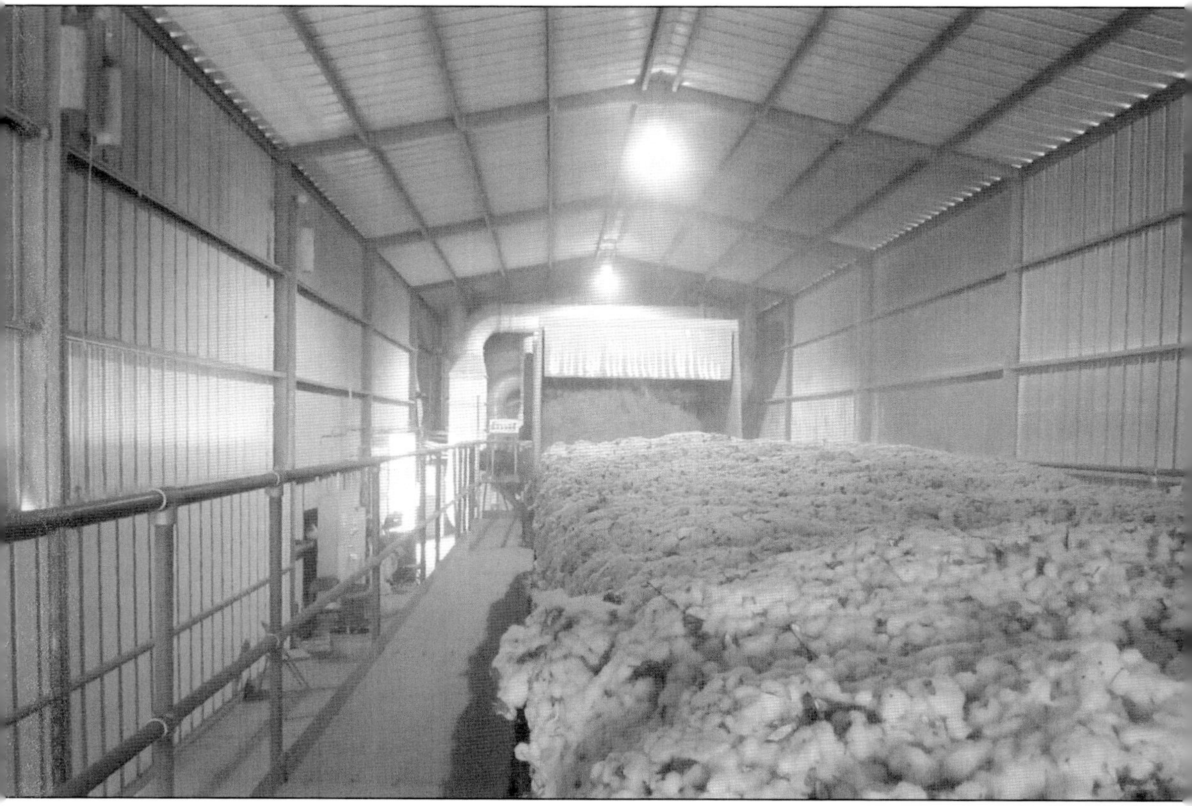

Trash, bits of dried leaves, stems, bolls, and cottonseed can account for up to 30 percent of the module by weight. The ginning process removes most of these by-products, which have a value of their own. (Photograph by and courtesy of Jack Becker.)

Six

Cotton Research Development and Cotton products

Cotton products affect life in a multitude of ways and show up in unexpected places. Cotton and cotton by-products are in what people eat and wear; they keep individuals cool in the summer and warm in the winter. They feed pets and help keep humans healthy, clean, and looking good. Cotton by-products are even in the currency used every day. The Texas International Cotton School and the Fiber and Biopolymer Research Institute (FBRI), both associated with Texas Tech University, are researching new ways to produce higher-quality cotton products and find new uses for cotton, including the use of fibers in protective wear for the military and police.

Not all cotton research and development is done in laboratories on university campuses. In fact, farmers living on the South Plains, who continue to work long and hard to develop better, faster, and more economical ways to produce quality cotton products, do most of the development. The South Plains farmers were the first to develop disease-resistant and storm-proof cotton, to improve cultivating methods, and to invent planting and stripping machinery. Area gin operators worked to improve the ginning process, which helped to market a cleaner and more desirable product. Many South Plains farmers work closely with companies such as John Deere and hold patents on equipment used all over the world.

The Littlefield Denim Mill is another example of how constant innovation and improvement strengthens the demand for cotton apparel. Through employees' own hard work and the upgrading of its machinery, the Littlefield mill is able to weave denim using polymer threads. This innovation makes it the largest producer of denim in the United States and one of only four such mills in the country.

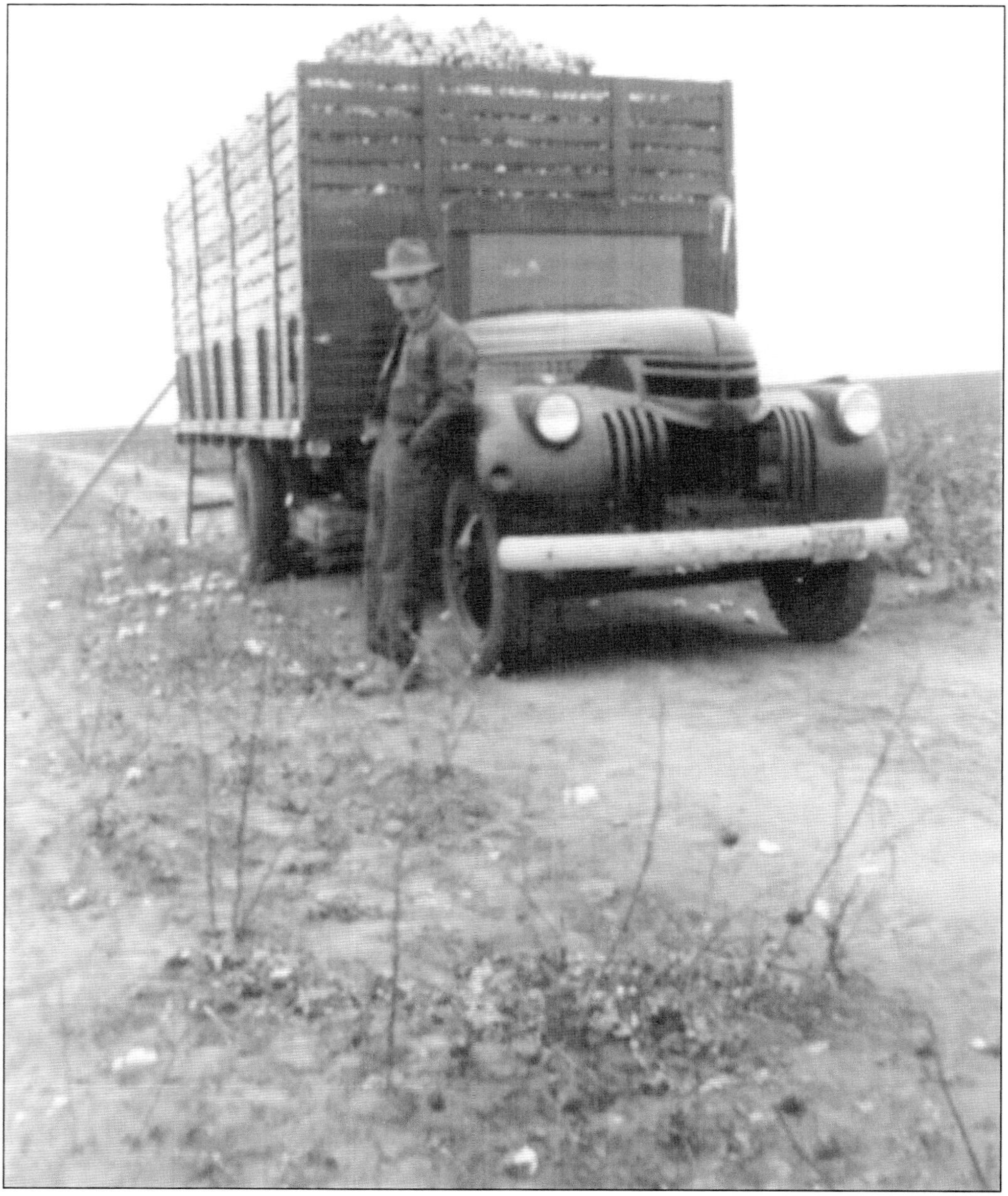

Lubbock County farmer Powell Adams stands beside his truck in 1960. The cotton in the truck is equivalent to four bales. Hoping a bigger truck would decrease downtime at the gin, Adams modified the truck by increasing the height of the sides so it could hold more than the standard cotton truck. (Courtesy of Carol and Powell Adams.)

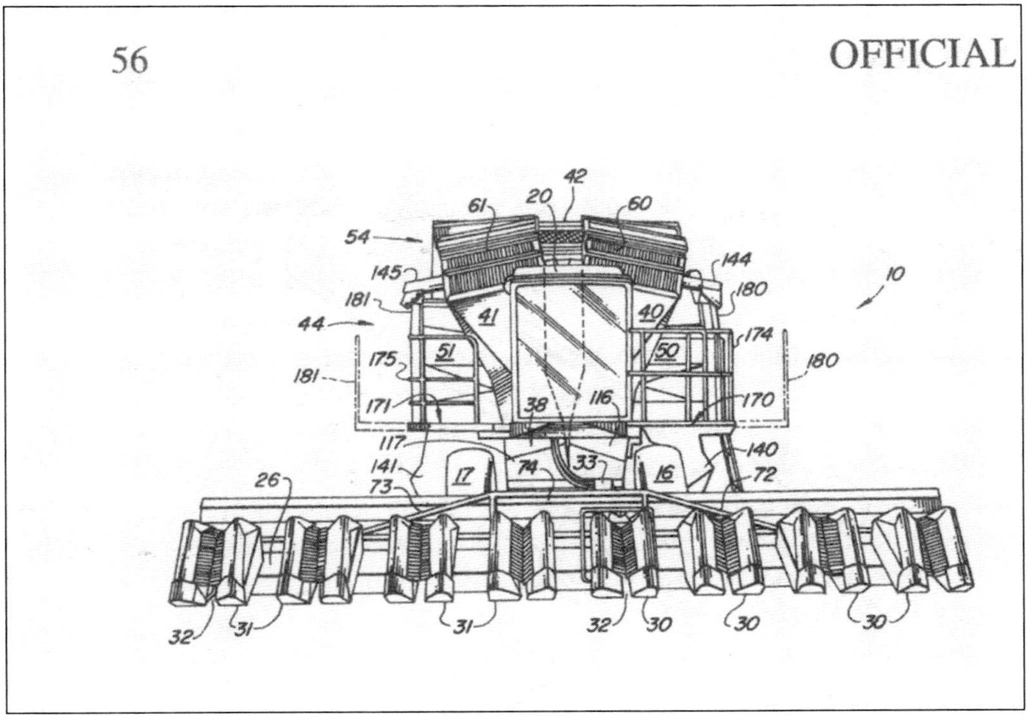

Never underestimate the capacity of South Plains farmers, as their ingenuity comes to life through constant contact with their equipment. The winter months give them an opportunity to seek new ways to improve production. These photographs show just one of the many patents obtained by farmers from the South Plains—in this case by Buzz Vardeman, who patented a high-capacity cotton harvester that includes up to eight brush-type units mounted on a cross-auger system. The system has the ability to move material inwardly toward a central location. From there, the cotton is conveyed to the rear of the harvester and into two baskets. (Both images courtesy of the United States Patent and Trademark Office.)

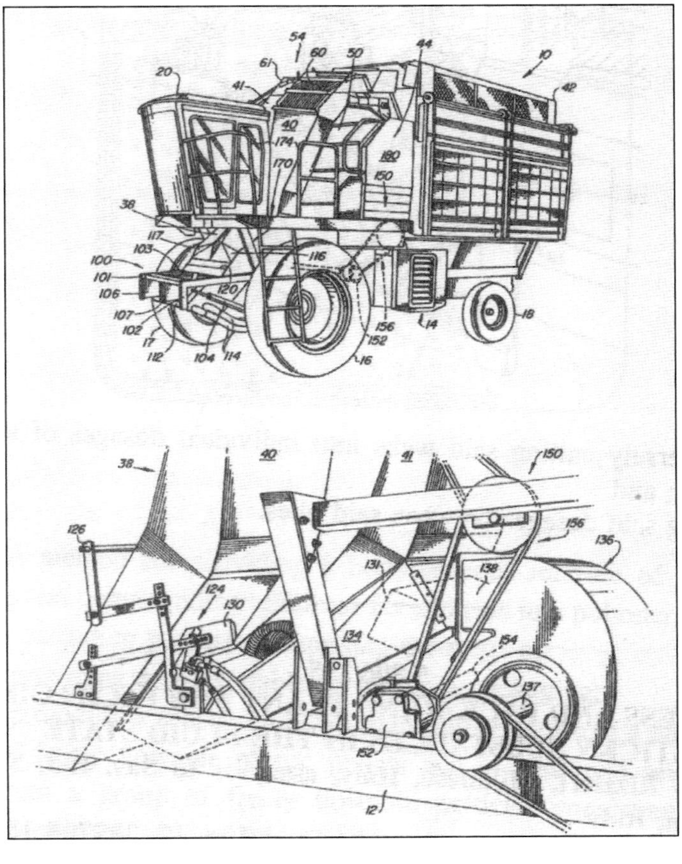

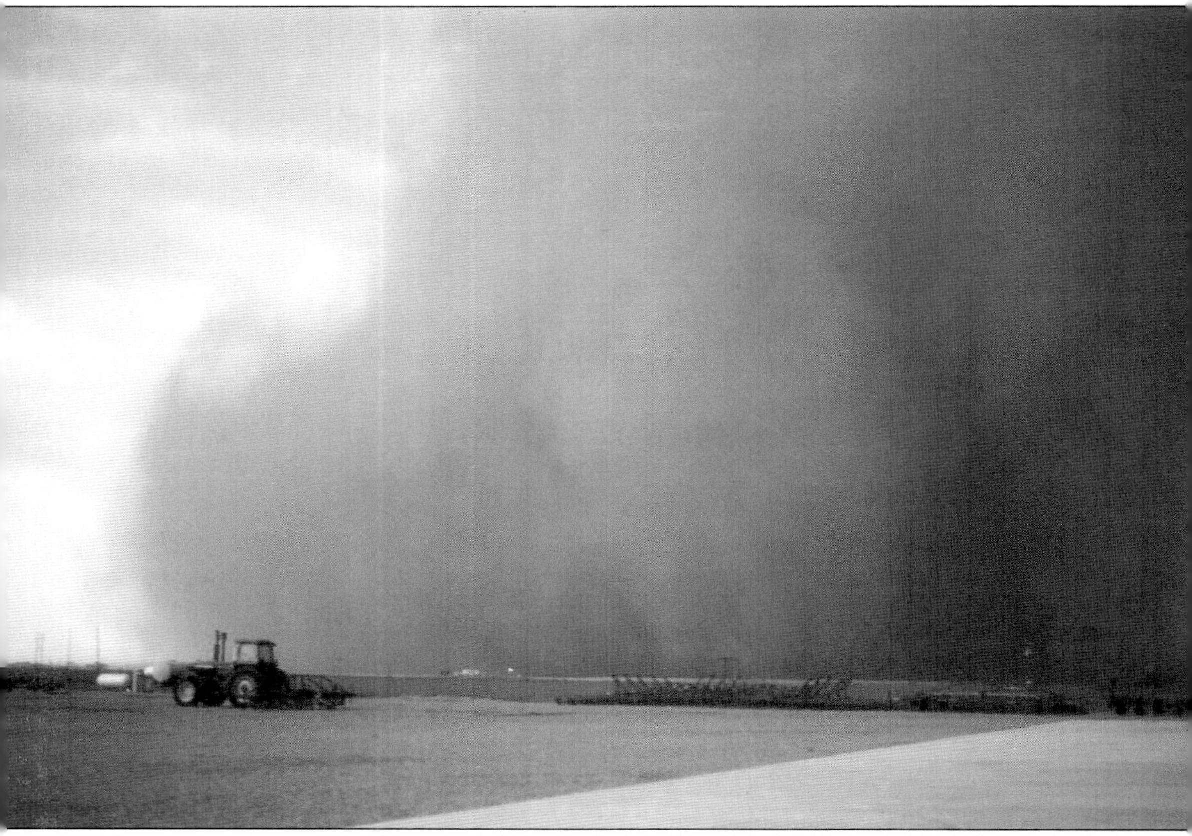

Cotton farming in West Texas can be a challenge. Unpredictable weather conditions such as drought, hailstorms, early or late frost, blowing sand and dust, and high winds make farming on the South Plains interesting. Farmers attempt to shield their crops from extremes in the weather, but there is no getting away from this 1991 sandstorm. (Photograph by and courtesy of Vardeman Farms.)

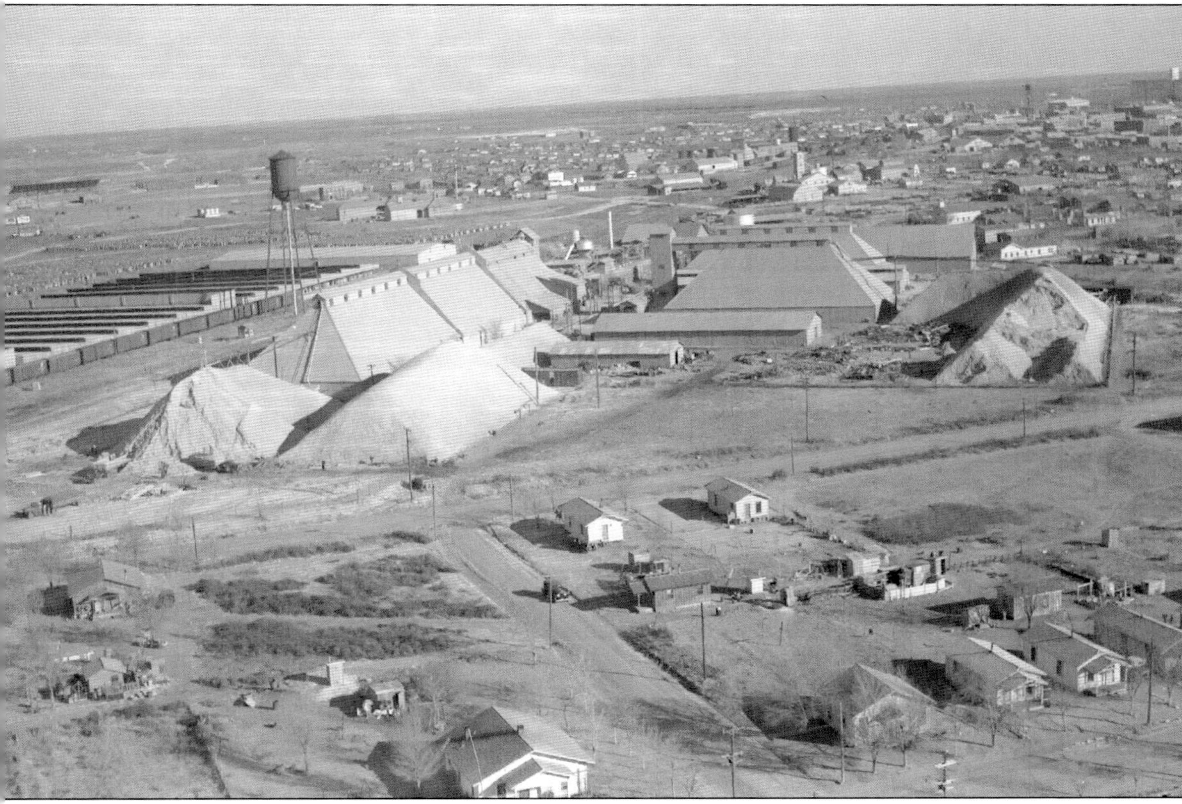

Several large piles of cottonseed are seen from a low-flying plane as they wait for processing at a Lubbock cottonseed process plant in 1930. This harvest was so large that the seed had to be stored outside. (Photograph from the Winston Reeves Photograph Collection, courtesy of the Southwest Collection/Special Collections Library, Texas Tech University.)

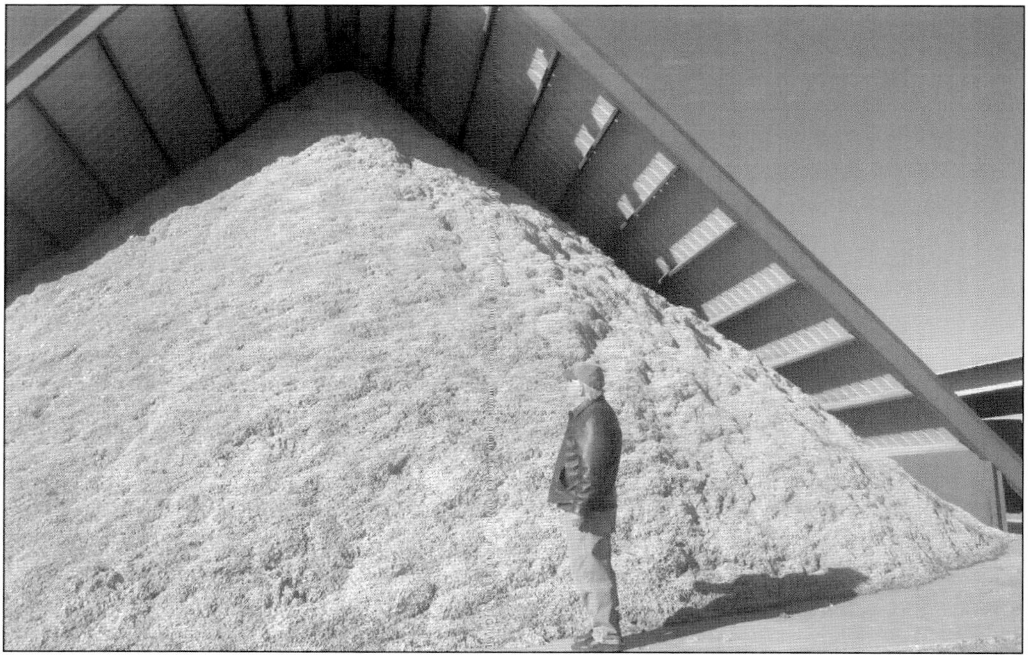

Jack Becker stands in front of the pile of cottonseed behind Buster's Gin. Cottonseed is used for making such products as cottonseed oil, organic fertilizer, and animal feed. This cottonseed awaits shipment to a large dairy in the panhandle of Texas near Muleshoe. In 2011, the price of cottonseed rivaled the price of lint. (Photograph by and courtesy of Innocent Awasom.)

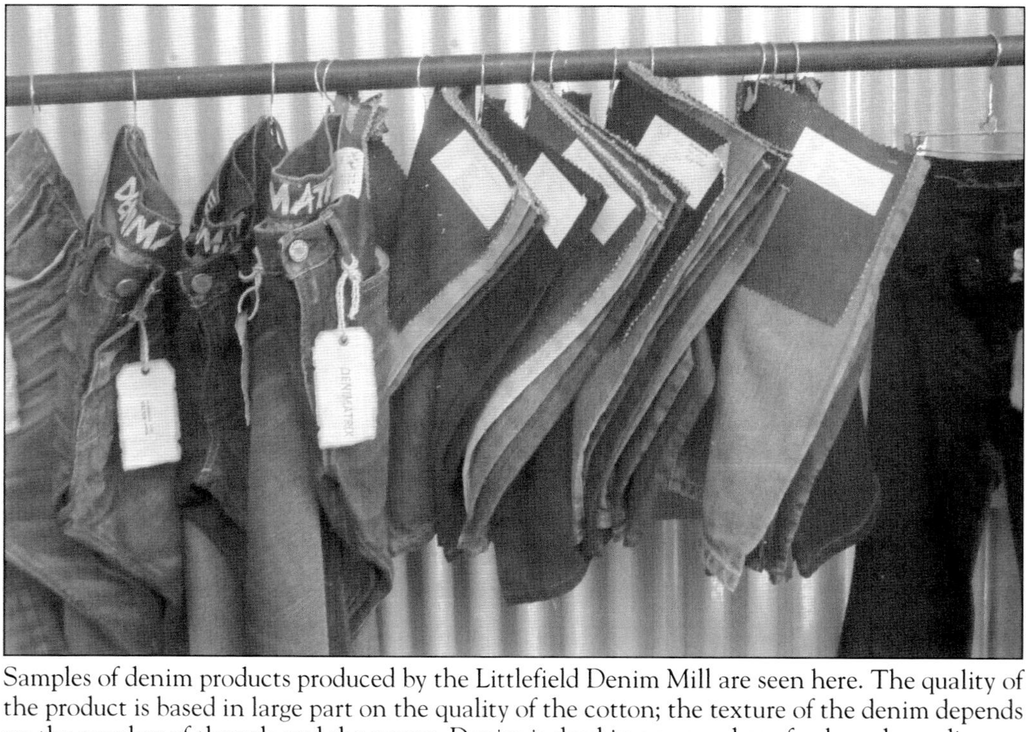

Samples of denim products produced by the Littlefield Denim Mill are seen here. The quality of the product is based in large part on the quality of the cotton; the texture of the denim depends on the number of threads and the weave. Denim is dyed in any number of colors, depending on the customer's wants and needs. (Photograph by and courtesy of Cynthia Henry.)

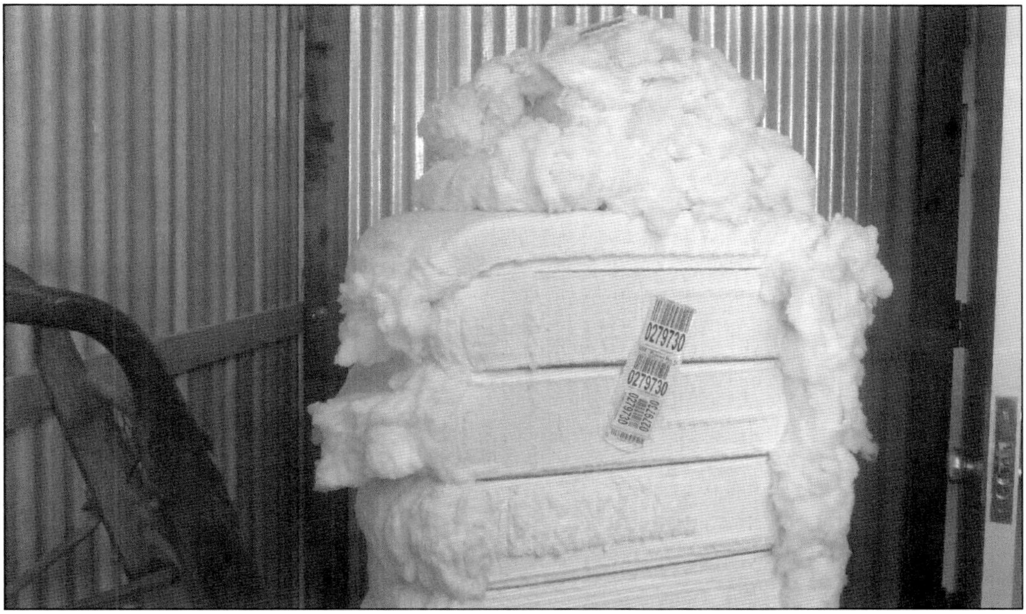

A cotton bale arrives at the mill weighing approximately 500 pounds. A permanent identification number provides important information about the cotton—indicating its grade, the farmer who grew it, where it was grown, and when it was harvested. This information is useful for accounting and quality control purposes. (Photograph by and courtesy of Cynthia Henry.)

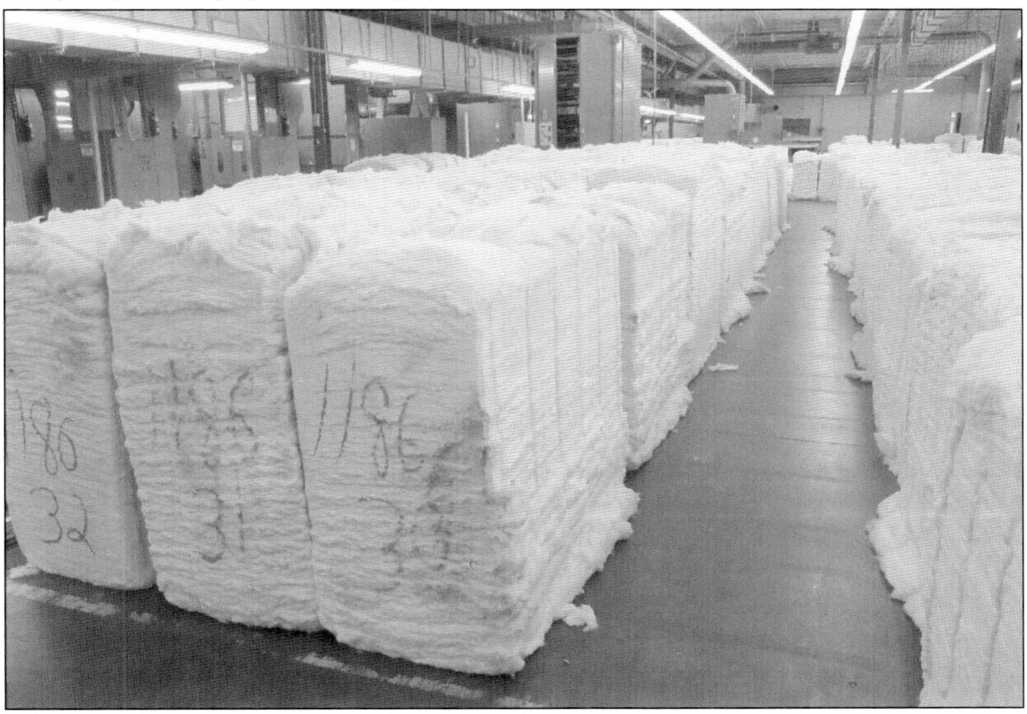

When cotton arrives from the gin, cotton from the same farm is stored together. This image shows bales 30–32 from Farm 1186. The cotton in these bales is similar in grade and quality and will be processed into yarn of the same strength. This process helps to insure uniformity of product. (Photograph by and courtesy of Cynthia Henry.)

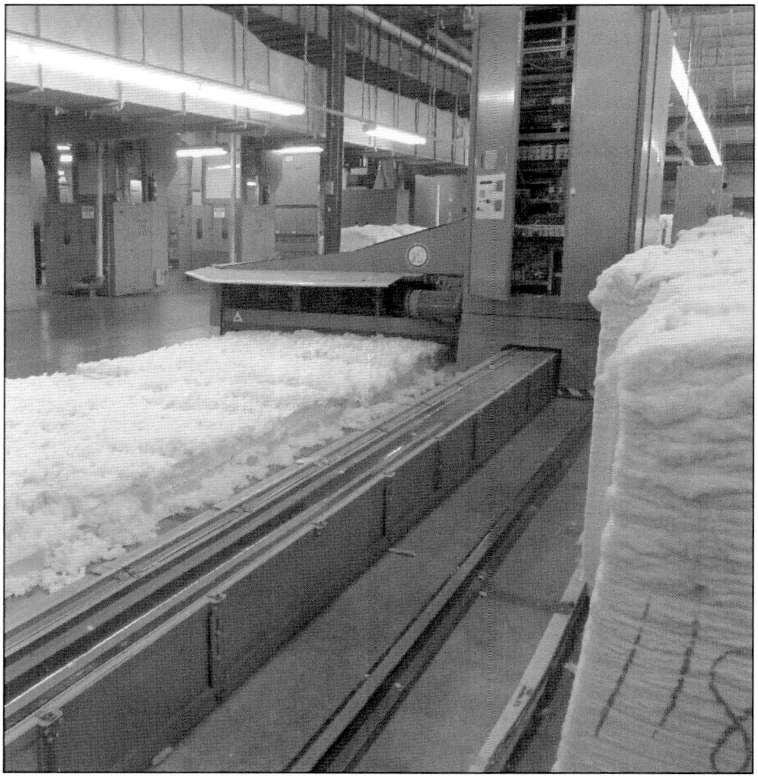

Cotton bales are arranged on the floor according to grade. Every product the mill produces requires a different mixture of cotton. The upright machine in the upper right picks up the cotton and blows it up and over to the machine on the left, which blends the cotton. (Photograph by and courtesy of Cynthia Henry.)

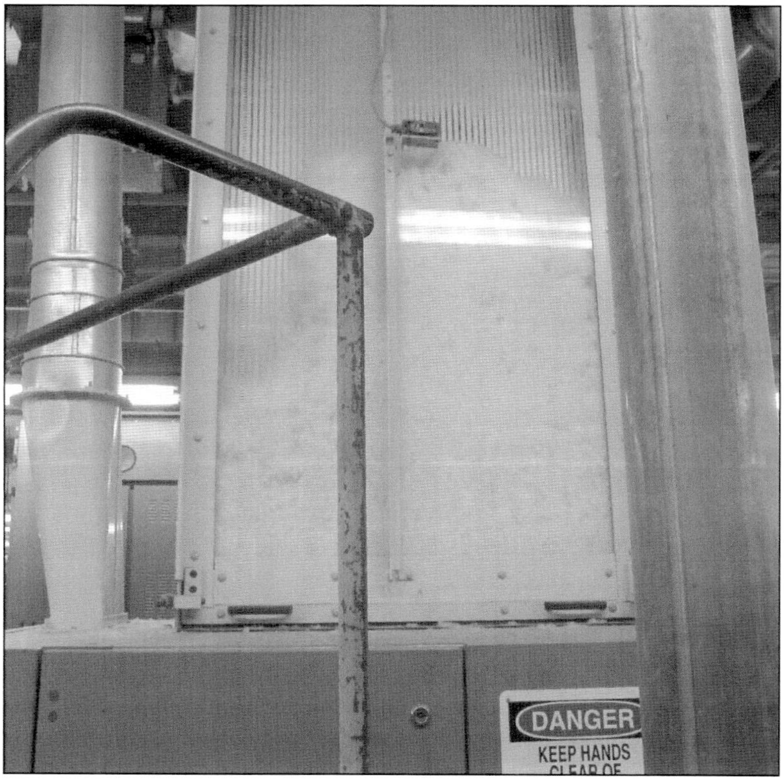

In this image, different grades of cotton are mixed together and given a final cleaning. Moisture is added to the cotton, helping the cleaning process. Later, it is blown dry and blended with other grades of cotton. At the end of this process, the cotton is spun into threads. (Photograph by and courtesy of Cynthia Henry.)

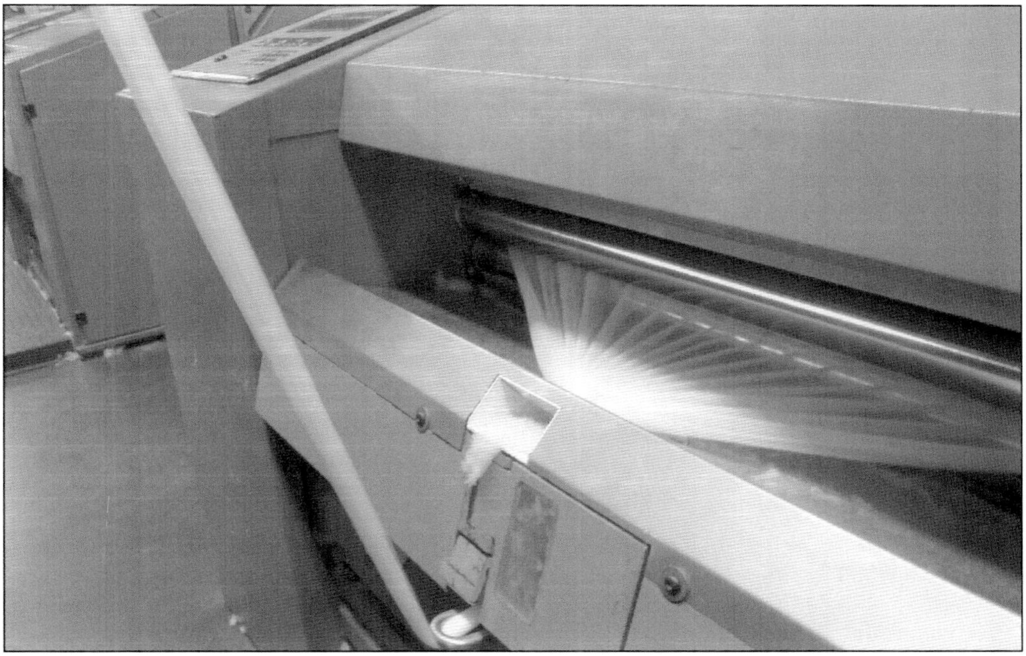

After cleaning, the cotton fibers are formed into threads called slivers. These large, fluffy slivers will be milled until they more closely resemble the thread used to produce cotton products. Traditional spinning, or ring spinning, is used to weave denim cloth. This cotton will be ring-spun into a pair of blue jeans. (Photograph by and courtesy of Cynthia Henry.)

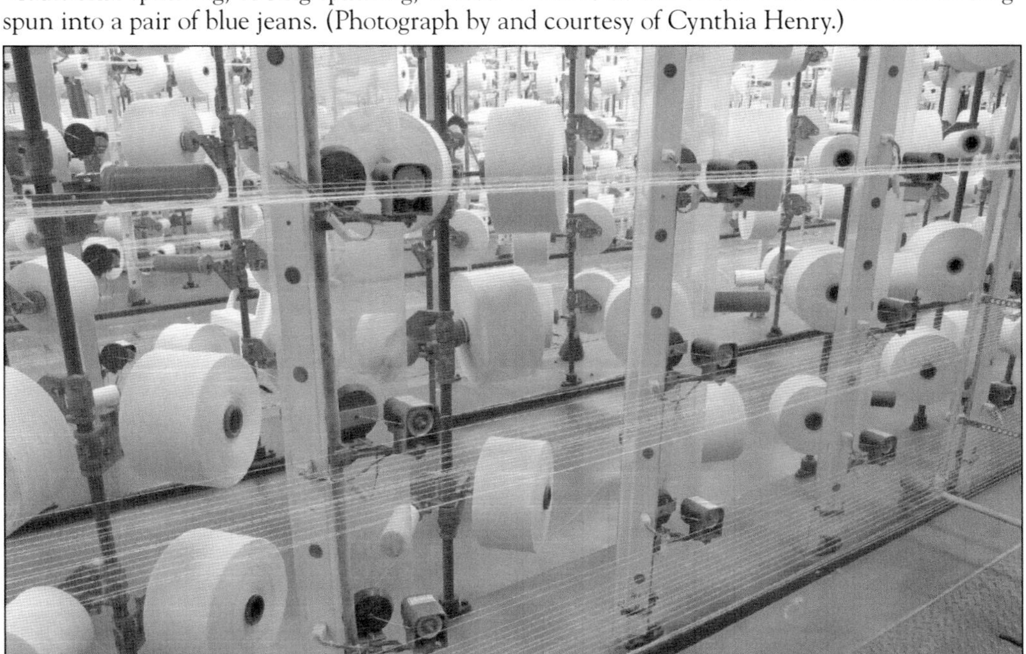

The cotton is continuously milled until it reaches the correct size and strength. Different products require threads of different size and strength, so the thread is spun to fit the needs of the customer. After milling, the thread is spun around these large spools in preparation for the dying process. (Photograph by and courtesy of Cynthia Henry.)

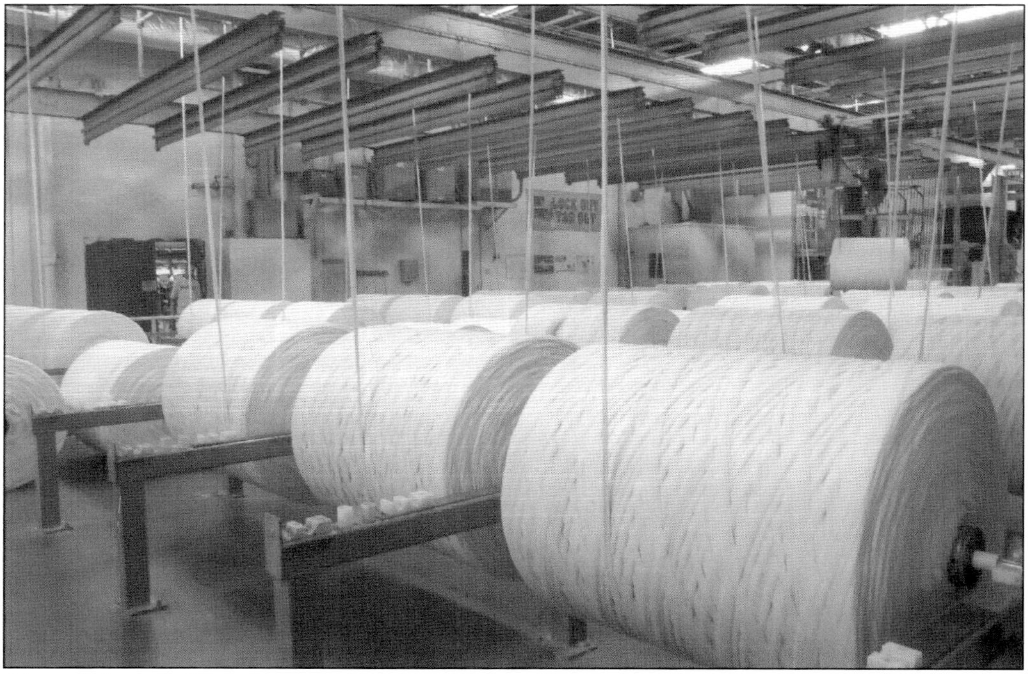

Threads from different warp balls (pictured) are woven together in preparation for the indigo dyeing process, which colors it. Each one of these warp balls can send cotton to a different dye vat or to the same one. Indigo and black are the colors used most in dyeing denim jeans. (Photograph by and courtesy of Cynthia Henry.)

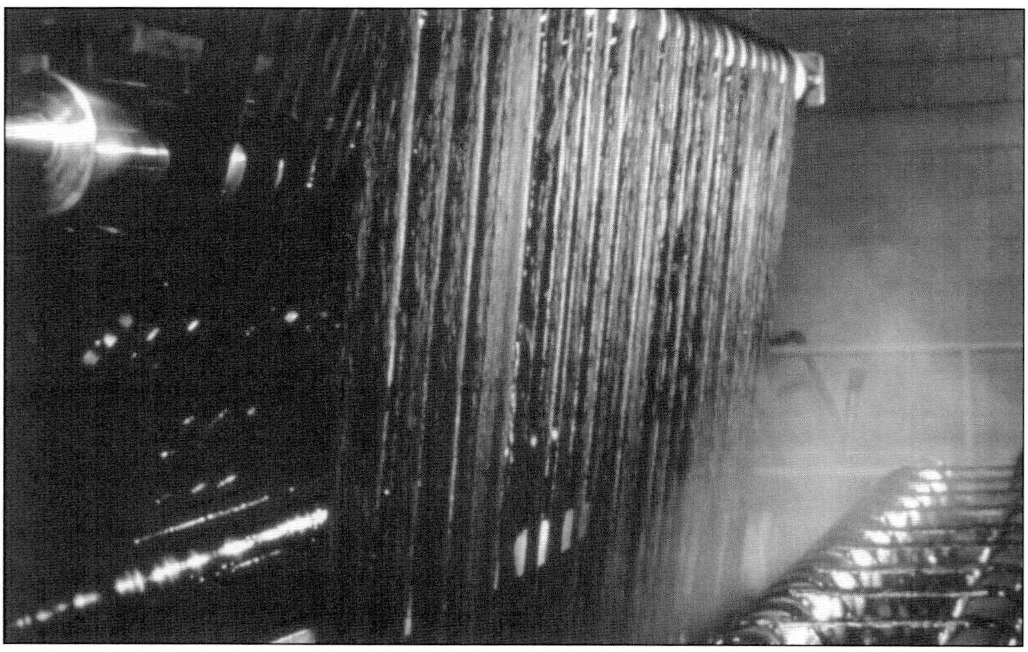

Dyes can be either man-made or natural. A sulfur solution floats on top of the dye vat to prevent oxidation, allowing the dye to work properly. Notice the threads have been separated before dyeing. As the threads move up and out of the vat, excess dye is removed. (Photograph by Lynette Thompson Wilson, courtesy of Plains Cotton Cooperative Association.)

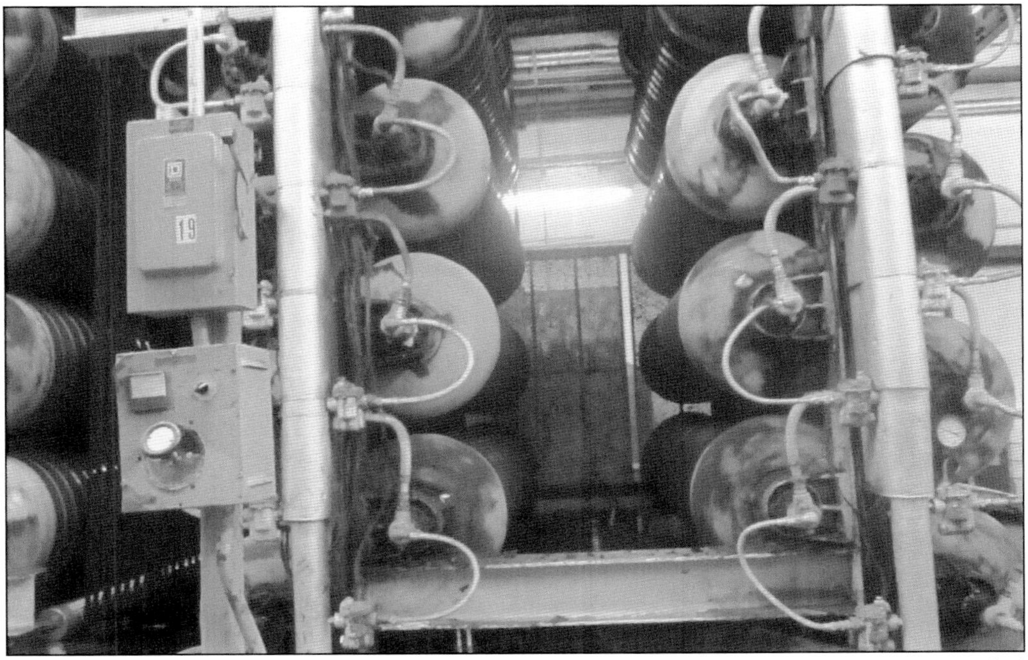

The dyed threads are sent through a set of machines, where they are heated in a very controlled manner. Afterwards, they are dyed and dried again. In a final step, the threads are coated with wax to add tensile strength to the threads. After washing out the excess wax, or slashing, the cotton is ready for weaving. (Photograph by and courtesy of Cynthia Henry.)

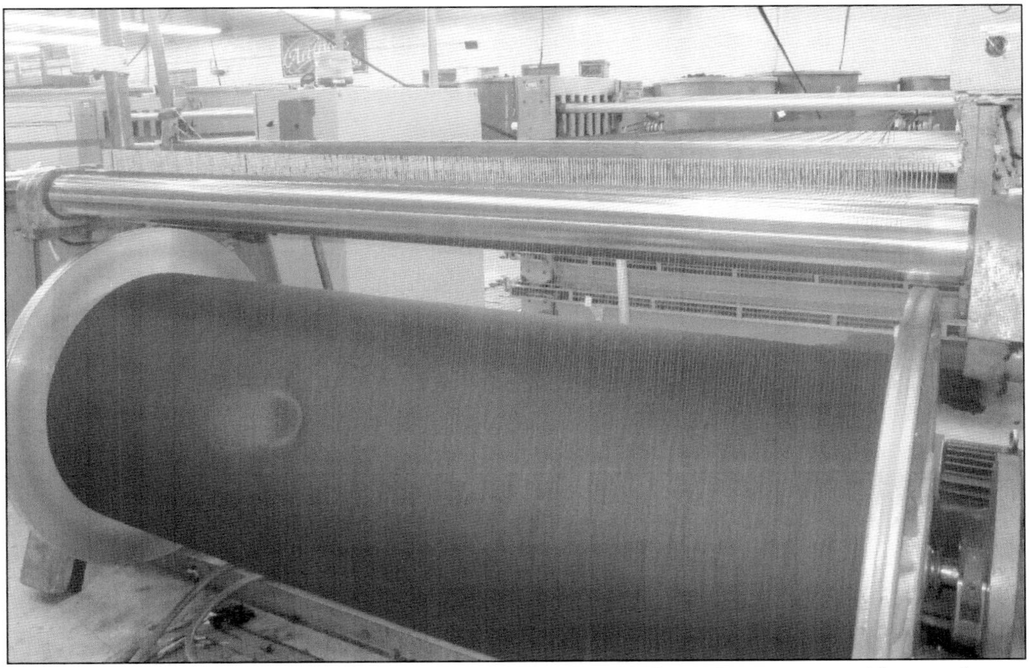

Denim thread is fed from a giant spool into the weaving machine. Yarn is weaved by interlacing the threads longitudinally and laterally using dyed and naturally colored yarn, respectively. Denim cloth is woven into a distinct pattern—one over, two under. The cotton, dye, and weave all go into making quality denim cloth. (Photograph by and courtesy of Cynthia Henry.)

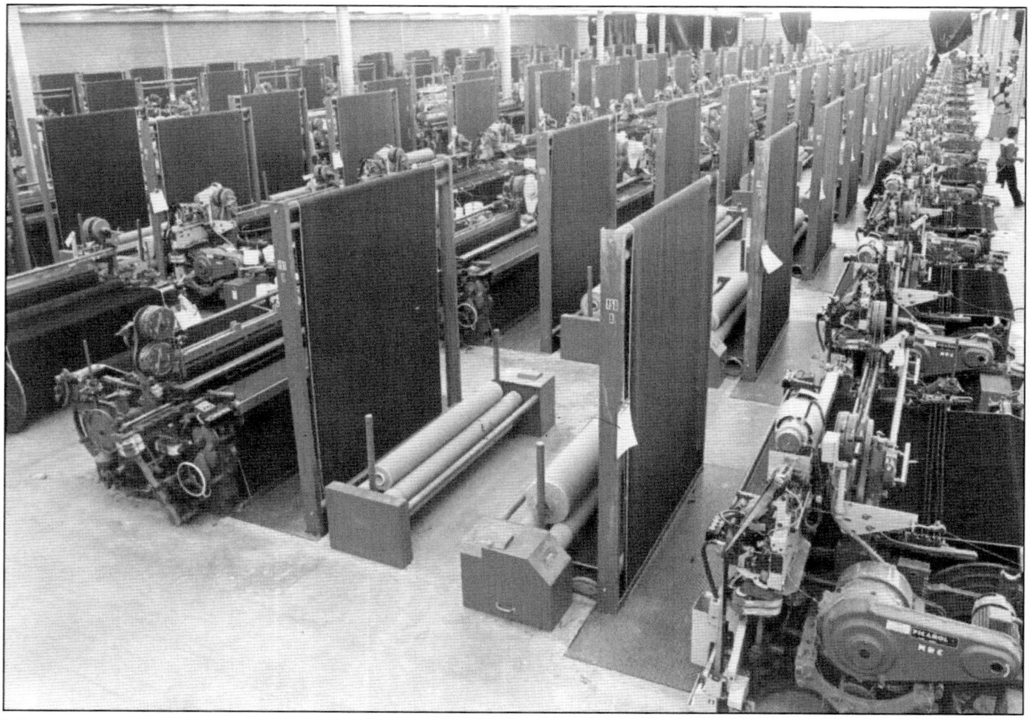

The cotton-weaving room is seen here in the 1980s. The large round objects are bolts of denim cloth, which has completed the milling process and has been rolled onto the large spools. The large spools of denim will soon be made into a pair of jeans either in Littlefield or more likely elsewhere in America. (Photograph by Lynette Thompson Wilson, courtesy of Plains Cotton Cooperative Association.)

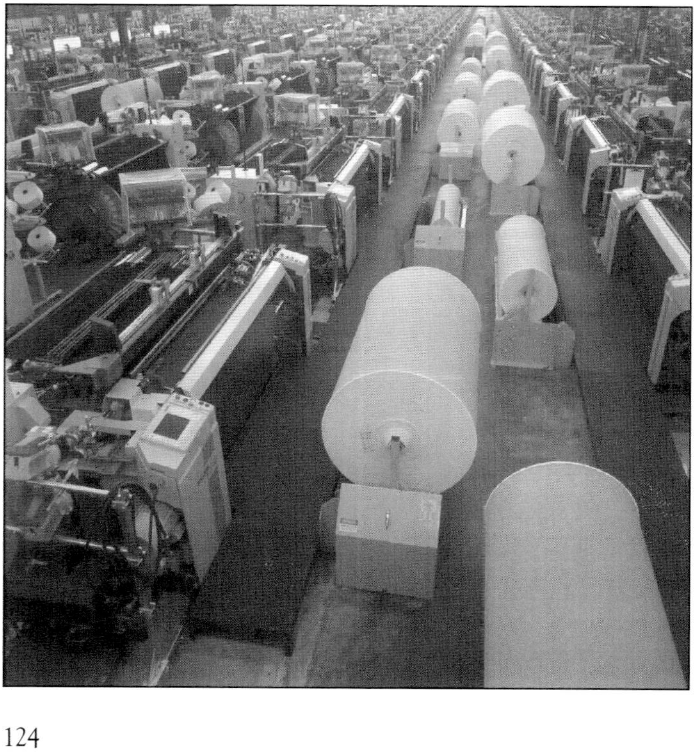

After weaving is completed to the desired specifications, the fabric is rolled onto giant spools. Since the ends of the cloth will unravel in the milling procedure, it must undergo one final process: it is immersed in a finishing solution and then pulled to the proper width, skewed, and dried. (Photograph by Lynette Thompson Wilson, courtesy of Plains Cotton Cooperative Association.)

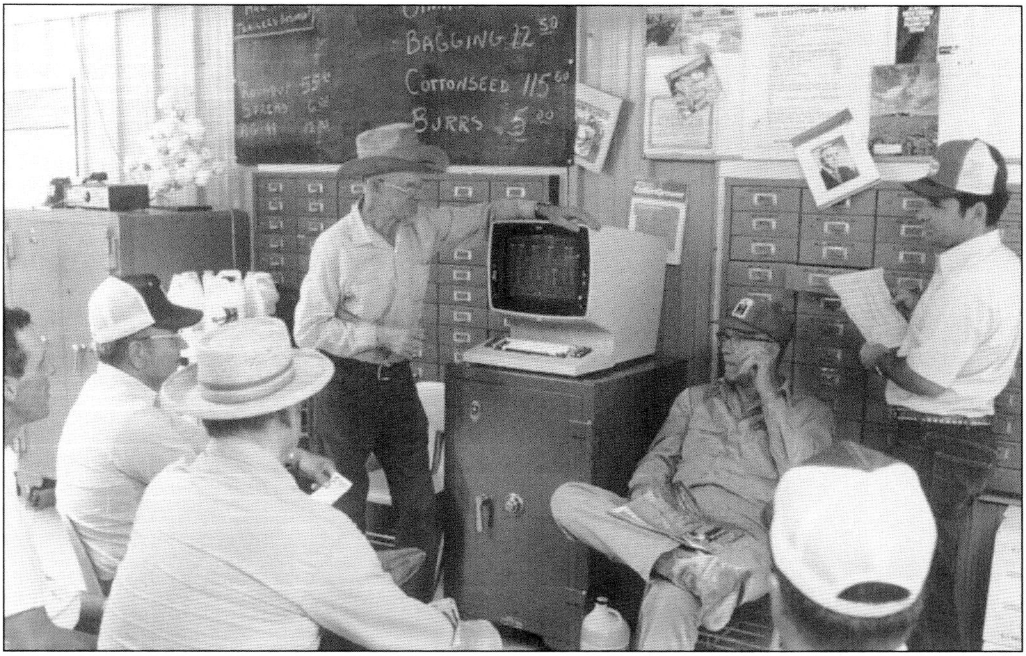

The TELCOT terminal at Lubbock Cotton Growers' headquarters is seen here in 1978. Among the men in the photograph are manager Gene Beck and member farmers Buzz Vardeman, Bill Piercy, Dean Vardeman, Keith Vardeman, and Bill Marshall. The terminal served as an electronic bulletin board where producers and subscribers got real-time global marketing data and farmers could sell their crops collectively. (Photograph by Lynette Thompson Wilson, courtesy of Plains Cotton Cooperative Association.)

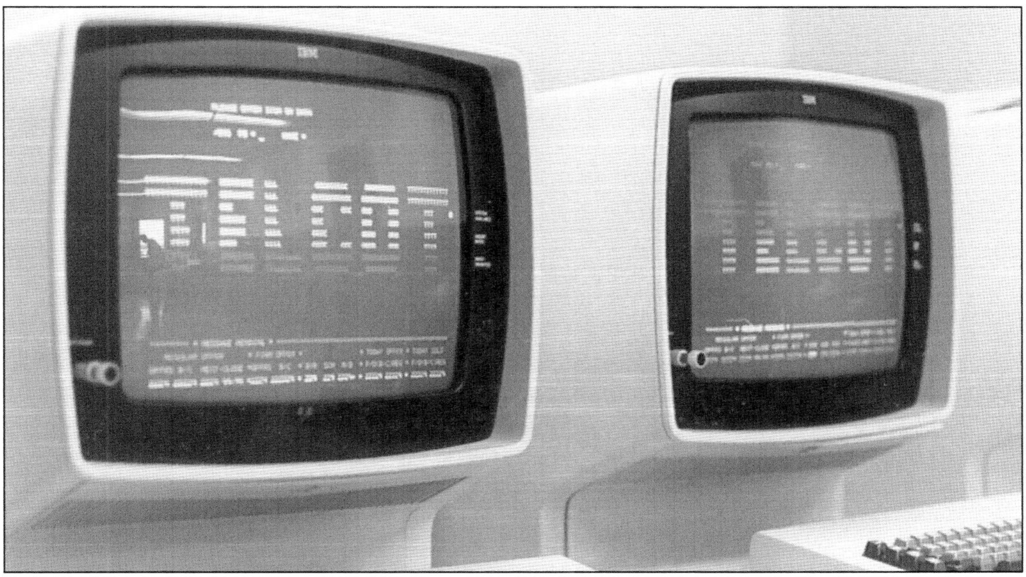

TELCOT is a registered trademark owned by PCCA and is an electronic marketing system. It was developed in 1975 to facilitate the marketing of cotton. Showing worldwide competitive prices in real time, remote terminals installed in 15 cotton-buying offices in Lubbock, Dallas, and Memphis connect to a central computer database at PCCA. (Photograph by Lynette Thompson Wilson, courtesy of Plains Cotton Cooperative Association.)

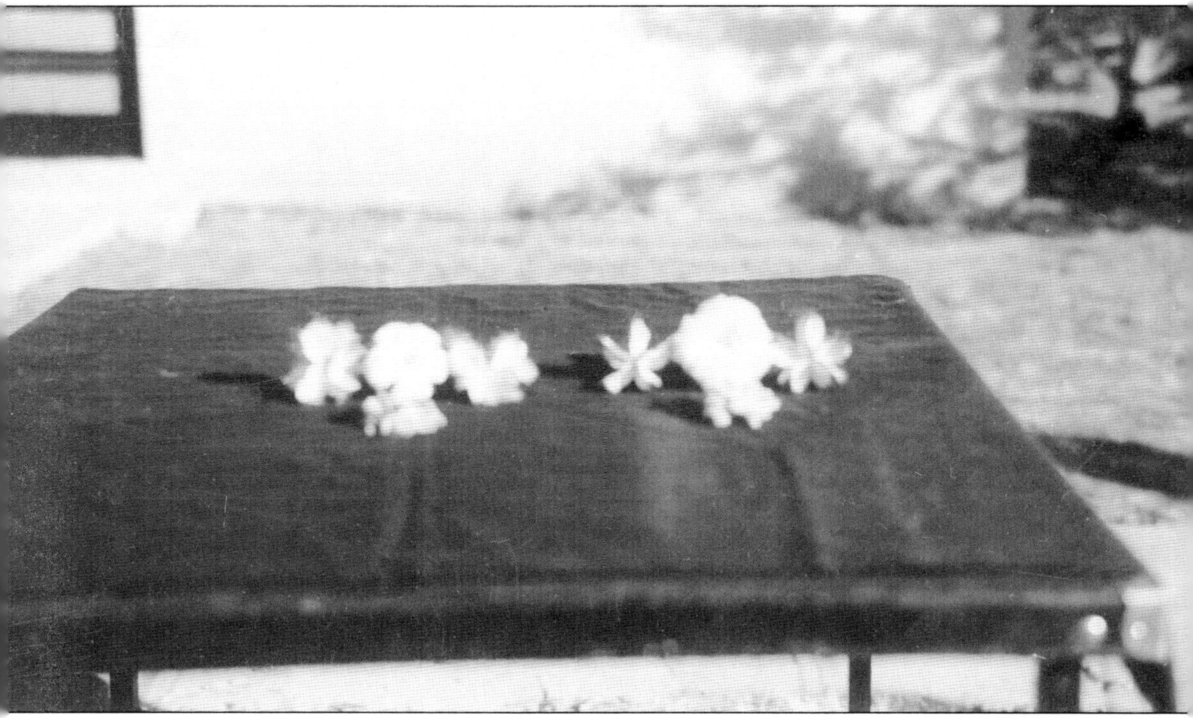

Two varieties of cotton with storm-proof boll characteristics, where the lint adheres to the boll without linters, are seen here. The cotton on the left, with two open burs and a pile of seed, is from a pure dominant variety, while the cotton on the right is from an intermediate species. (Courtesy of the Texas AgriLife Research and Extension Center – Lubbock, Texas.)

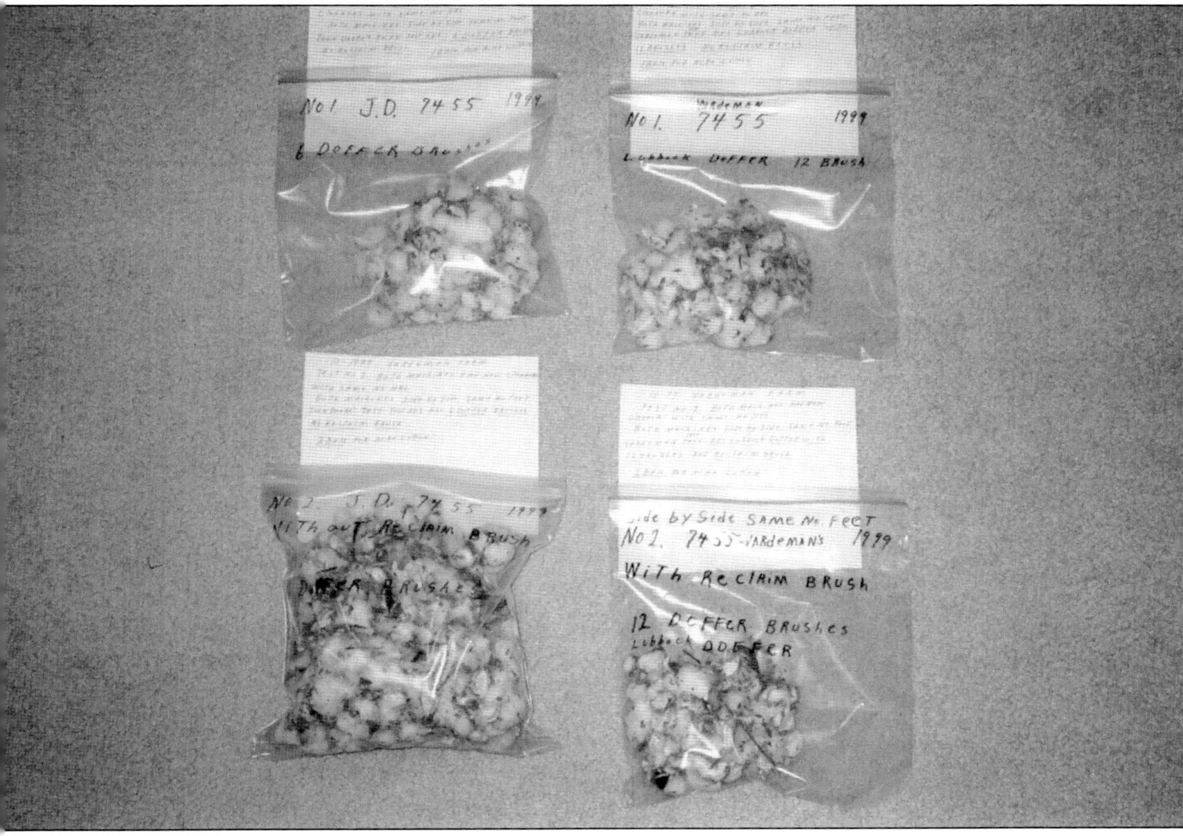

These plastic bags hold cotton from a John Deere 7455 stripper equipped with a new type of cleaner developed by Buzz Vardeman in 1999. His tests have shown that the new cleaner works. Vardeman performed the test on his farm by driving the stripper the same distance down four rows of cotton. Each test represents a different arrangement of brushes used in cleaning cotton. (Photograph by and courtesy of Vardeman Farms.)